Susanne U. Schultz
"Failed" Migratory Adventures?

Culture and Social Practice

Susanne U. Schultz holds a PhD from the Faculty of Sociology at Bielefeld University, where she is an associated research fellow at the Center on Migration, Citizenship and Development (COMCAD). Her research focuses on (return) migration and West Africa. She currently works in the area of migration and Africa at the Bertelsmann Stiftung, a German think tank, focusing on legal pathways and political cooperation.

Susanne U. Schultz

"Failed" Migratory Adventures?

Malian Men Facing Conditions Post Deportation in Southern Mali

[transcript]

I acknowledge support for the publication costs by the Open Access Publication Fund of Bielefeld University. Additionally, the German Association of Female Academics (Deutscher Akademikerinnenbund e.V.) contributed financially to the publication.

Bibliographic information published by the Deutsche Nationalbibliothek
The Deutsche Nationalbibliothek lists this publication in the Deutsche Nationalbibliografie; detailed bibliographic data are available in the Internet at http://dnb.d-nb.de

First published in 2022 by transcript Verlag, Bielefeld
© Susanne U. Schultz

Cover layout: Maria Arndt, Bielefeld
Cover illustration: Susanne U. Schultz
All photographs by Susanne U. Schultz
Translation from Bambara: Birama Bagayogo, Bamako
Copy-editing & proofread: Stephen Curtis, Bath UK

Print-ISBN 978-3-8376-6009-8
PDF-ISBN 978-3-8394-6009-2
https://doi.org/10.14361/9783839460092
ISSN of series: 2703-0024
eISSN of series: 2703-0032

Contents

*To all those in Mali, Germany, and elsewhere
who supported me and offered me their time,
their intimacy, and their wisdom.*

Abbreviations

AEI	Afrique-Europe-Interact
AJRECY	Association des Jeunes Rapatriés d'Espagne du Cercle de Yanfolila
AME	Association Malienne des Expulsés
AMRK	Association des Migrants de Retour de Kayes
ARACEM	Association des Refoulés d'Afrique Central au Mali
AVR	Assisted Voluntary Return
CIGEM	Centre d'Information et Gestion des Migrations
DGME	Délégation Générale des Maliens de l'Extérieur
ECOWAS	Economic Community of West African States
EU	European Union
EUTF	European Union Emergency Trust Fund
FRONTEX	frontières extérieures [European Border and Coast Guard Agency]
GAM	Global Approach on Migration
GAMM	Global Approach for Migration and Mobility
GWP	Gallup World Poll
HDI	Human Development Index
IOM	International Organization for Migration
MMEIA	Ministry of Malians Abroad and of African Integration
MNLA	Mouvement national de libération de l'Azawad
NGO	Non-Governmental Organization
OFII	Office Français de l'Immigration et de l'Intégration
PONAM	Politique National de Migration du Mali
SAP	Structural Adjustment Program
UNHCR	United Nations High Council of Refugees

Foreword

The past two decades have witnessed growing attention to forced mobility as *refoulement*, i.e., deportation in the wake of growing immigration restrictions and the externalization of migration control to places of transit and origin countries of migration. The growing restrictions and attendant securitization attest to the significance of the universalization of the nation-state form: *refoulement* is regularly taking place not only from Europe to Africa but also from some African states to others. Susanne U. Schultz's study contributes to the rapidly emerging field of deportation studies with a focus on various types of forced return as a form of what she calls "legally produced violence" in the wake of what the late French sociologist Abdelmayek Sayad termed initially unsuccessful *"emigration-aventures."* Deportation as a process has an impact upon the condition of irregular migrants and, in this case, on the post-deportation condition.

Susanne U. Schultz frames her investigations around supposedly "failed" migratory adventures, thus pointing toward the ambivalence of failure and success as reflected in the migration experiences of both young and older men from various regions of Mali. The experience of "failure" is interrogated as a notion that is materially, emotionally, and morally charged in its social dimensions. The study suggests that failure may eventually turn out to be "a productive category." This finding provides one of the answers to the main question: how do the forced returnees (*refoulés*) deal with deportation?

This rigorous study pushes us to rethink the scope and the consequences of forced returns in the lives of migrant workers, their families and communities. Susanne U. Schultz's way of tracing the processes of forced return points to a research line sufficiently rich to inform a research agenda for years to come, and her book offers a multi-perspectival analysis which considers the experiences of forced migrants in addition to the usual views of governments. This makes it a rare and convincing exemplar of providing reflexive knowledge on (return) migration, something that is badly needed if better policies for European–African transnational social spaces are to be devised.

Bielefeld, November 2021
Thomas Faist

Acknowledgements

The political paths of ethnography from the field to the final book are to be followed prudently, for you never know where you may end up. This has been a long, sometimes turbulent, but very enriching journey and a true phase of transformation. I want to thank all of those who advised and supported me on the way and enabled me to arrive here.

Above all, I am deeply indebted and full of thanks to the people who made up my field – all the respondents, acquaintances, and people I met, who shared their stories and invaluable insights with an often overwhelming openness and warmth that has, in part, lasted until today. Among them, I want to especially thank the self-organized groups of former deportees, the AME and ARACEM in Bamako and Kita, AMRK in Kayes, and AJRECY in Yanfolila, who welcomed and integrated me immediately, and provided me with indispensable contacts. Without all of them, this work would not have been possible or would be completely different.

A workshop with an enriching group of anthropologists and Africanists of different ages and levels of experience provided me with an insightful and comforting starting point for entry into the field of southern Malian lifeworlds post deportation. For this I was, and remain, very grateful. The German–Malian research institute Point Sud in Bamako acted as my base throughout the fieldwork. This much appreciated, fruitful environment brought me into contact with a number of Malian doctoral students; together we passed long hours discussing and drinking tea, and I was able to report to them my "fresh" impressions from the field. There, I was introduced to Birama Bagayogo, who became an indispensable advisor and friend in collaborating on my research and much more. I am deeply grateful for his constant assistance, support, and inspiration that has continued until today.

Back "home," I was generously supported by the Bielefeld Graduate School in History and Sociology (BGHS), which allowed me to pursue my research topic in the first place. Throughout, the BGHS has been an inspiring and supportive environment in intellectual as well as social terms. A warm thank you to everybody there! My supervisor, Thomas Faist, was an invaluable support throughout this doctoral journey. I very much appreciated our thoughtful exchanges, the "work in progress" discussions in our (back then) Vlotho research class and in his colloquium. Many thanks are due as well to the colleagues in the working group "Sociology of Transnationalization" for their support, time, and advice.

I am also deeply grateful to Dorothea Schulz, who co-supervised my work after thoughtfully scrutinizing whether my approach and output would fit into her domain. Her colloquium in Cologne has been incredibly helpful and a perfect anthropological and mostly (West) Africanist embedding for exchanges on my work: Another big thank you to all her colleagues for reading my manuscripts, providing insightful feedback, sharing and exchanging their work and lives. I was able to meet and engage with enriching scholars on this journey at academic events, workshops and conferences, and, importantly, was associated with the Bayreuth International Graduate School of African Studies (BIGSAS), all of which contributed greatly to developing this research.

Finally, I want to thank my family, who have always supported me, my friends, who were there when needed in the ups and the downs, my partner, who joined in supporting this journey for the last few meters, and, not least, my thoughtful copy-editor, who provided the finishing touch. My deep and warm thanks to all of you.

Bielefeld, January 2022
Susanne U. Schultz

Chapter 1
Introduction: Toward embedding "failed" migratory adventures in southern Mali

It is a hot and dry December morning in the main square of a hub city in southwest Mali. I am here with a group of activists from Mali and Europe in order to participate in and document an event organized by a transnational activist network. Together with community representatives and bereaved families we have come to commemorate the deaths of migrants in the Mediterranean – their "martyrs," as some call them. In this region there are communities with long histories of mobility and migration that take many forms and established practices regarding them. Everybody here has some relation to being on the move, whether through previous or prospective migratory experience of their own, or as a relative, acquaintance, or dependent of a migrant. The numerous chairs set out under sun canopies on the square are still empty. It is early Saturday. The commemoration event, which was preluded at first light by the sacrifice of an ox at the imam's house, will start soon.

As we pass through the square and observe the site, people start to arrive. They are mostly men, middle-aged and young, who come and sit. After a little while, the chairs are filled. More official representatives of the city and members of the bereaved families take their places in the broad main stand flanking the square. We sit with them in the shadow of the canopy as the event is rolled out. As we shortly learn, a large majority of the men seated on these rudimentary chairs typical of the locality have previously been deported.[1] They are what people commonly call refoulés[2]: former adventurers (anciens aventuriers) who "have not made it."

---

1   The term "deportation" here refers to different forms of forced return, including push-backs, *refoulements*, expulsions, repatriations, and, importantly, transit or emergency returns. My intention is to emphasize the often coercive and above all involuntary nature of these returns without focusing on legal differentiations. This derives from my observation that legal terms are sometimes arbitrarily or dissimilarly used by (Malian and other) representatives of authority and above all by the returnees themselves (cf. Alpes, 2020, 2017; Kleist, 2017a).

2   A term that literally translates as "people who have been pushed back" and that deportees and other "involuntary" returnees most often use to refer to themselves. I will deal with this

Most of them were forcibly returned from the Maghreb states externally bordering the European Union (EU), that is, from Libya, Morocco, Mauritania, or Algeria; others come from Gabon or the two Congos. Few of those who are here have been forcibly returned from European states directly; only a small number have come from Spain, France, Germany, or, most recently, Italy. Many of the latter prefer to stay in Bamako, Mali's capital city. Together with the few from Germany and from other West African countries, the former migrants and deportees form an international crowd to commemorate and value the migrant "heroes," who went out for the well-being and betterment of their communities expecting to return "in triumph" (Latour, 2003). Now they are presumed dead; they cannot even be buried according to the Muslim rule (cf. Sylla & Schultz, 2020).

The day is primarily an occasion to express and share mourning. Several of the parents burst into tears when offered the chance to bring in their testimonies describing the difficulties they have faced. But, in addition, the families and civil society actors are able to express their political discontents, challenging the "neoliberal state," "international donors," and the "development" regime. In their introductory speeches during the main commemoration, representatives of the local authorities harshly denounce the attitude of the Malian government regarding the treatment of Malians abroad. They appeal for agriculture to be properly valued as that would retain "the valid arms on the spot" (field notes, 12-19-2015, in other words "keep fit and effective workers in the country"), and avoid young people "being forced" to leave. The activists' declaration places the central responsibility squarely on the EU, denouncing the political and economic inequalities of restrictive border protection policies and their corollaries, the extinction or distortion of many migrants' lives (Afrique-Europe-Interact [AEI], Mali Section, December 18, 2015, unpublished statement). The Europeans' established discourse on "irregular" migrants will eventually legitimize these policies, including deportations, dividing those on the move into desirables and undesirables (Agier, 2011). Even if it took place out of sight of most participants, the ritual sacrifice element was of central symbolic significance for commemorating the absent, dead bodies. It allowed the dead to be integrated in the "normal" order of a funeral practice, thus ensuring "their rest and salvation," and recovering something from the great loss caused by the politically externalized borders (see Sylla & Schultz, 2020, p. 5).

This situation is a snapshot of the contemporary state of the global deportation regime (De Genova & Peutz, 2010) and of the unequal practices in place at its externalized borders. It marks a very specific historical moment at which border controls, mobility restrictions, and deportations have created everyday realities of

---

term in more detail shortly. Stefanie Maher (2015) makes similar observations in Senegal. For further explanation see the subchapter headed "Everybody is a *réfoulé*" (p. 33).

death, abuse, trauma, and destruction. Not only have the "migratory failures" produced by these restrictions and forced returns had devastating consequences for individuals within these communities, the expectations of a better life and development for all, in terms of potential economic and social mobility, have been reversed. Albeit a deportee has some chance of continuing and potentially finding new opportunities, a shipwrecked young man cannot be brought back to life. More concretely, the death of a young breadwinner can imply the loss of social status for an entire family and the impossibility of achieving the economic goals expected from the migratory project (see Bredeloup, 2017; Koenig, 2005). The repercussions are substantial and hard to redress. Against this background, contestations and responses evolve far beyond this region of southwest Mali with its long-established migratory patterns and cultures. While experiences are collectively shared and publicly expressed, an individual "failure"[3] through deportation may still be received ambivalently by the community. After deportations, the collective imaginary of success through migration may be particularly contested.

Hazards, survival, and loss in adventure – the emblem of returning empty-handed

Salif's[4] account captures this central ambivalence of returning to one's community involuntarily and with empty hands very well. He comes from a village close to where the commemoration I have just described took place and thus allows me to dive straight in to the micro level of my study. His story illustrates the entanglement of the different political, economic, social, emotional, moral, and cultural dimensions at stake. Now in his late forties, the father of eight children and husband of two wives, Salif is someone who embodies not only the suffering and hardships of the adventurous journey, but the financial loss it can entail as well. All the money Salif earned between 2008 and 2010 in Libya while working on a construction site was lost when the rubber boat he was in went adrift in the open Mediterranean and was finally returned by the Libyan Coast Guard. His journey ended in an odyssey through various prisons. He recalled:

---

3   Throughout this book, the term "failure" will be set in inverted commas to underline the relative stance I take towards this morally and emotionally charged judgment, as I will explain below. Particularly in the case of deportations, an unwanted return is to be seen first of all as the result of a politico-administrative measure that is potentially economically driven.

4   The names of the respondents have been changed to preserve their anonymity, and information relating to individuals has been partly modified. For the same reason, the deportees' villages and living and working places will not be named specifically and are only roughly characterized.

Yes, the motor broke. We had one day and two nights when the motor was good, but on that second day, the motor broke down. We spent nine days like that on the water, without motor. This was the water that would help us to get anywhere. We were 152 persons in the Zodiac. And 70 people died in the water. (Salif, 11-1-2015)

The water "that would help [them] to get anywhere," water full of hope and promise turned out to be full of desperation and misery, hardly traversable by Zodiac, a small rubber boat often used to transport people without legal papers over the Mediterranean to enter Italy, Spain, or Greece. The Zodiac becomes a microcosm of the horrors of an unequal world experienced in the suffering and death of the migrants and in the helplessness and despair that follow the conviction that originally persuaded them to get into the boat. It embodies the violence and distress as well as the hope on the high seas that live on in many *refoulés'* memories. At the same time, it represents the contingencies deciding over death and life. The survivors were captured; their journeys were disrupted and reversed. Having lost everything, Salif had to return with empty hands. He had invested all his money in this journey of hope. He forfeited a fortune. He laughs a little bitterly, when recalling his arrival back in the village, but the picture he draws has two sides to it:

It is a pity, but it is a pleasure, and also disturbing, the money that you've lost and you spent eleven days on the sea and you saw the people die and you are not dead and when you have met your family again, that's a pleasure. But it's a pity for an adventurer to lose all his money like this without gaining anything, and return and start with the hardship here. That's a pity. (Salif, 11-1-2015)

Many men, young ones and older ones,[5] venture out, like Salif, to "search for money" (Bambara: *warignini*)[6] in their youth in order to grow, become someone (*ka kè waritiguiyé*), and contribute (*ka gwa dèmè*) to their families. Their migratory journey is called "the adventure" (French: *"l'aventure"*) in large parts of West Africa, as I will shortly elaborate further. But this short episode points up what I call the ambivalence of the "failed" migratory adventure. Salif feels obliged to return to the narrow social space of the village and to the hardships he had left behind. He

---

5   "Young" or "younger" men refers in emic terms to those aged between 16 and about 40, and very much relates to a person's capacity for mobility and migration and thus for actively contributing to the family income; "older" refers to men outside this broad category.

6   Bambara is the main local language in Mali and the one most frequently used in newspapers, media, and politics as well. I will provide more information on the language and translation of my research in Chapter 3. French is the official language of Mali and is also frequently used in everyday communication. Throughout the text, terms in Bambara and French will appear in italics. The annex includes a Glossary for the main Bambara terms used, and some French equivalents.

considers it a pity, a shame, for an "adventurer" to return without the thing he adventured for. Still, it's a pleasure to be back with the family alive and well.

This book will showcase emic conceptions of peoples' leaving and their often forced and unwanted returns on the one hand, and their going on after deportation on the other as revealed in deportees' (retrospective) narratives and everyday practices. My aim is to develop a differentiated picture of supposed breakdown and "failure" after deportation, showing how it can be a productive category for some people as well, and an indicator of how to go about one's life. This introductory chapter is intended to provide the reader with a theoretical and contextual base for the analysis to come. First, I briefly explain what makes Mali a particularly interesting research setting. Second, I lay out the central question dealt with in the study, which derives from an instance of a supposedly "failed" adventure, and describe my major aim in tackling it. This gains substance in a third section where I introduce the main theoretical lines I have followed and summarize the concepts and terminology that emerged from my research. I then close this introductory chapter by providing an outline of the chapters to come.

The specificities of (post-)deportation in Mali

There are a number of reasons that make Mali an extraordinarily interesting place to study situations and conditions after deportation in general and so-called "failed" adventures in particular. In Mali, the different social, political, economic, and cultural dimensions as well as the relevant actors who are affected by and respond to the global deportation regime intersect in very particular ways. As the country has longstanding cultures of migration (Hahn & Klute, 2007) and different forms of mobility, expatriate Malians constitute a quarter to a third of the country's population. Conversely, Mali has also become a country of immigration and transit for many people journeying northward. In 2008 it was strategically selected by the EU as a pilot country to implement its new approach to migration and development in a place of transit toward the Mediterranean and the outer shores of Europe. Throughout the last few decades, Mali has been impacted by high numbers of forced returns, starting from the time when many African states gained their independence. Meanwhile, the country has never implemented large-scale deportations itself.[7]

Apart from that, Mali has developed a specific political context, favorable to the establishment of civil society engagement (Lecadet, 2017; Siméant, 2014). In light of the size and importance of the segment of its population living abroad, the *Association Malienne des Expulsés* (AME; the Malian Association of Expellees) was founded in 1996 by a number of former deportees from different African and European countries politically inspired by the movement of the *sans-papiers* in France (cf. Lecadet, 2018, 2011; Cissé, 1999). Over the years, the organization has gained a critical role in the debate on deportations in Mali and beyond and been involved in the reception and reintegration of deportees. It was the organization's activist presence that called my own attention to post deportations in Mali as the flipside of the EU border externalization regime in the nexus of migration and development. I found all these entanglements highly interesting. They demanded more insight and analysis.

Today, there are generations of deportees in Mali, particularly since the externalization of the EU's borders into the African continent received a major new push in the follow-up to the so-called "refugee crisis"[8] and the issue of transit returns became particularly virulent (Alpes, 2020; Zanker & Altrogge, 2019). Since then, deportations, including transit returns, have become an ever more public phenomenon in the country, debated first of all on radio and television, in the newspapers, and at public events. Though the commemoration described at the beginning of this chapter was in itself a unique event, it has to be seen as part of a process of commenting on and contesting national as well as international (migration) policies through civil society actors and former deportees in particular. Today it may no longer be rare, for instance, to see deportees as spokespersons at public events, such as debates about the meaning of migration, return, and opportunities in society, organized by a Malian radio station at the French institute

---

7   Mali and Tanzania have been unique in this regard on the African continent, though lately the situation has been changing. Individual cases of deportation have been reported from Mali, and the country has been involved in transit returns as well (see Chapter 2). Similarly, Tanzania is said to have been involved in forced repatriations of Burundian refugees: https://www.amnesty.org/en/latest/news/2019/09/tanzania-confidential-document-shows-forced-repatriation-of-burundi-refugees-imminent/, accessed 31 October 2021.

8   While the "refugee crisis" dates back to the protracted situation in which millions of refugees from the Syrian civil war arrived in the Middle East and Turkey and decided to journey on, it was mostly the dilapidated boats setting out from the Libyan coast "full of Africans" and the increasing number of shipwrecks in the Mediterranean that imprinted our image of and approach to this "European crisis."

(*l'Institut français*), or an academic workshop aiming to engage in the public debate on migration[9] (cf. Lecadet, 2018).

Meanwhile, one can now speak of collective experiences of deportation rather than experiences of individual "failure" – as Plambech similarly finds for Nigeria (2018) – and a certain "normalcy" in deportations (Galvin, 2015). Increasingly, these are becoming collective memories of (post) deportation, too, though deportees may still react with shame and may easily be stigmatized (cf. also Plambech, 2018, 2017; Drotbohm, 2015; Dünnwald, 2011; Lecadet, 2011). We know too little about these interrelations and conditions post deportation, above all about individual social experiences and the practices that develop afterwards, particularly over the longer run and in different geographical contexts. This book aims to contribute to filling these gaps in our knowledge. In all this, Mali serves as a particular case of experiencing and reacting to (post) deportations.

Toward the topic and question: "failed" migratory adventures under post-deportation conditions in southern Mali

Within this debated, contested, and simultaneously devastating setting, this book will develop and critically question the concept of the "failed" migratory adventure on the basis of narrative representations (collectively) experiencing and dealing with situations post deportation and the practices developed to help people cope with them. At stake are social, emotional, and material interrelations and perceptions, which often center on loss of money and thus failing the expectations of one's kin. All this indicates what I call the "ambivalence of the 'failed' migratory adventure."

Literary reminiscences – the "failed" hero?

The term "adventure" conjures up a series of literary motifs of the hero who went out into the wilderness and came back broken, unrecognizable, but also changed and enriched in some way, such as the ancient Greek hero Odysseus, the prodigal son in Jesus's parable recorded in St Luke's Gospel, and the medieval knight Parzival (Percival), in a romance written by the knight-poet Wolfram von Eschenbach in Middle High German (13th century). Siddhartha, the rich and sheltered Indian prince who later became the Buddha, is another example. Siddhartha lived years

---

9   Programme Point Sud 2019, Récits et débats locaux sur la migration. Dits et non-dits de l'expérience du départ et du retour, 2-6 October 2019, Point Sud Bamako, Mali, Rapport; see online : http ://pointsud.org/wp-content/uploads/PPS-2019-R%C3%A9cits-et-d%C3%A9bats-locaux-sur-la-migration-Bamako-Rapport.pdf, p. 5, accessed 31 October 2021.

of ascetic apprenticeship in mostly solitary withdrawal in the Indian wilderness, which brought him eternal wisdom and enlightenment in the end and became the origin of Buddhism. Eventually, all of them grew wiser. They went out to search for something and come back as heroes, but "failed" in one way or the other as a result of the obstacles and trials they had to overcome, before they returned differently than expected, but bringing back something more precious than what they had set out to find. Siddhartha Gautama founded a new religion; Odysseus was eventually recognized, reintegrated and could govern his kingdom well; Parzival had to acknowledge his God-given culpability and sinfulness, his unconscious guilt for the death of his mother and his relative Ither. Eventually, however, after passing through numerous *âventiures*[10], he found the Holy Grail and was received into the circle of the knights of the Round Table (cf. Schwietering, [1944]; 1946, pp. 18ff).

None of these heroes was forced to return, they struggled on to achieve their goals, enduring years of suffering and apprenticeship. The heroic masculine qualities of courage, bravery, steadfastness, and persistence are intrinsic to the stories. Similarly, some migrants continue the struggle when they come back, or refuse to return because they have been unable to live up to the social expectations of a considerable income and contribution to the family that were placed upon them, even though return, if only perhaps for a visit, is the ultimate aim of many (see, e.g., Hernandez-Carretero, 2015; Le Courant, 2014). Deportations come as radically unexpected, unprepared for, and most often deeply unwanted interruptions to their quest. Even if there are substantial differences between them and the literary heroes, the deportees too originally went out to search for something. Their years of suffering before, during, and after deportation also make up a true phase of transition and becoming. Furthermore, former adventurers may show dedication and courage after deportation similar to that of the literary and religious heroes, a theme that will be particularly developed in Chapters 6 and 7.

Like Odysseus, for instance, whose 10 whole years of struggle had rendered him unrecognizable by the time he made it home, many returnees and their social circles report how the former's experiences made them unrecognizable after deportation – physically, but also mentally. They have to recover, to find themselves again and get back to their lives. I will develop this process of arrival, and what deportations can do to people along with presenting their narrative depictions of experiencing deportation in the first analytical chapter. In Kafka's story "Homecoming" (Kafka, 1971), the returned son never verifies whether he is recognizable. He stops in front of the closed door of his parents' house, feeling more and more alienated the longer he stands there. The reader is left with the impression that he

---

10   In Middle High German; Old French *aventure, avanture*). The New High German term "Abenteuer" finally developed from this. See online: https://de.wikipedia.org/wiki/Aventiure, accessed 31 October 2021.

will turn around and walk away. Possibly, his time of being away and what happened in between cannot be overcome.

Deportees who have stayed abroad for a long time and far away have the greatest difficulties in finding their way back into their previous lives. They have changed "too" greatly. Some immediately take to the road again in such a situation. Migrants who return of their own volition and well prepared after long periods of time in faraway countries may report a similar change in mind, body, and perception (e.g., Konzett-Smoliner, 2015). Odysseus is finally recognized and reintegrated. Eventually, many deportees are too, even if their traumatic experiences and memories keep impacting them and they did not return as expected. In this sense, references to literary motives of adventure, heroism, and return can be a fruitful source of inspiration and analytical understanding of migratory journeys and their forcible, involuntary interruptions. These motives accompanied my thinking in the further development of the book. First, though, I will throw some light on the relevant local and emic conceptions.

The migratory adventure

In West and Central Africa, the "adventure" (*tounkan*, literally: "going to the wilderness") is the term mostly used to describe migration and departure abroad. Central aims of the migratory adventure are described as striving for social (financial) responsibility, above all for the sake of the family, and becoming independent, "someone" (*ka kè waritiguiyé*), and globally connected. The term captures the different facets of risk, success, and potential "failure" implicit in such an undertaking, referred to elsewhere as "high-risk" or "irregular" migration. The term apparently originates from the time of French colonization and was formerly used for all forms of migration. "*Emigration-aventure*" was how Abdelmayek Sayad (2004) referred to the experience of Algerian emigrants to France in the 1960s, for instance. It implied a necessary process of getting along ("*débrouillardise*") as an individual, in which you had to learn to rely on yourself and which was, not least, a form of learning and making a career.

The migratory adventure in Mali builds on former pilgrimages into the wilderness – "the first collective or individual experience of a man. [...] Weeks of walking through the forests, savannah, and soils [that] reinforced his masculinity" (Dougnon, 2012, p. 152) – thought of as an initiation into social adulthood. The wilderness has now been replaced by bigger cities or faraway countries, though the journey's function as a "rite of passage" partially remains, as it involves facing risks, violence, or even death.[11] The migratory adventure, not necessarily toward Europe,

---

11   Similar ways to adult- and manhood building on rites of "initiation" can be found in Cameroon, for instance, where "bushfalling" commonly refers to going abroad against all obstacles

to gain economic, social and personal success, is "reinterpreted, as a prestigious, 'initiatory,' value-giving experience" (p. 162). Since the 1960s, the migratory voyage, or "the adventure," has been a part of local culture and a popular theme in music, literature, and everyday life in Mali (Dougnon, 2013, pp. 39ff). In this context, mobility is intrinsically connected to masculinity, economic success, socio-cultural recognition, and families' livelihoods. According to Sylvie Bredeloup (2017, p. 139), the adventure is seen as the "spice of life" and an "appreciated lifestyle" by migrants who describe their lives as "more intense and more dignified," "turbulent and fast moving," and themselves as young and courageous, differentiating themselves from those who are "bored and dreaming of a better life at home." Scholars also use the term "adventure" for clandestine migration (e.g., Streiff-Fénart & Poutignat, 2014) or for mobility more generally (Bruijn et al., 2001), besides discussing its function as a *"rite de passage"* and in the process of becoming "a man" (Stock, 2019; Pian, 2009, pp. 44ff), which can only be achieved through suffering. In all this, the adventure is in itself deeply "ambivalent." Janneke Barten concludes from her research on migratory relations in Malian families that it is "something positive and exciting, on the one hand, and something dangerous and not very desirable, on the other" (2009, p. 9). All this reminds one of the literary figures described above, but much of it is readily accepted, as I will show throughout this book.

Meanwhile, migration and the migratory adventure have attained a highly symbolic value in Mali. Migration has become a "fetish" phenomenon, a kind of "a god-thing" (Bazin, 2008), due to the importance of the income it generates and the political construction put upon it (Lima, 2005; Quiminal, 2002). In this context migrants are constructed as "local builders" (Soukouna, 2016), as adventurers (Bredeloup, 2008), and ultimately as "martyrs" (Sylla & Schultz, 2020). For instance, the Malian singer Fatoumata Diawara in her popular song *"Clandestin"* describes the tragedies of today's global inequalities and the existential need for migration on the part of many (2011): "But we call them Men of Adventure" (*Dòw ko olu ma tunkannadenw*),[12] she sings, praising them. In the neighboring Ivory Coast, it is furthermore a common belief that you cannot be civilized if you do not migrate, and migratory journeys have become the "ultimate act of consumption" (Newell, 2012, p. 186; see also Chapter 5 of this book).

Consequently, and again by analogy with the literary heroes, the return of the adventurer, the warrior (*"le guerrier"*), is supposed, as Éliane de Latour (2003) explains, to be voluntary, triumphant, and heroic in the collective imaginary. Returning allows one to realize oneself, to repay one's "debt of life" towards one's parents, as well as to support projects undertaken by one's close family and friends, so that

---

and returning successfully (Alpes, 2017), while in Sierra Leone the civil war became a means of initiation for young men who joined rebel groups (Jackson, 2005b).

12

success can bring even more advantage and prestige (p. 187). The returnee is supposed to be a hero indeed.

Deportations and the supposed "failure" of the migratory adventure

Restrictive migration policies and multifold borders are what interrupt, stop, redirect, or reverse these migratory journeys (Drotbohm & Hasselberg, 2015) converting them into "new confinements and modes of exploitation" (Glick-Schiller & Salazar, 2013, p. 190). Deportation is generally understood as a legal, political, and socio-economic measure involving the forceful removal of a migrant from a national territory to another country (cf. Drotbohm & Hasselberg, 2015). There is a tendency to consider it as forced removal by air, but research is increasingly considering cross-border removal by land as well (Sylla & Cold-Ravnkilde, 2021; Alpes, 2020; Kleist, 2017a; Mensah, 2016).

Deportations and involuntary returns produce the opposite of the heroic homecomings expected. They violently cut the journey to potential economic success and socio-cultural recognition. Particularly in the West African context, deportations are to be seen in relation to the adventurers' deep social embedding and relationality, before, during, and after the journeys (cf. Pian, 2010, p. 97). Here, the extended family plays a significant role in any aspect of life: West Africans experience themselves not as "having" relationships but as "being" relationships (Piot, 1999), an idea that I will develop, particularly in Chapter 5, and consciously construct their families across (inter)national and continental boundaries (cf., e.g., Drotbohm, 2015, 2009). Deportations thus produce potential "failures" in light of the collective expectation of success and a triumphant homecoming. Against this background, the informants portray themselves as distressed and empty-handed, like Salif: at best with a plastic bag shuffling from the airport to some relative in Bamako. This powerful image emblematically embodies the drama of the unwanted return. As Éliane de Latour puts it: "Failure on the journey is worse than immobility on the spot: from being poor at the start, the warrior becomes poverty-stricken" (Latour, 2003, p. 187; transl. S.U.S.),[13] though in fact such a symbolic and charged depiction does not adequately mirror the realities on the ground.

"Failure," like the term "adventure," emerged in my research as an emic term first of all. Former deportees and their close contacts speak of "l'échec" or "maloya," the Bambara word for shame. More often, deportees and their circle will say "mon objectif n'était pas atteint" ("My objective was not attained"), or "je n'ai pas réussi" ("I did not succeed"), or, more explicitly, "j'ai échoué" ("I failed"), "c'était un échec" ("It was a failure"). However, the line taken by most of the men is that tounga man ja ("the travel did not work out") and "there are other ways of getting on" (Chapters 5 and 6).

---

13   S.U.S. stands for the initials of the book's author Susanne Ursula Schultz.

From the respondents' descriptions, the potential for "failure" is deeply connected to luck, "*la chance*," (Bambara: *kunna dija* or *gèrè sèkè*), which, in turn, is related to an adventurous mode of trying and seeing within the tension between fate, destiny, and human agency that I discuss further in Chapter 7. Interestingly the medieval term "*âventiure*," used to describe Parzival's journeys, starts from a basic meaning of "chance" and "fate" (from the Latin *adventura* "that which will/should happen").[14] All of this indicates the openness and unexpectedness of the migratory adventure.

For theoretical purposes, it helps to consider academic literature on conceptions of "failure" more broadly. "Failure" is mainly discussed as a phenomenon of the "unsecured temporal perspectives of modern societies," (my translation) related to insecurities, uncertainties, and risks (John & Langhof, 2014, p. 7; Appadurai, 2016). "Failure" is based on the expectation of success, is its opposite in the moment success is missed. René John and Antonia Langhof, however, locate a potential learning process in envisioning "failures" as means of securing the future (2014, p. 7). Arjun Appadurai goes further in his theoretical conceptualization introducing the normativity of "failure," (2016, p. xxvii), which "may be the only thing about it that is truly universal." In any other respect, failure, its measurement, meaning, and means of coping with it (e.g., through risk assessments or by externalizing failures to technological devices in modern, capitalist societies), is prone to change according to historical, cultural, and social factors. Its human-made, normative conception, in accordance with which we behave and act, however, eventually links to questions of the social order (Simmel, [1908] 1958). Appadurai sums up:

> Yet failure is a bigger mystery than it at first appears to be. The most important thing about failure is that it is not a fact but a judgment. And given that it is a human judgment, we are obliged to ask how the judgment is made, who is authorized to make it, who is forced to accept the judgment, and what the relationship is between the imperfections of human life and the decision to declare some of them as constituting failures (Appadurai, 2016, p. xxi).

It is this deep morality of "failure" and the judgmental behavior based on normative and hegemonic conceptions which can cause emotional extremes of stigmatization, shame, and social (self-)exclusion for deportees. Such social mechanisms have been prominently discussed in deportation studies not least as inciting processes of re-emigration or social distancing (cf. Hasselberg, 2018; Khosravi, 2018; Plambech, 2018; Alpes, 2017; Bredeloup, 2017; Drotbohm & Hasselberg, 2015; Schuster & Majidi, 2015; Drotbohm, 2012).[15] Some literature on the consequences of deportation tends to draw an extreme image of such "failures." Mamoutou Tounkara (2013),

---

14   Later it is reinterpreted as a test the hero has to pass.

15   This needs to be differentiated from theories on return from neo-classical economics and the new economics of labor migration, which center on the failure/success paradigm. This has

for instance, analyzed the narratives of Malian deportees from France whom he interviewed in the rooms of the AME. He was overwhelmed by everybody speaking about "failure" ("*l'échec*"). All his interviewees had returned about six months previously and stayed in Bamako afterwards, indicating that they could not return to their villages as they did not want their family to know about their unsuccess – in other words, in order to save face (see Chapters 4 and 5). Sylvie Bredeloup, who uses Tounkara's study to make her point, appears similarly dramatic in depicting "the moral experience of the migratory adventure" (2017) in which "failure" plays a central role in people being rejected by their communities. It picks up the central aspect of morality in migratory expectations. Stigmatizations in relation to (gang) criminality and violence, which create radical forms of social exclusion, have been specifically discussed in the Latin American post-deportation context (see Chapter 4).

The use of the term "failure" in speaking about deportations links not least to political and public discourses. Even the international media report on stigmatized and socially excluded deportees as a common narrative. In the Malian context, where my research took place, these are to be seen as extreme cases, however. There were people who were reported having been socially excluded. Indeed, as Tounkara shows, particularly those returning from Europe often did not want to go back to their home villages or would simply visit them from time to time, although this trend has recently shown signs of altering. Nevertheless, one cannot speak of a general exclusion from society (cf. also Maher, 2015).[16] Without aiming to downplay the gravity of what may happen in such situations, I want to outline how these depictions are too one-sided, and to provide a more differentiated picture of the Malian context, particularly in regard to what develops over time in rural and urban milieus. Civil society representatives too speak of "failure" and shame very explicitly, mostly when they want to highlight the political cruelty of the administrative act of violating migrants' rights. At the same time, they clearly mean the opposite when they say such things as "it is not the end of the world" (field notes, 10-20-2014).

---

been taken further by the structural approach to return migration, which links the individual experience of the migrant to the context of return (cf. Cassarino, 2004, pp. 2ff).

16   The temporality and locality of deportations play a critical role in the post-deportation experience and situation, a theme that I will develop throughout this book. Against this background, Tounkara's work needs to be seen in relative terms. It shows a specific piece of post-deportation reality since the author carried out his research mostly from France, also with regard to the way that he set up contacts with former deportees in Mali. Interviews were conducted exclusively on the premises of the AME, mostly with Malians who had recently been deported from France and who preferred to stay in Bamako instead of returning to their home villages.

In this sense, "failure" can be seen as an integral part of being. It has repercussions, but one mostly goes on. Consequently, "failure" and success can be "two sides of the same coin" (Voirol & Schendzielorz, 2014, p. 27) or "provisional containers for one another" (Appadurai, 2016, p. xxv; see Chapter 7). All this very much seems to resemble deportees' conceptions as I will show. Against this background, the analysis of what this judgmental "failure" is and means in this specific time and cultural context, and moreover, how people cope with the defined and perceived "failures" of their migratory adventures after deportations, is highly interesting for understanding more about people's social lifeworlds in light of the effects of the global deportation regime in southern Mali.

Central questions, aims, and contentions

Against this background, the central question I attempt to answer in this book is: How did the deportees that I met, interviewed, and accompanied in Mali, cope with having been deported and with the situation in which they found themselves back "home," even years after their return?

From this a number of related questions developed as I worked on my study: What does deportation do to former deportees? What are people's socio-economic perspectives and their strategies, and what is their everyday life like after deportation? In what ways are they socially embedded or disembedded? How does a deportation affect a person's life over the long term?

Overall, I am interested in doing two things. First, in finding out whether the literal mass of people who have experienced deportation in the last few years has contributed to a change of discourse as well as of social and political practice in Mali; second, and most importantly, in revisiting the global horizons of migratory success.

The aim of this work is thus not a stark focus on "failure" itself. The data collected and the results analyzed showcase a very specific historic, political, social, cultural, and economic setting post deportation in southern Mali. The ambivalent and potentially "failed" migratory adventure developed as a central analytical lens that enabled a better understanding of the social dimensions that deportees narrate and that I could observe. The book thus goes beyond the individual level of return and deportation and links to the social dimension as well as the historical and structural context, entangling dominant discourses and paradigms.

My main contention is that we cannot speak of sheer "failure" when talking about deportations and involuntary returns. Even if normative conceptions are fundamentally shattered, they continue to have an impact .So we need rather to see the ambivalence of the situation and the experiences and practices it engenders. As a first step, deportation is defined as an administrative and political structural intervention. In a second, "judgmental," social implications come into play. Finally, such supposed "failures" may be specific moments (conjunctures), where subjectivities and agency develop. Consequently, a perceived "failure" may spin off new energies and motivations for courageously going on, working hard, and standing one's ground. The following chapters will analyze narrative and practical accounts given under (post-)deportation conditions and examine their effects and reactions to them in their social, emotional, and material dimensions in different places and in a broader context, besides considering what they may imply in the long run.

Everybody is a *refoulé*

The supposedly "failed" migratory adventures that I analyze below, encompass repatriations – self-induced, though mostly unwanted (for reasons such as a political crisis, sickness or injuries, lack of money, family problems back home, to name but a few) – and unscheduled returns without having obtained the objective aimed at, *refoulements* over the border, deportations by air or over land. Many of the people were deported in trucks from the North African interior on ways through the desert and set down close to the Malian border; others were turned back while they were on their way to Europe – or from a European country itself, after a certain time on the move, in a country of destination abroad, or just after leaving their country of departure. The majority were already on boats – crossing the Mediterranean (from Libya, Morocco, Algeria or Tunisia) or the Atlantic Ocean (from Mauritania or Morocco). They were forced to return due to bad weather conditions or technical problems such as the motor breaking down, as in Salif's case; others were literally lost at sea. Alternatively, and often in addition, boats were intercepted by patrols and escorted back to shore. Furthermore, migrants may have been deported immediately on their arrival in the Canary Islands, Malta, or Italy (cf. Hernandez-Carretero & Carling, 2012, p. 410). In all these cases, former deportees most often speak of themselves as "*refoulés*" in everyday language, no matter where they came back from and how. This may even refer to those who returned through a program of "assisted voluntary return (and reintegration)," increasingly seen as the more humane and flexible alternative to deportation (see Chapter 2). The exact legal status and condition of return are not decisive in the end.[17]

I differentiate between deportations from other African countries, particularly those in North Africa, and deportations from Europe with respect to their symbolic meaning and the specific power imbalances inherent in them (cf. Walters, 2002; see also Chapter 4). Deportations from France, for instance, were perceived

---

17   This differs from the terminology of "state-induced" returns (Koch, 2014), which would imply deportations, repatriations, as well as "assisted voluntary" and so-called transit returns.

from the beginning as a direct colonial continuity (cf. Lecadet, 2016). The increasing trend of intra-African deportations, *refoulements*, and repatriations, including transit returns, particularly from North Africa, connected with the externalization of EU borders to the African continent has not so far been sufficiently analyzed and researched in depth and through micro-level ethnographic studies.[18] This book will make a contribution to this strand. Often those returned from Europe are referred to as *expulsés*, a term specifically applied in activist terminology. It builds on a process of self-designation leading to collective action, mainly advanced by the AME, in which the absent, almost shameful figure of the expelled migrant has become an actor capable of taking part in public debate (cf. Lecadet, 2018). Everyday language, however, and media representations do not necessarily differentiate in a similar way: terms are often used interchangeably.

Embedding research situations post-deportation in Mali

This book belongs within the literature of deportation and return, which has come to a number of unambiguous findings in recent years. Even if they concern human beings in a political field, however, most of these studies have not found a way to enhance the broader debate or political practice. I will briefly summarize some of the relevant examples.

The study of deportations is an interdisciplinary field developed from border and security studies within the last 20 years (Coutin, 2015). Deportation is discussed as a measure to implement penalties against immigrants through detentions and forced returns (Drotbohm & Hasselberg, 2015) that has become increasingly normalized in the Global North, particularly in the "deportation nation," the United States (Kanstroom, 2012), in European countries, above all the United Kingdom (Gibney, 2004), in Australia (Schuster & Bloch, 2005) and in many other countries. Matthew Gibney coined the term "deportation turn" (2008) to capture "recent government successes in boosting deportation" that "bypass or avoid violating liberal norms" (p. 148). Meanwhile we are said to be living in an "age of deportations" (Boehm, 2016), characterized by a "culture of deportation" highlighting the criminalization of migration and the making of border policy.[19] Deportations are thus

---

18   Extant examples include the work of Nauja Kleist (e.g., 2017) on accounts given by deportees from Libya in Ghana, as well as the on-going research on return and reintegration experiences in the Gambia by Judith Altrogge (cf. Zanker & Altrogge, 2019) and, lately, the work on emergency returns from Libya and Algeria (e.g., Alpes, 2020) as well as by Almamy Sylla and Signe Marie Cold Ravnkilde (2021).

19   Cf. the related internet platform for information and mobilization: http://cultureofdeportation.org/, accessed 31 October 2021.

usually differentiated from other forms of return, most importantly other state-induced ones such as "Assisted Voluntary Returns" (AVRs).

Anderson et al. (2011) assert that deportations have become a constitutive practice reaffirming the normative boundaries of "who is a member and who has the right to judge who belongs" (p. 547) in an international system of independent states. Deportations are thus inherently connected to the development of the modern nation; they manifest its territory and build states' sovereignty (cf. Walters, 2002; De Genova, 2002).[20] Importantly too, deportations often serve a purpose in symbolic politics.[21]

For a long time, however, deportations have been viewed as a phenomenon of the Global North's attitude toward the Global South, reversing supposedly established migratory pathways. This is reflected in contributions by researchers and participants at academic events. Nevertheless, the history of deportations on the African continent dates back to the 1960s, the years in which many states gained their independence, and needs to be seen as a postcolonial legacy with emergent states inheriting the "Western" concept of the modern nation-state (for more on this subject, see Chapter 2). This has barely found a place in academic discussion so far.

In 2006 Nathalie Peutz called for an "anthropology of removal," taking into account the different aspects and phases of deportations. Notwithstanding, expulsions are mainly discussed as stirring internal debates in liberal societies (cf. Lecadet, 2013), while the impact on the social and political life of the countries from which the expelled migrants originate, or through which they pass, has attracted relatively little attention. This underlines the Eurocentric bias in the deportation literature. Academic work has mainly focused on the earlier stages of deportation: on the resistance against it (e.g., Daphi et al., 2017; Nyers, 2015, 2003), the established state practice (e.g., Ellermann, 2013, 2009), or the perils of a deportation experience (e.g., Hasselberg, 2016; Fekete, 2005). Studies of conditions after deportation have increased in number recently and most often follow ethnographic accounts and highlight the micro level of analysis (cf. Khosravi, 2018). It became clear through my own research, in fact, that in-depth ethnography appeared to be the most satisfactory way to grasp the complex social, emotional, moral, and material entanglements and dynamics that accompany deportations. As I shall further explore in my chapter on methodology, it appeared increasingly critical to immerse myself to some degree in social lifeworlds post deportation, including elements of

---

20   The genealogy of deportations goes back to the slave trade (Walters, 2002).

21   The "deportation gap" (Rosenberger & Küffner, 2016) indicates that more persons are supposed to be deported than can actually be removed.

participatory and action research, in order to grasp the gist of what these social dimensions imply.[22] But much more in-depth research is needed.

Stephan Dünnwald (e.g., 2017; 2011) and Clara Lecadet (e.g., 2018, 2011) are those who have done most research on post-deportation situations in Mali so far. They both started with the AME, on and off, accompanying the organization's work over several years, thus playing a major role in researching the political and social space after deportations in Mali between 2008 and 2011, a time marked by a high number of deportations from Europe. They provided an in-depth insight into the self-organization of deportees in Mali; they also roughly developed the social dimension post forced return as well, in some cases in Kayes and Yanfolila, but mostly in Bamako. Lecadet gave a sketch of the overall deportation regime at that time and the massive number of returns of Malians and other Africans in transit at the borders of Mali and in Bamako. Even if my work goes more into the fine-grained social dynamics, above all in rural areas, and the political situation has changed since their time with ever more collective responses to deportation, their work importantly informed this study and will be referenced time and again. The more recent work of Almamy Sylla (2019) more specifically analyzes the reintegration trajectories of Malian repatriates from the Ivory Coast and Libya between 2002 and 2017 in an impressively thorough and comprehensive way. Even though it deals with a specific case, his work and our collaboration have substantially influenced my thinking; it is therefore integrated and referenced accordingly.

Deportability and deportation as a process over time and space

My work focuses on the continuation of deportation as a process long after an actual deportation has taken place, impacting former deportees and their social circle often many years later. Deportation studies have highlighted some of the temporal and spatial effects of deportations in terms of their processual character: deportations may start long before an individual is apprehended, "through the myriad practices that make someone vulnerable in the first place" (Coutin, 2015, p. 674) and render actors "deportable" (De Genova, 2002). Furthermore, the transnational impact of deportation "continues long after an individual is returned, through the difficult process of readjustment, the ripple effects on family members and the continued prohibition on re-entry" (Weber & Powell, 2018, p. 206).

---

22   In anthropology there has been a general debate about the constant ambivalence of proximity: the insights gained through getting close up or "going native," on the one hand, as against the alienation or even menace generated by strangers. This has been clearly changing with the rise of more participatory methods (see Lachenmann, 2010, p. 19 or Breidenstein et al., 2013). For more on this, see the discussion in Chapter 3.

Nicholas De Genova's term "deportability" (2002) has fundamentally shaped the discussion of deportations through drawing attention to the constant potentiality of being deported which eventually shapes a "condition of everyday life of migrant 'illegality' creating fundamental insecurity eventually rendering 'undocumented' migrant labor a distinctly disposable commodity" (De Genova, 2002, p. 438) and thus facilitating migrants' exploitation on the labor market. In this sense, deportations have become a "crucial strategy for contemporary neoliberal capitalism" (Khosravi, 2018, p. 4) and reproduce global social inequalities and injustices (p. 6), differentiated exclusions and inclusions, related to broader processes of "social expulsions and marginalization" (p. 12) before as well as after deportations. A condition of undocumentedness, at least as inscribed in a person's memory and emotions, may continue to have an impact after an actual deportation, as I will develop here.

Consequently, deportations are more than "simple" (Peutz, 2006) or "discrete" (Coutin, 2014, p. 4) events, and deportation is a "process that spans over long periods of time and geographical areas" (Hasselberg, 2018, p. 16). Nyers (2003) identifies a "transnational corridor of expulsion," which evolves between the waiting areas, the detention facilities, and the deportation flights, while Heike Drotbohm and Ines Hasselberg speak of the "deportation corridor" which relates to this space between leaving and arriving as well as all the different actors involved (2015).[23] Others have described deportations as side events (Galvin, 2015; Schuster & Majidi, 2015; Bloch & Schuster, 2005), which mostly relates to the frequency of deportations and a certain everydayness about them, which may allow better strategies of survival and coping. Deportations from North African countries are not necessarily an everyday phenomenon for returnees; still they seem to carry a certain element of "normalcy" in the cases investigated.

Re-emigration is often seen as a consequence of deportation (e.g., Alpes, 2017; Schuster & Majidi, 2013; Dünnwald, 2012), in that the latter creates a space of what could be termed a space of forced mobility. Others have theorized deportation as one point in the migration cycle (Kleist, 2017a; Cassarino, 2016, 2014, 2004).[24] From my research it appears that many deportees effectively try to re-emigrate, while others talk about leaving again, but never do so in the end. Many deportees are

---

23 Deportation is not limited to the encounter between the deported person and the deporting nation-state. Rather it involves a variety of people and institutions, from deportees, their families, and communities to civil servants, border agents, immigration lawyers and judges, prison and immigration detention staff, bureaucrats, civil society organizations, security personnel, activists, and the media (cf. Hasselberg, 2018, p. 16).

24 In this context, a migration cycle refers to the whole process of migration, from emigration, via immigration to another country to return to one's country, considering the relevant circumstances in each of these phases (Cassarino, 2016). See further Chapters 4 and 5.

thus immobilized after deportations, unable to re-emigrate due to migratory constraints, lack of money or the family expecting them to stay. There is a large space of immobility after deportations as well. Talking about a new adventure becomes a constitutive part of their being and of the everyday, as I will show.

So far, research has focused mainly on people encountered shortly after a forced return and on the organizational structures involved, besides being based above all in urban areas. The work of Heike Drotbohm greatly contributes to the study of the social dimensions of, and transnational ruptures caused by, deportations from the United States to Cape Verde, also over the longer term (2016, 2015, 2012, 2011). Likewise, the recent ethnographic studies by Nauja Kleist on Ghana (2017a, b, c), in parts of Sine Plambech's work on Nigerian women (2018, 2017) or by Stefanie Maher on *refoulés* in Senegal (2015) explore the social dimensions of life after deportation in West Africa. But studies of the complex in-depth social dimensions of deportations in urban and as well as in rural areas and set a longer time after deportation in Mali do not exist so far. Above all a perspective on rural contexts after deportation is badly needed, as "deportation is not the end of a 'problem,' but the start of a new and ongoing dilemma for individuals, families, and the wider community" (Pereira, 2011, p. 11). Temporality becomes a central dimension, as well as age. I will show how this links in with immobility and re-emigration after deportations.

Structure and aims of the book

In the following chapters, I intend to tell a particular Malian story of situations after deportation, using as my analytical lens the ambivalence of what I term the supposedly "failed" migratory adventure. By following the narratives and everyday practices of former deportees and their social circles, my book will extend our knowledge of the everyday lives of people in these situations, especially who live in the southern Mali. It focuses on the "space of immobilization" after deportations as well as their long-term impacts. In the Malian context, although deportations create multiple ruptures, they are integrated into patterns both of circular and social mobility and of remaining on the spot. So, in the end, the book is about renegotiation, navigation, and repositioning after deportation.

Chapter 2 provides an overview of the historical, social, economic, political, and cultural context of the selected case to enable the analytical results of the study to be better understood and situated. I will describe the history and setting of migrations in Mali, as well as the role that deportations have played from pre- to postcolonial times ending with the latest developments in EU border externalization measures up to the recent Valletta process. Along with that, I will sketch the particular reactions to deportations by different actors, including former deportees, which make the Malian case specific.

Chapter 3 develops the methodology of the study, describing how the field site was defined and data were generated. A central place is reserved for discussing specific positionalities in order to understand what I was able to research and what I was not, including the how and why. Further, the chapter reflects on the methods I used and the analytical steps I followed, concluding with further thoughts on the specific kind of ethnography necessary for operationalizing my central research question: how deportees deal with having been deported and their situation back "home," even years after being returned.

Chapters 4 to 7 constitute the main analytical part of this study. Chapter 4 empirically sets the reader inside conditions post deportation through deportees' remembering and narrating their deportation experiences after their arrival and later on. It aims to enable an understanding of what these mostly unexpected and violent acts do to former deportees (and potentially to their social circles), revolving around different aspects and accounts of suffering. Using selected cases, I will show the social suffering caused by the process of deportation from North African or European states, plus how deportees experience it on the basis of their own agentic accounts.

Chapter 5 centers on the main narrative of suffering after deportation condensed into the loss of money and the emblematic "empty hands" that follow supposed "failed" migratory adventures. By focusing on the role of money and its social meaning in southern Mali, it reveals the meanings of contributing, reproduction, and the management of social and emotional relations after deportation, based around the concept of shame in light of (unfulfilled) expectations and strategies of silence, talk, and gossip over time.

Chapter 6 focuses on the everyday practices of going on under conditions post deportation, through hard work, courageous engagement on the spot, and, most importantly, (re)interpretations of the suffering one has experienced. All these are strategies to enable one to eventually recover or renegotiate one's masculinity post deportation. On that basis, the last analytical chapter, Chapter 7, centers on the cosmological as well as everyday notion of "*la chance*," (*kunna dija*) which serves as the final means of sense- and future-making in the face of deportation, eventually opening up a potential space for new chances and even new (collective) imaginings. The concluding chapter summarizes the study's central results, also dwelling briefly on two remaining aspects: sociological ambivalence in light of the "failed" migratory adventure and the political dimension and what remains to be done.

Overall, the book provides an exemplary ethnographic view of the deportation regime at work in southern Mali and, by fleshing out this particular Malian example, it builds a basis for further engagement by deportation studies in how this regime can have a profoundly transformative effect on the society at large and what shape that transformation will take.

Chapter 2
Contextualizing and historicizing deportations and situations post-deportation in Mali

To understand and situate situations and conditions post deportation it is indispensable to sketch the specific historical, social, economic, political, and cultural context around mobility, immobility, and deportations in Mali. This chapter provides an overview, first by presenting some basic facts and figures about Mali, then by describing the history and setting of migration, plus the role that deportations play – taking into account aspects of pre- to post-colonialism, the Malian crisis and current situation, and the latest developments in EU border externalization up to the recent Valetta process and the new reality of transit returns. Juxtaposed with this, I sketch out the particular space in which the political and social dimensions of (post) deportation in Mali are contested and handled both from an official state perspective, and, more importantly, from that of civil society actors and former deportees. Finally, I offer a more detailed description of the areas of Kita and Bamako, the sites of my field research, with respect to their political economy of mobility and immobility histories.

Mali, migrations, mobilities, and immobility

Mali is a semi-arid, landlocked country in the Sahel zone with an estimated population of about 21.1 million[1] covering an area of 1,240,192 sq. km. It has a very young population, with a median age of 16.3 years and life expectancy of about 58.9 years, and a high population growth rate (2.97% in 2021 estimated)[2] but with a decreasing fertility rate of 5.9 children per woman in 2021. It is also a low-income

---

1   See online: https://worldpopulationreview.com/countries/mali-population, accessed 31 October 2021.

2   See online: https://www.migrationpolicy.org/country-resource/mali, accessed 31 October 2021.

country with a multidimensional poverty rate of 68.3%.[3] While the political crisis in the north of the country (ongoing since 2012) has had a substantial impact on its economy, Mali's Human Development Index (HDI) of 0.434 has been slightly, but continuously, increasing since democratization in 1990, though with a short period of stagnation during the outbreak of the crisis. Ranked 184th out of 188 countries in total by HDI, it is considered one of the poorest countries in the world. Its economy is chiefly based on agriculture, largely at subsistence level, and mainly in the south of the country, while the dry north is a region of cattle breeding. Mali is rich in resources, above all gold, which creates employment in the service sector, although the income is mainly exported abroad and the population has little benefit from it. Droughts and climate change pose major risks for the country's agriculture sector and food security. Further, the economy is vulnerable to raw material price fluctuations in world trade and exchange rates (World Bank, 2021).[4] Industry is rather weakly developed and even decreased after the overthrow of the first Malian president Modibo Keita (1960–68). Of the overall population above 15 years old, 64.2% are employed while 65.3% of all workers are employed in the agricultural sector. The largest share (90.5%) of the non-agricultural economy is to be found in the informal sector, which has developed since the first Structural Adjustment Programs (SAPs) were set up by the International Monetary Fund and the World Bank in the 1980s (Brand, 2001, p. 43). Youth unemployment (15–24) stands at 24.8% and the proportion of young people who are neither in school nor employed is 34.0%.[5] The average schooling expectancy in Mali is 7.6 years, with a low average literacy of 33.1% (2018). The illiteracy rate is thus almost 67% and is higher among females than males. Mali is an ethnically highly diverse country (CIA, 2020)[6], most of whose inhabitants belong to the regional Mandé family of ethnic groups in Western Africa who speak any of the many related Mandé languages of the region.[7] About 94% of the population is Muslim, about 3% Christian, and 0.7% Animist by belief.

---

3   See online: http://hdr.undp.org/en/countries/profiles/MLI, accessed 31 October 2021.

4   See online: ttps://www.worldbank.org/en/country/mali/overview#1, accessed 31 October 2021.

5   Vulnerable employment constitutes a total of 89.6% of all employment.

6   Ethnicities are distributed as follows: Bambara 33.3%, Fulani (Peuhl) 13.3%, Sarakole/Soninke /Marka 9.8%, Senufo/Manianka 9.6%, Malinke 8.8%, Dogon 8.7%, Sonrai 5.9%, Bobo 2.1%, Tuareg/Bella 1.7%, other Malian 6%, from members of Economic Community of West Africa 4%, other 3% (2018 est.). See online: https://www.migrationpolicy.org/country-resource/mali, accessed 31 October 2021.

7   Besides Mali, various Mandé groups are found in Benin, Burkina Faso, Côte d'Ivoire, Gambia, Ghana, Guinea, Guinea-Bissau, Liberia, Mauritania, Niger, Nigeria, Senegal, and Sierra Leone.

Histories of migration, mobility, and immobility

Migration in Mali has grown (historically) and been characterized by circular migration cultures, nomadism, and ritual journeys (Hahn & Klute, 2007; cf. Massey et al., 1993), together with the migratory adventures and emerging, dynamic transnational spaces of today (Manchuelle, 1997). The high mobility of the population (cf., e.g., Hahn, 2004) is thus embedded in a large number of circular migratory patterns within the region and far beyond. According to Mirjam de Bruijn et al. (2001):

> These mobilities encompass all types of movement including travel, explorations, migration, tourism, refugeeism, pastoralism, nomadism, pilgrimage and trade. In these forms, mobility is essential to many people and is even a means of survival for some. It is culturally and socially embedded in society and in each individual's actions. Being mobile, or living in a culture where many people are mobile, is a fact of life and with it goes an enormous cultural, social and economic flexibility.

Reasons for migration are many and complex; migration, as repeatedly shown by research, is to be seen as a process (Faist et al., 2021; Stock, 2019, Carling & Schewel, 2017; Castles, 2010; Carling, 2002).[8] While in most Malian social groups male-dominated migration formerly meant pilgrimage into the wilderness, during French colonization "migration for prestige dominated, where cultural values prioritized imported items like umbrellas, cloth, perfume." This was followed by "survival migrations" after two major droughts (1973 and 1984) when people had to leave in order to earn their living abroad; first within the subregion, largely to urban areas, later to Europe (Dougnon, 2013, p. 37). Children, particularly boys, are trained from early on, first of all through (often internal) labor migration (Dougnon, 2012, p. 144). Many young boys in Mali grow up with the desire and expectation of leaving home, both to study and also, potentially, to support their family (Hertrich & Lesclingand, 2013, p. 181). Today's migrants, still mostly men, are driven by the desire to go "on an adventure" (Bredeloup, 2008), catalyzed by a lack of prospects at home and the search for a better life (Jónsson, 2007). Although female labor migration can also be a path to adulthood, it is rather seen as a personal project involving strong expectations of learning and obtaining life skills (Hertrich & Lesclingand, 2017, 2013). A negative social judgment, which used to attach to solitary adolescent female migration, seems to be weakening in places where "girls take the lead"; moreover there

---

8   As Carling and Schewel (2017) explain, it is well-nigh impossible to say what drives a migratory decision or aspiration to leave: it might be individual desires or particular constraints, while an expressed preference for staying may even be an adaptive psychological mode or a proactive acceptance (p. 14). In any case social and cultural approaches to migration should not neglect the structural factors which lead to widespread forced migration, (im)mobilities and expulsions (Khosravi, 2018; Sassen, 2016; Hammar et al., 1997).

seem to be new lines of solidarity emerging between female generations (ibid.). Their urban experience may entail a new scale of worldliness and consumption against the experiences and values brought by male labor migration (Hertrich & Lesclingand, 2017, pp. 81ff). On an international scale, women mainly follow the paths taken by their husbands (Konaté, 2012). However, there are reported cases of single female adventurers as well (see further Chapter 6).

Two patterns of Malian migration were central under French colonialism. With the regional establishment of the colonial regime in the second half of the 19th century (cf., e.g., Amselle, 1987), *navetanes* were often forced, regular and seasonal, circular and above all rural-to-rural migrants who went to large-scale sites of peanut production in the Senegambia; *tirailleurs*, on the other hand, were French military personnel recruited during the two world wars to serve in the fight against Germany – "cannon fodder," as one prominent postcolonial critique put it (Lecadet, 2016; Mann, 2003). The *navetanes* became an established migratory form over all of southern Mali and beyond during the 20th century, building the basis for other types of mobility and labor migrations (cf. Dougnon, 2012; Koenig, 2005a; Amselle, 1978). In this sense, colonial (coercive) labor migration policies built on existing, comparatively large-scale migration for employment in all British and French colonies of West and Central Africa, rather than initiating it. The emblematic expression of "returning empty-handed" dates back to those seasonally or circularly migrating *navetanes*, expressing their fear of returning *"avec les mains vides"* (with empty hands) and without success to their communities (Gary-Tounkara, 2008, p. 87), not fulfilling the expectations they had raised. Back then already some extended their stays until they had earned enough, while others never returned (cf. Pollet & Winter, 1976, p. 138).

After World War I, self-initiated migrations by young men and the practice by families of sending off of a son to supplement the household income from elsewhere in the region increased, though it was soon criticized by the colonists bemoaning a shortage of labor in some places. From the 1930s on migrations became more urban and of longer duration (cf. Koenig, 2005a; Clark, 1999). Some people settled in other countries and, for example, became major actors in the diamond and the business sector in Congo Kinshasa, Congo Brazzaville, Cameroon, and Angola, subsequently setting up bases to build up real recruitment networks for new migrants.

The dominant intraregional mobility pattern in West Africa was, and still is, a North–South movement from the landlocked Sahelian countries of Niger, Burkina Faso, and Mali to the more prosperous agricultural or urbanized zones in the southern or coastal states (Côte d'Ivoire, Liberia, Ghana, Nigeria), or to Senegal and the Gambia in the West. After independence in the 1960s, economic development, infrastructure works, a growing transportation network and an increasing demand for labor – likewise for cash – influenced the labor migration to rural and more importantly urban areas, often along the coast (van der Land, 2015, pp. 64f; cf. Konate & Gonin, 2016; Hummel et al., 2012; Bakewell & de Haas, 2007; Hahn, 2004).

By the beginning of the 1970s, the Congos, and Cameroon had become hubs of Malian immigration in light of economic constraints caused by cyclical droughts (1973–1984) and the repressive political regime under Moussa Traoré (1968–1991) that forced many people to leave seeking alternative possibilities of earning an income and greater freedom. Together with large numbers of migrants from the Sahel and other West African countries, Malians became extensively engaged in Côte d'Ivoire in the trade in kola nuts thus linking the Malian savanna to the Ivorian (rain) forest (Lovejoy, 1980, p. 125). With economic and political crises in several West African countries (Ghana: 1966; Senegal: mid-1970s; Nigeria: 1973), during the 1980s and early 1990s Côte d'Ivoire became the main migration hub in the region and has remained one of the countries hosting the largest share of Malian immigrants ever since.

It is important to mention at this point the Soninké, an ethnicity originating from the upper Senegal river and living mainly from the production of grains, who developed an "entrepreneurial spirit" (Meadows, 1999, p. 209) in their (economic) way of life in precolonial times. As a result of extensive archive visits,[9] François Manchuelle (1997) gathered evidence to show how their labor migration had roots in old patterns of trans-Saharan trade with Western Sudan established at least since the thirteenth century. It was the gradual disappearance of the locally rooted slave trade in Senegambia, which sparked off a system of seasonal migration or outmigration to complement and enable their agricultural production (Manchuelle, 1989). Abundant literature exists investigating their "traditional" migratory networks and the dynamic transnational spaces encompassing not only the subregion but also other African countries as well as the Global North (e.g., Lima, 2015; Cisse & Daum, 2009; Rodet, 2009; Quiminal, 2002; Manchuelle, 1997, 1989; Chastanet, 1992; Pollet & Winter, 1971). Since the 1950s, 85% of all Black African migrants to France have originated from the Soninké ethnic group (Meadows, 1999, p. 208). In Mali today, the majority of Soninké still live in the administrative region of Kayes, of which the circle of Kita is part, the area in which a large part of the research for this present book took place (see the penultimate subsection of this chapter). Even in the present day the Soninké serve as an almost mythical model for other migratory groups and individuals in Mali and beyond.

From the administrative and political point of view as well, migration increasingly became a central theme in Mali and within the region. While the first Malian president, Modibo Keita, followed an external policy of African Unity, opening the

---

9   Even if he has been criticized on the grounds that his "use of evidence is both impressive and problematic" (cf. Meadows, 1999, p. 208).

borders to other incoming nationals, his policy for his own population was one of "back to the land" (cf. Gary-Tounkara, 2008, see further Chapter 6), aiming to restrict its mobility. Under the following president, Moussa Traoré, migration was reevaluated and integrated into the national policy and identity, making migrations agents of "national reconstruction" (cf. Lecadet, 2016). In the 1980s, Malian ambassadors and consulates started to organize a category of Malians abroad (*Maliens de l'extérieur*) – about a decade earlier than other migrant origin states – defining conditions not only for Malians who wanted to return, but also for those who remained abroad with respect to integrating them into the "nation," most importantly through consular identity cards that granted a number of rights. In 1982 the fifth conference of Malian ambassadors was held in Bamako, partly on the question of the conditions of stay for Malians abroad but also in order to think about measures for those wanting to return (ibid., pp. 175f). In the face of increasing deportations, however, post-return measures such as training for reintegration or the allocation of land proved insufficient. Some development projects by Malians abroad for their home communities went "beyond mere satisfaction of domestic needs" (Keita, 2013, p. 217) by contributing to community infrastructures. In 1991, after the transition to democracy, the High Council for Malians Abroad was created to show appreciation and support for the economic and political implications of this migration, its settings, and to institutionalize development associations (Gary Tounkara, 2013, p. 48). These efforts were also supported by France, although at the same time they became increasingly subject to restrictive measures.[10] Since then, Malians abroad have represented an essential economic and political complement to Malian realities and engaged in the mobilization against deportations as well.[11]

In 1975, the long history and practices of mobility, seasonal migration, and nomadism in the Sahel region were institutionalized in the Economic Community of West African States (ECOWAS), an area of free mobility and circulation of cross-border ethnic groups (Camara et al., 2011). The liberal immigration policies in this context supported regional migration (cf. van der Land, 2015). With the worsening of political and economic situations and insecurities in the 1980s, as well as the civil wars in Sierra Leone (1991–2001), Liberia (1989–1996 and 1999–2003), Guinea (1999–2000), and Côte d'Ivoire (2002–2007 and 2010–2011), new destinations, such as Gabon, Libya, Botswana, South Africa, other Maghreb states and

---

10   In the early 1990s, France developed a scheme to assist development efforts by Malian (and other) migrants and migrant associations that has been known as *codéveloppement* since 2002. Gradually this assistance became linked to two procedures: stopping migrants from leaving and giving incentives to irregular migrants to return home. An office of the French OFFI (*Office français de l'immigration et de l'integration*), was established in Bamako, assisting returning migrants and their projects. This program is said to have never worked well or had the intended effects on a broader scale (Dünnwald, 2017, p. 90; Daum, 2005).

11   See further subchapter "Reactions to deportations and returns in Mali".

increasingly European countries, became more and more attractive (ibid.). Since the 1990s migrations from everywhere in Mali have been directed to the Maghreb and Europe in particular. Furthermore, this has been fueled by economic cuts experienced through the SAPs, the devaluation of agricultural products, and the increasing globalization of technology (Bruijn et al., 2001). But the conflict and civil war in Libya in 2011, the Malian crisis, the recent refugee crisis and the Valetta process[12] that followed have again changed migration patterns.

Today, Mali is considered to be a country of emigration, transit, and immigration. Three to four million Malians are said to live abroad (about one-quarter to one-third of the population), most of them in West and Central African countries – which makes them a substantial share of the population of their respective host countries (about 70% within West Africa alone; Ballo, 2009). Statistics from the Malian department responsible for migration issues reveal that 5,474,048 Malians were living in African countries other than Mali itself in 2015, which represents 96.68% of all Malians abroad (DGME, 2015).[13] Immigrants to Mali originate mainly from other West African countries too, principally from neighboring Guinea Conakry, Côte d'Ivoire, Burkina Faso, and Senegal; many transit migrants pass through or stay temporarily on their way to Europe, and many of them are from Central African countries (field notes).[14] Mali's net migration rate (2015–2020) is -2.1 migrants/1,000 population.[15] Remittance inflows constituted 5.9% of gross domestic product in 2019 and totaled about US$ 1,022 billion.[16] Even so, most mobility takes place within the country and the region. The urban population today is thought to be 43.1% of the total population (2019), with a 4.86% annual rate of change (2015–20 est.; CIA, 2020). According to the UNHCR report September 2021, however, 401,736 persons were still displaced internally due to the conflict that has been going on in the north of Mali since 2012; 606,617 have returned. In addition,

---

12   The Valetta process was a direct follow-up to the European "refugee crisis." Inaugurated by the EU and international organizations, it aimed to develop strategies for managing migration with African countries. Since then migration has become an ever more restricted issue, and deportations, above all in the form of transit and emergency returns, have risen substantially, see the section "Recent deportation regimes and reactions"(pp. 64ff).

13   It needs to be added that these data may not include irregular migrants without papers, so the number of Malian migrants, particularly in European countries is most likely higher.

14   See online: https://mali.iom.int/fr/rapports, accessed 31 October 2021.

15   See online: https://mali.iom.int/en/facts-and-figures, accessed 31 October 2021. Nevertheless, numbers differ and the migration policy institute puts the net migration rate at-3.17, estimated for 2021, based on the CIA World Factbook: https://www.migrationpolicy.org /country-resource/mali, accessed 31 October 2021.

16   See online: https://www.knomad.org/data/remittances?page=15, accessed 31 October 2021.

140,098 fled to the neighboring states of Burkina Faso, Mauritania, and Niger and of these 82,507 have returned.[17]

Overall, only a relatively small percentage of West Africans migrate to European countries (about 25%), and some go on to North America and increasingly to Asia (SVR, 2020; MIF, 2019). The number of migrants entering Europe is thus very small. With increasing migratory restrictions, migration towards the North has become largely irregularized; in many cases migrants are suspected of travelling to Europe long before they ever reach European shores (see, e.g., Karakayali & Rigo, 2010). More than half of the sub-Saharan Africans apprehended at the external European borders in 2014 came from West and Central Africa (Carling, 2016). Moreover, 73,000 West and Central Africans applied for asylum in Europe in the same year. Malians constituted the largest number of people crossing borders undocumented[18] (9,789, ibid.) and accounted for more than 10,000 asylum applicants between 2008 and 2014, the highest number, with Nigeria and Gambia, and after Gambia the largest number relative to the overall population (Carling, 2016, p. 32f; see also Dembele, 2010). This was also represented in the Mediterranean shipwrecks, which increased in number in 2014 and 2015 and eventually set off the "refugee crisis."[19] Among the 800 people lost at sea on April 19, 2015, were 184 Malians. However, refugees from Eritrea, Ethiopia and Somalia have altered the composition of the migrant population crossing the Mediterranean in recent years.

As mentioned in the introductory chapter, West African and Malian migration and deportations can only be thought of in relational terms. Socially, culturally, and historically engrained, migration and mobility constitute a substantial part of family livelihoods for some groups, as well as an option to leave uncertainty behind and to seek more generally for opportunities (Kleist, 2017b; Gaibazzi, 2015a, Hahn & Klute, 2007, Bruijn et al., 2001). Thus, seasonal and circular migration and moving with cattle still constitute (coping) strategies for rural households to diversify and secure income in Mali and a strategy for (flexible) adaptation to environmental and climatic conditions as well (van der Land, 2015, p. 59; Hummel et al., 2012; Bruijn et al., 2001). In this sense, migration and mobility have been shaping the country

---

17   See online: https://data2.unhcr.org/en/country/mli, accessed 31 October 2021.

18   Many migrants do not reveal their nationality or do not carry any documents with them.

19   Deaths of migrants have been recorded since 1993, with the loss of 34,500 lives up to 2017 (Dubuis, 2017). The post-Gaddafi period was one of the deadliest with 13,545 lost at sea alone (see IOM, "Missing Migrants" project). The figures for shipwrecks in the Mediterranean are often vague, thus simply indicating the actual number of fatalities. The blog "Fortress Europe" offers an unofficial estimate of the number of missing persons lost in the Mediterranean since 1988.

as motors for social change and vice-versa (cf. Castles, 2010).[20] It is due to their economic significance, that migrants are constructed as "local builders" (Soukouna, 2016), "adventurers" (Bredeloup, 2008), and eventually "martyrs" in the context of recent shipwrecks (cf. also Sylla & Schultz, 2020). At the same time, migratory and mobility constraints, and particularly deportations, have been shaping people's lifeworlds in essential ways, as this study will show.

Histories of African deportations

Most Malian migrations took and take place within the African continent; the same holds for Malian deportations. Since the first days of Mali's independence and even before, its people have faced deportation from other African states, European states, the US in part, and again and again on a massive scale from Saudi Arabia (Lecadet, 2011, p. 118; cf. also Boyer, 2017). Conversely, Mali itself has never officially implemented large-scale deportations until today (Sylla & Schultz, 2019), even if it started to engage in transit returns of other African nationals to their countries of origin under the aegis of the International Organization for Migration (IOM) in recent years (Alpes, 2020).[21] At the same time, Malian society has shown a tremendous capacity to reintegrate its citizens.

Deportation has become an instrument that has enabled African states to express and confirm their national sovereignty since independence. It is thus a constitutive part of all new African postcolonial nation-states (Sylla & Schultz, 2019), insofar as it decides who belongs to a particular state and who does not (cf. Anderson et al., 2013). This has to be seen within the context of a new demarcation of national boundaries, the emergence of independent nation-states and the setting up of regulations governing immigration, as well as, initially, the different employment opportunities offered by different countries and, later, the general economic recession (Adepoju, 1984, p. 427).[22] In total, the period 1960–2000 accounts for 44 events of expulsion in Africa, with about half of all sub-Saharan African countries expelling their immigrants en masse at least once (Adida, 2010, p. 86).

---

20   The link between social change, transformation, and migratory behavior should not be neglected: "the whole notion of mobility as presented here turns the supposedly rupturing effect of travelling on its head: through travelling, connections are established, continuity experienced and modernity negotiated" (Bruijn et al., 2001, p. 2).

21   Moreover, since 2018, single cases of international staff have been expelled from or asked to leave the country due to critical political statements, cf. e.g., https://www.jeuneafrique.com/868300/politique/mali-expulsion-du-francais-christophe-sivillon-chef-du-bureau-de-la-minusma-a-kidal, accessed 31 October 2021.

22   In countries like Congo Zaire, Côte d'Ivoire and Uganda deportations of non-nationals were common practice (Adida, 2010, pp. 86f).

Importantly, during the colonial period, the French empire, after annexing the territories of French Sudan, was already deporting resisting community leaders to other territories under its rule.[23] Unlike deportations in the post-colonial period these deportations were targeted at political figures who opposed colonial practices, not at migrants, and they were carried out within the borders of the same colonial empire – in this case the French – with a view to containing or transporting rebellious initiatives against the established order.

The first Malians were expelled from neighboring Senegal (which, together with Mali, constituted the French colonial territory "*Fédération du Mali*" from 1958 to 1960; cf. Rodet & County, 2018), and from the former Belgian Congo in 1964[24]; other countries took up this practice: Ghana in 1969, Nigeria in 1983, Angola in 1996, Libya from 1990 to 2000, Equatorial Guinea starting from the 2000s, and not least Gabon, which carried out deportations of several hundred in 2015 (Daou, 2016; field notes).[25] From the mid-1980s on, these expulsions increasingly took place in the context of economic crises and were legitimized for xenophobic and domestic political reasons as well as to assert the foreign policies of the states involved. Ghana and Nigeria can serve as examples of countries that, in time, introduced anti-migration policies against so-called 'illegal migrant workers' or 'aliens.' Particularly notable were the deportation of 500,000 "aliens," among them Malians, from Ghana in 1969 (most of those affected were Nigerians, cf. Adepoju, 1984, p. 430) and the expulsion of more than two million "illegal" immigrants from Nigerian territory within a few weeks in January 1983 (Gary-Tounkara, 2015).[26] Since Malians for the most part did not possess any papers, they could hardly be detected and even less deported. With the economic crisis in the 1980s the Ivorian economy too faced a severe recession, which led to the hardening of the conditions of residency. In the wake of the conflict of 2002, the concept of *ivoirité*[27] was particularly propagated and more than 200,000 Malians were repatriated as a consequence of

---

23   This was the case of Samory Touré who was deported to present-day Gabon, Cheick Hamala Hamahoulah deported to France (Hamès, 1997), and the Canton chief Siaka Traore of Sirakélé (present-day circle of Koutiala) also deported to France.

24   By a Decree-Law of 19 August 1964, Congolese authorities forced thousands of West Africans, who had become fundamental part of the diamond sector, to leave.

25   See online: https://maliactu.net/mali-immigration-illegale-le-mali-accueille-ses-129-rapatries -du-gabon/, accessed 31 October 2021.

26   At the peak of the wave 1.5 million people were deported, including 700,000 Ghanaians, 180,000 Nigerians, 150,000 Chadians, 120,000 Cameroonians, 5,000 Togolese and 5,000 Beninese from Nigeria (Gary-Tounkara, 2015, p. 30).

27   Since the mid-1990s, *ivoirité* has been aimed at the comprehensive political and material exclusion of a large part of the population living in Côte d'Ivoire, disenfranchising them on the basis of their national, linguistic and religious affiliations. This exclusion policy has since been pursued by various governments.

armed rebellions (Sylla, 2019; Calenda, 2014a; Outarra, 2010; DGME's databases). These policies clearly contradicted the often-propagated notion of West African integrity, institutionalized through the ECOWAS and UEMOA (*Union Economique et Monétaire Ouest Africaine*).

Despite the high numbers involved in the West African case, deportations from European countries, particularly from France, carry a specific symbolic value, that weighs far more even if the numbers involved are far smaller (for more on this topic see Chapter 4). The first "European" deportations of Malian nationals took place from France in the 1980s, to be followed by deportations from Spain in the 1990s. Since 1945 the French National Office of Immigration (ONI) had been recruiting mostly unskilled migrant workers as a "cheaper workforce" for the country's reconstruction after World War II, not least as a kind of "dividend" for the French colonies' participation in the war. But following the economic crisis of 1973 undeclared foreign workers in France were no longer able to obtain residence permits, and a selective regularization procedure was introduced (Siméant, 1998, p. 27). The official labor immigration of Africans into France stopped in 1974. Increasing deportations were one of the consequences. In 1986, 101 "undocumented" Malian immigrants were deported from France on a charter flight, causing serious disturbance among the population in Mali as well as in France (cf. Lecadet, 2011). In summer 1996 almost 300 undocumented migrants, mainly from Senegal and Mali and many of them minors, took refuge in the Church of St. Bernard in Paris. The situations of some of whom were not even irregular (Siméant, 1998; Lecadet, 2011). The brutal clearing of the church and subsequent deportations (Garot, 2016) gave birth to a strong international movement against the "inhumane conditions of expulsions and deportations." The figure of the *tirailleur* was reactivated in this *sans-papiers* movement that cumulated in the protest at St. Bernard's church. The deportees were constructed as a direct colonial continuity, recalling the war debt owed by the West to its former colonies (Lecadet, 2016, p. 174f.).

The case of Libya and progressive EU externalization

Libya has been the country most prominently involved in deportations of Malians on the African continent. When it nationalized its oil companies in the 1970s, the country urgently needed workers. The recruitment of Malians began under an agreement signed in 1980 (The Employment Convention of 12 December 1980 between Mali and Libya), making Libya an ever more attractive destination in light of the economic slowdown in West and Central African countries (Sylla, 2019).[28]

---

28 These Malians originated mainly from the Sahelian and Saharan regions with cultural affinities with Libya, such as the Tuareg.

Some migrants saw the country as an "easy" means of entry to the European continent, as became particularly evident with the strengthening of EU border controls from the 2000s. Under these circumstances, Libya increasingly began to act as an outpost of EU migratory control executing forced returns at its land borders and imprisoning migrants suspected of intending to continue on to Europe. On the basis of agreements between Libya and EU member countries, principally Italy, in the context of FRONTEX (*frontières extérieures*) operations, about 2,670 Malians were deported between 2002 and 2008 (Ballo, 2009, p. 120). In Mali, the Libyan position was perceived ambiguously. While Libya had otherwise been acting as a strong promoter of the African Union, it now was criticized for its discriminatory treatment of its "African brothers."

Libya had, in fact, been using expulsions of migrant workers as political and diplomatic instruments in its relations with other African states (Sylla, 2019) since 1985. Some 80,000 Tunisian and Egyptian migrant workers and about 7,000 Malian migrants were expelled between 1985 and 1987 (Bensaâd, 2012, p. 88; Jamana, 1987). Although these expulsions were intended to destabilize African countries with a differing political outlook, they were less discussed and mediatized than those of the 2000s. Most significantly, the earlier deportations were not carried out with the support of external, non-African international actors (most importantly the EU), which made a great symbolic difference.

In 2006 FRONTEX, the European Border and Coast Guard Agency, began one of its first operations, stopping and "pushing back" small vessels departing from the Senegalese or Mauritanian coasts for the Canary Islands (Dünnwald, 2012).[29] The Cotonou Agreement with the African, Caribbean, and Pacific Group of States (ACP countries; 2000) had systematically introduced the issue of migration (including return) into cooperation between, among others, the EU and African states. Moreover, the Rabat Process, implementing the new Global Approach on Migration (GAM, 2005)[30] and constituting the framework for the EU's cooperation with third countries in the area of migration and asylum, had a clearly restrictive agenda, even though it included a link between migration and development. Since the early

---

29   The Council Regulation (EC) 2007/2004 of 26 October 2004 led to the establishment of the European Agency for the Management of Operational Cooperation at the External Borders of the Member States of the European Union (Frontex), a regulation, which has been amended since, most recently in 2019. The agency's mission is to promote, coordinate and develop European border management in line with the EU charter of fundamental rights and the concept of Integrated Border Management. See online: https://frontex.europa.eu/about-fron tex/who-we-are/origin-tasks/, accessed 31 October 2021.

30   After the revision of the GAM in 2011, the European Commission issued the Global Approach for Migration and Mobility (GAMM) with a further emphasis on strengthening the external dimension of EU migration policy. See online: https://ec.europa.eu/home-affairs/orphan-pag es/glossary/global-approach-migration-and-mobility-gamm_en, accessed 31 October 2021.

2000s, return policies have become an integral part of the policy instruments of the EU and its member states for combating unauthorized migration (European Commission, 2005, p. 2). Return has likewise been defined as "the process of going back to one's country of origin, transit or another third country" (European Council, 2002, p. 29). Migrants' conditions post-return or post-deportation were not taken into account. During this normalization process, "mixing return with expulsion or readmission has become commonsensical" (Cassarino, 2016, p. 219). In the course of it, migrants have been increasingly dispossessed of their rights and aspirations (Cassarino, 2004). Moreover, a previously discussed paradigm of return migration linked to development has been neglected. But with the recent Valetta process and the increasing incidence of "assisted voluntary returns," above all in the form of transit and emergency returns from North African countries (Alpes, 2020; Zanker & Altrogge, 2019), this has been changing – as I will shortly show.

In view of the growth in north-bound mobility from the late 1990s, the political instruments described above have been used to transform parts of North and West Africa into transit zones en route to EU territory. Libya, Morocco, Tunisia, Algeria, Mauritania, and Senegal were enlisted to prevent unwanted irregular migrants from reaching Europe, and eventually to return them (Gary-Tounkara, 2015; Bredeloup, 1995). Consequently, a large number of deported Malians returned from the countries bordering the Mediterranean. Malian migration statistics estimate that 91.8% of the Malians expelled between 2002 and 2012 were removed from other African countries, while deportations from Europe represented no more than 6.6% of all deportations during the same period (MMEIA, 2014, p. 55). This possibly reflects "the strong vulnerability of Malian migrants to regime instability in the region" (Calenda, 2012, p. 12). The following table shows the continuation of this pattern:

TABLEAU SYNOPTIQUE DE RECONDUITE DES MALIENS DE L'EXTERIEUR PAR PAYS AFRICAINS DE 2002 A MARS 2014

Année	Total	Afrique du Sud	Guinée Konakry	Rwanda	RD Congo	Congo Brazza	Tunisie	Centrafrique	Zambie	Gabon	Kenya	Mauritanie	Côte d'Ivoire	Guinée Equatoriale	Algérie	Mosambique	Angola	Maroc	Libye
2014	1 807	0	0	0	0	0	0	1 797	0	8	0	0	0	0	0	2	0	0	0
2013	297	1	0	0	0	24	0	0	0	9	0	0	0	0	0	0	8	0	255
2012	744	0	26	2	19	0	0	0	0	9	8	120	0	45	0	2	86	1	426
2011	33 164	1	0	0	0	20	831	0	0	9	5	0	1 881	0	7 346	1	19	9	23 042
2010	598	1	0	0	0	11	2	0	0	20	1	0	0	14	351	0	2	4	192
2009	848	0	0	0	0	0	2	0	0	2	2	0	0	0	559	18	28	9	228
2008	881	0	0	0	0	0	0	0	0	73	3	2	0	0	0	127	12	0	664
2007	1 047	0	0	0	0	0	0	0	0	0	2	0	0	7	0	3	19	152	864
2006	133	0	0	0	0	0	0	0	0	0	0	76	0	0	0	0	0	8	49
2005	2 335	0	0	0	0	0	0	0	1	0	2	0	0	0	276	0	78	1 289	689
2004	18 956	0	0	0	0	0	0	0	1	4	2	11	17 561	152	410	0	501	6	308
2003	22 732	0	0	0	0	0	0	0	1	4	0	0	22 676	0	0	0	22	0	29
2002	67	0	0	0	0	0	0	0	0	0	0	0	0	0	0	0	0	0	67
Total	83 609	3	26	2	19	55	835	1 797	3	138	25	209	42 118	218	8 942	153	775	1 478	26 813

Table 1 (see p. 54) presents an overview of forced returns of Malians abroad from African countries from 2002 to March 2014. (Source: DGME/MMEIA; taken from PONAM [2014])

As the table shows, the repatriations and forced returns in the context of the crises in Côte d'Ivoire (2002-2004) and in Libya (2011) stand out dramatically, even if numbers are to be taken with caution and to be seen rather as indicators than as strictly accurate. Simultaneously, the EU policies of externalizing migration and border controls gave rise to a further phenomenon whereby many of the candidates for emigration to Europe were kept in a situation of "forced" or "involuntary immobility" (Jónsson, 2007), either in their respective transit zones, or back in their Malian villages after deportation, or before they even left.

Under the authoritarian Libyan regime of Muammar Gaddafi from 1990 to October 2011, practices such as imprisonment, extortion of property, the use of migrants in militias, and expulsions became an everyday phenomenon. But the collapse of the regime in 2011, ongoing war and partly anarchic conditions, brought the numbers of involuntary and forced returns to an unprecedented peak (see Table 1). While local human rights organizations and journalists have been documenting abuses for years, it is only recently that international organizations and Western media have revealed the ever more brutal practices of human trafficking on migratory routes and torture (cf. Schultz, 2018). It was CNN broadcasts of images of Libyan "slave markets" during the summit of the African and the European Unions (AU–EU) in Abidjan in November 2017 that sparked off a bulk push of so-called "Voluntary Humanitarian Returns"[31], though these were not necessarily perceived as voluntary (cf. Alpes, 2020). Simultaneously, these detention centers provided an important financial windfall for brokers and heads of networks facilitating irregular migration. With the 2019 bombing of a detention camp that killed 60 jailed migrants (Macé, 2019), the centers more and more became symbols of a protracted conflict.

Reactions to deportations and returns in Mali

In contrast to the deportation practices that characterize other African states, Mali has directed its diplomacy towards the realization of an ideal of African unity and citizenship since its independence and, until the transit returns of today, has never carried out large-scale returns itself, and has devised its own methods of managing incoming deportees. Its cautious attitude towards deportations results in part from its dedication to Pan-Africanism and African socialism, but there is a fear too that the communities of Malians living abroad would suffer the countereffects

---

31   See online: https://www.iom.int/news/voluntary-humanitarian-returns-libya-continue-reinte
gration-efforts-step, accessed 31 October 2021.

of deportations, as would the Malian economy (cf. Sylla & Schultz, 2019). Last but not least, the history of the policy of hospitality towards strangers implemented in Mali for centuries has had, and still has, a considerable impact (Lecadet, 2016, p. 178). At the beginning of the 1970s, for instance, a group of Malians living in the former Belgian Congo was forcefully returned, and the then president Moussa Traoré offered them the choice of a place to settle. They elected to stay in Badinko, a village about 150 km southwest of Bamako located on the railway line to Dakar, with fertile lands. Since then, the small train station has changed significantly due to the settlements that followed and the investments and remittances sent by the population abroad, the descendants of the former migrants. Today, the modern city clearly differs from other surrounding villages (field notes, 11-3-2015).

Possibly, this example was inspired by the model of integration of migrants from Paris, who returned in the 1970s, though "voluntarily," to set up agricultural projects supported by the French government in light of sudden migratory restrictions.[32] This included grants for business start-ups as well as training in the management of agricultural cooperatives and agricultural innovations (see Nouvel Observateur, 1983; cf. Sow, 1987). While these reintegration processes were carried out on the basis of the monopolistic perspective typical of the French and the Malian (welfare) states, those undertaken in democratic and liberal Mali after 1990 adopted the perspective of the civil society actors who were replacing the state in the domain of social assistance. The voluntary or rather "constrained returns" from France (Quiminal, 2002) that were increasing during the 70s were more and more supported by the migrant development associations that started to emerge at that time. Since then, returning pensioners have become an ever larger phenomenon; officially they receive support from the French state, but this, however, is only partially realized (ibid.).

A clear differentiation was and is made between so called "high-skilled" and "low-skilled" migrants: while the high-skilled, who may have migrated legally, are regarded as contributing to the development efforts of the state and are dubbed, or raised to the rank of, "local builders" (Soukouna, 2016), low-skilled migrants are more often perceived as receivers of public goods (cf. Zanker & Altrogge, 2019). Highly educated Malian emigrants living in Europe, North America, and Japan, for instance, are encouraged by the Malian State to come to teach in public universities

---

32   Similar initiatives were undertaken by the French government to encourage first- and the second-generation emigrants to return to their "fatherland" during the economic crisis in the mid-1970s as a complement to the new restrictive migratory measures.

as part of an inter-university exchange program called *"Programme Tokten"*[33]. Contrariwise, deportees who are mostly "low-skilled" can potentially end up in severe social, economic, and institutional conditions after their return. Trajectories after deportations are thus deeply impacted by the policies and practices of the state that deports as well as the one that receives.

Meanwhile, the (re)integration of former deportees into society is above all a task for different civil society associations in Mali, though new initiatives by the state, the EU, and above international organizations such as the IOM, have been introduced lately, in the context of the Valetta process, that again engage the state. The AME (*Association Malienne des Expulsés* – see Chapter 1) was founded in 1996 as a consequence of the *sans-papiers* movement at St. Bernard's Church in Paris and 10 years after the "Charter 101" of the first large deportation from France – a connection which was constructed by the AME as a direct continuity and legacy (cf. Lecadet, 2016, p. 180). In addition to dealing with humanitarian assistance to the small but increasing numbers of returnees from Angola, Gabon, and Mozambique, as well as from Asian and American countries, it protested against the treatment suffered by Malian migrants abroad during the process of expulsion and on their return and reception in Mali. From the start, the AME's activities were thus politicized – pioneering interventions in the management of post deportation and the integration of deportees (Sylla & Schultz, 2019; Dünnwald, 2017; Lecadet, 2016, 2013, 2011; Gary-Tounkara, 2013). For instance, before, deported Malian migrants were imprisoned upon their return and accused of "illegal migration" by the Malian public authorities.[34] The protests, organized by the AME and other associations, are said to eventually have led to the abolition of this practice. While the contemporaneous context of democratization in Mali provided the political base for civil society organizations to intervene increasingly in social and economic domains, it favored a soft disengagement of the State (cf. Kasfir, 1998; Ceesay, 1998). In addition to the growing co-development activities of migrants' associations abroad, which will be further discussed elsewhere (Keita, 2013), these associations have played, and continue to play, an important role in mobilizing against deportations as well.

---

33   TOKTEN (Transfer of Knowledge through Expatriate Nationals) is a program that was established in 1977 by the United Nations Development Program in Turkey and operates in dozens of countries. It was launched in Mali in 1998; see online: https://www.globalgiving.org/projects/improve-education-in-mali/, accessed 31 October 2021.

34   This state practice of imprisoning expelled and deported migrants was also a legacy of the socialist regime in Mali which aimed to retain *"bras valides"* (capable hands) in Mali to bolster socio-economic development there (cf. Lecadet, 2016). After its creation, the AME's pioneering act was a support march in Bamako in 1997 to demand the release of 77 Malians expelled from France by the "36th charter Debré" and imprisoned by the Malian government (Lecadet, 2011, p. 120). Cf. http://www.expulsesmaliens.info/Historique.html, accessed 31 October 2021.

Furthermore, the expulsion of about 200,000 Malians from Côte d'Ivoire between 2002 and 2004, partially organized in the form of a massive repatriation by the Malian government, contributed to influencing policy perceptions and priorities as regards return migration. In the course of this, the number of expelled migrants, and the presence and voice of new organizations formed by returnees from Côte d'Ivoire increased notably, pushing the Malian government to take action (Sylla, 2019; Calenda, 2012; Ouattara, 2010). Even if these initiatives cannot be compared to the activist character of the AME mobilizations (Gary Tounkara, 2013), they contributed to setting up more return assistance and reintegration programs, especially during the last Ivorian crisis in 2011. Mostly this took the form of small-scale interventions (Calenda, 2014a, pp. 57f). The Malian population, above all families and civil society, but also the government, were engaged in the task of taking back their people. However, socio-economic reintegration was in most cases difficult or even impossible. Maybe the state was unable to recognize the skills of the returnees sufficiently and to create appropriate training and employment opportunities (Camara et al., 2011). Still, it was thanks to the Malian population's outstanding capacity for reintegration that no social conflict broke out and relations and migratory networks to Côte d'Ivoire have persisted until today. In reaction to the Libyan crisis, more associations formed, which were particularly political (Sylla, 2019, 2014; Gary-Tounkara, 2013). In addition, the International Organization for Migration (IOM), funded by European donors, started its activities in the field of larger-scale reintegration programs in this context (Aghazarm et al., 2012).

The rather "poor performance" (Dünnwald, 2017, p. 91) of Malian state institutions became clear in the incidents surrounding the shooting of migrants in Ceuta and Melilla in 2005 and the massive arrivals of forced returnees from Morocco, a result of the strengthening of the European borders in North Africa at that time. It was civil society and above all Aminata Draman Traoré, a renowned Malian intellectual, activist, and former politician,[35] who offered shelter to the returnees and coordinated public hearings and a protest movement together with the AME, ARACEM (l'Association des Refoulés de l'Afrique Central au Mali)[36], another organization of former deportees, and other groups. In spring 2006, moreover, the Polycentric World Social Forum was held in Bamako and brought in numerous activists and organizations from Africa, Europe, and other places. Migration and deportation were

---

[35]   She is a prominent critic of globalization and the economic policies of most developed countries. She takes a very critical stance on migration politics in her writings, particularly as regards EU policies against African migrants.

[36]   See online: http://aracem-mali.org/, accessed 31 October 2021.

central themes. Malian associations used the forum to connect to human rights associations, mostly from France.[37]

With these events, which became the subject of unprecedented media coverage (cf. Stock, 2019; Tyszler, 2019), a new type of response to the EU emerged at the level of migrant-sending countries through the activism of migrant associations, increasingly supported by groups from European civil society (Dünnwald, 2017). Their transnational struggle also built on the denunciation of neocolonial policies in Africa and of the criminalization of migration and mobility after 1990 (Korven-syrjä, 2017). The AME and other organizations in Mali and in other North and West African countries played a central role here. It preceded and accompanied the first wave of the EU externalizing its borders into sub-Saharan Africa and the setting up of the Center for Information and Migration Management (CIGEM) in Bamako (see below). The protests against the signature of readmission agreements with France – protests organized by the AME in collaboration with other migrant and civil society associations as well as with Malians abroad – were particularly significant. It is due to their pressure that the Malian government is said to have twice refused to sign these agreements: with France in 2009 (Soukouna, 2011) and with the EU in 2016/17 (Traoré, 2016).[38]

Recent deportation regimes and reactions

The paradoxical effects of the externalization of EU migration policies seem to have become visible in a very concentrated manner in Mali (Trauner & Deimel, 2013; cf. Dünnwald 2017, p. 89). In 2008 the EU established the CIGEM, its overall objective being to support the development and implementation of a Malian migration policy with particular emphasis on the link between "migration and development" (European Commission, 2011). The Center was the first of its kind on the African continent. The year 2008 also constituted a peak in European deportations, with 1,834 Malians being deported mainly from France and Spain, followed by 765 in 2009, and 335 in 2010 (Calenda, 2012, p. 8, based on Eurostat data). This had been preceded by a readmission agreement concluded in 2007 between Mali and Spain as part of a larger circular migratory agreement. Supposedly this was favored by the fact that Mali and Spain had no common colonial heritage (ibid., p. 12). The

---

37   A number of new associations were founded in this context, and the AME and ARACEM managed to get stable funding from the French Protestant Church-based CIMADE (*Comité Inter-Mouvements Auprès des Evacués*) and the German NGOs Medico International and Pro Asyl. This contributed to extending and transnationalizing their work quickly, and its gaining wider visibility in certain circles (Dünnwald, 2017, p. 91).

38   The latter refusal took place, moreover, in light of the recent shipwrecks, which became a subject of public debate (first, when on July 27, 2014, between 82 and 87 young Malians drowned off the coast of Tripoli; Coulibaly, 2014).

CIGEM became a center for managing the arrival and reception of deportees. It was a literal "market" of organizations in the field of migration and return (Wiedemann, 2010) that emerged around the funding offered for often newly founded, but eventually short-lived associations (field notes, 11-18-2014).[39] Five years later, they existed on paper only or in the persons, as it were, of a left-over president and secretary.

At the end of the CIGEM project in February 2015, the general impression of AME representatives and EU officials in Bamako was that the Center had "flopped" as regards achieving its objectives (field interviews, Bamako, 22 and 24 October 2014; cf. Andersson, 2014, 241ff). The basic criticism was precisely that it had acted as the receiver of returnees and deportees instead of creating jobs and promoting legal migration as previously announced (cf. also Feldman, 2012). Following the virtual failure of this pioneering experiment in managing migration in sub-Saharan Africa, the EU decided to marginalize the issue of migration as an area of intervention in Mali in its strategic agenda 2014–2020 (European Commission, 2015). After 2008 the numbers of expulsions from outside of Africa to Mali decreased again until rising to another peak with the expulsion of 307 Malians from France in 2016. This was mostly related to new protests at St. Bernard's Church in Paris against the conclusion of the readmission agreement between the EU and Mali in the aftermath of the European refugee crisis (DGME database, unpublished), mentioned previously. The data of the DGME barely show any further returns from European countries in this period, but this needs to be viewed with caution as many returns may not have been included.[40]

The "refugee crisis" of 2015 gave a new impetus to the EU's political orientation on migration in the region. It resulted in the establishment of PONAM, the new Policy on Migration in Mali, which in itself was one of the concrete outcomes of the CIGEM and the directives of the Valetta summit (see below). This renewed EU interest in migration inaugurated an ever more intense phase of externalizing its borders in response to the migration governance established in Mali. This consisted of collaboration between international actors (i.e., the French Office of Immigration and Integration, Technical Co-development Unit, the Spanish, Italian, Swiss, and German representations, the IOM and other United Nations entities)

---

39 Organizations such as AME or ARACEM refused to receive such funding.

40 Malian nationals who did not identify as such are not registered; moreover, deportations may pass "unnoticed" as states, France above all, are said to send back individual deportees on commercial flights without informing the authorities to create as little "noise" as possible (field notes, 1-8-2016). The same may apply to other European countries. The fact that numbers of deportations on and to the African continent are barely accessible or non-existent is at the same time an indicator of the global structural inequalities inherent in the invisible aspects of the deportation regime.

and Malian state actors, including the Ministry of Foreign Malians and African Integration (MMEIA), the General Delegation of Malians Abroad (DGME), and the
Agency for the Promotion of Youth Employment (Diombana, 2009). Moreover, the
Malian conflict, which was escalating in 2012 in the North, represented a turning
point in the management of deportations and migrations and in their effects on
the country. It led to an interim cessation of deportations not only from European
countries, but also from the Maghreb, Morocco, Algeria, and Libya, which all acted
more cautiously – apart from the fact that in Libya the state was nonexistent by
that time.

The conflict needs to be depicted more fully, since a number of factors led to
a complicated and protracted political situation, which has still not been settled
to date but has even worsened again (cf. Schultz, 2021a; Klatt 2020; Bergamaschi,
2013; Lecocq et al., 2013; Soares, 2013; Hagberg & Körling, 2012): The conflict between the Tuareg (the largest ethnicity in the region of Azawad in the north of
Mali) and the government about more autonomous rights had escalated several
times since 1963 (1990, 1994–2000, 2006, and 2012),[41] but had never been resolved.
This goes back to the division of the mainly Tuareg-inhabited territory through
post-colonial nation-building and the definition of state borders without including Tuareg interests. The Malian state has never been able to provide sufficient
infrastructure on its territory, especially in terms of education, health, and road
construction. In fact, in the north and north-east of the country it was conspicuous by its absence. Terrorists exiled from Algeria found refuge in centers in the
north at the end of the 2000s. Weapons came from Algeria, as well as from Libya.
With the outbreak of the Libyan conflict in 2011, a spread of Islamist ideas by returning fighters followed. This exacerbated a tense situation marked by increasing
droughts, poorer soil for livestock, and high youth unemployment. "Traditionally,"
Islam in Mali follows a tolerant Sufi direction.[42]

The Tuareg uprising in early 2012 was followed by a coup d'état, in which units
of the Malian army revolted against the government of Amadou Toumani Touré in
Bamako. The National Movement for the Liberation of Azawad (*Mouvement national
de libération de l'Azawad*; MNLA) took advantage of the power vacuum to proclaim
the independent Tuareg state of Azawad. Within a very short time, the MNLA had
conquered the main cities of the north. The intervention of Islamist groups in-

---

41   See online: https://www.bpb.de/internationales/weltweit/innerstaatliche-konflikte/175842/m
     ali, accessed 31 October 2021.
42   The rise of Islamic organizations such as the very popular, also Sufi-based, movement Ansar
     Dine led by Chérif Ousmane Madani Haïdara, and the success of certain Islamist groups,
     shows a diverse, complex, and shifting Islamic landscape in Mali (cf. Soares, 2013). See online:
     https://culanth.org/fieldsights/islam-in-mali-since-the-2012-coup, accessed 31 October 2021.

ternationalized the conflict.[43] Thousands of people fled to the south of Mali or to neighboring countries. At France's insistence, the UN Security Council provided for an African-led military mission called MINUSMA.[44] When the Islamist groups quickly advanced towards Bamako, however, the Malian interim president Traoré requested an urgent military intervention by France, which started in January 2013 and was successful, though the Islamist fighters were not defeated completely. On international insistence, quick democratic elections were held that made former Prime Minister Ibrahim Boubacar Keita (IBK) president in August 2013.[45] Mali, which had for long been an international "donor darling," celebrated for its alleged successful transition to and implementation of democracy, within short time became the subject of international humanitarian aid actors and military operations (Bergamaschi, 2016, 2013; Lacher, 2013). While, the humanitarian actors have partially left in the meantime, the presence of security and military personnel continues to characterize the country's situation, also regarding migration and deportations, even if France, meanwhile, seems to be on the verge of changing its "counterterrorism" strategy and building local forces towards more autonomy (Tull, 2021).

The official peace process, consolidated in 2015 and signed by relevant groups and parties under international supervision in Algeria, is viewed positively in principle by the population despite doubts about its success. However, the government and international actors have been unable to succeed in pacifying the north on account of the complex crisis and security situation. Since 2015 the conflict has decentralized and intensified: centers of "whites" in Bamako as well as international security forces have become targets of Islamist attacks. Jihadists from the north infiltrated groups of the Fulbe ethnic group who live alongside the Dogon in central Mali, who, in turn, radicalized themselves as a rebel group. In the background are old feuds over land and resources. The conflict has spread across the borders into Niger and Burkina Faso, and now also into western Senegal.[46] Since 2019, ethnically motivated rebels and jihadist groups have increasingly attacked

43   These were mainly Al-Qaeda in the Islamic Maghreb and Ansar Dine ("Defenders of the Faith" – the latter not to be confused with the religious movement led by Chérif Ousmane Madani Haïdara). The more secular MNLA quickly lost its influence. The Islamists forced their fundamentalist interpretation of the Sharia on the population in the occupied cities. Old cultural goods, religious monuments, and African Islamic writings were destroyed.

44   The United Nations Multidimensional Integrated Stabilization Mission in Mali, see online: https://minusma.unmissions.org/en, accessed 31 October 2021.

45   Despite ambivalent performance and increasing involvement in corruption scandals, IBK was re-elected in 2019.

46   See online: https://globalriskinsights.com/2021/01/conflict-moves-west-in-mali-towards-the-senegalese-border/, accessed 31 October 2021.

central Mali's population. In some places, brutal massacres have occurred.[47] In the absence of the state, the groups offer the population protection from Islamist and reciprocal threats. With a disillusioned population, economic difficulties, dehydration of soils, and a lack of prospects, young men in particular are joining the new Islamist and rebel groups in these areas (Benjaminsen & Ba, 2019). Again, many people have been internally and internationally displaced. The situation in central Mali coincides with a dramatic drought and thus a food crisis.[48] The latest survey by the German Friedrich Ebert Foundation (FES) in March 2020[49] confirmed security, youth unemployment and poverty as the biggest challenges facing the country. In addition, many are more pessimistic about the coming years than before.[50] In fact, on 18 August 2020, another coup d'état by the military junta CNSP (National Committee for the Salvation of the People) under Colonel Assimi Goita incited the fall of the government under President IBK. It had been preceded by civil society protests since June 2020 expressing people's discontent. The COVID-19 crisis was the last straw (Schultz, 2021a). Since then, the country has been in a transition process toward a new government and supposed political stability, though this was upset by another coup d'état, in May 2021, which brought back Colonel Goita as leader and reinforced criticisms of the military dominance in the process.[51]

This political crisis in the Sahel has heavily securitized migration management and cooperation. All this is mirrored in the current responses and EU instruments, and the increased EU influence on migration, flight, and deportations. Meanwhile, facilitating migration has become criminalized, which has made transit migration more dangerous and the business of migration facilitation more lucrative (Faist et al., 2021, p. 78ff). The UN military forces, the French "Barkhane" mission (since August 2014) and the G5 Sahel Joint Force (Mauritania, Mali, Niger, Burkina Faso,

---

47   See online: https://www.france24.com/en/20200117-mali-foulani-dogon-ethnic-clashes-jihad ist, accessed 31 October 2021.

48   See online: https://www.lemonde.fr/afrique/visuel/2021/01/24/dans-le-centre-du-mali-des-vi llages-rases-par-les-violences-et-la-famine_6067424_3212.html?s=09&fbclid=IwAR2o3rAXSJ HoWoyXIuwHsWXO2U8wtlAIbuxgvKKeopNJg9oijLaTJPpyw-g, 31 October 2021.

49   The FES is a political foundation, close to the Social Democratic Party in Germany.

50   While the peace process, consolidated under an agreement of 2015 and signed by a large number of relevant groups and parties under international supervision in Algeria, is generally seen as positive, the population has little confidence in its success. This may relate to its abstract nature for large parts of the population (Goldberg, 2018). The *Dialogue National Inclusif* (DNI: national inclusive dialogue), a week of workshops and debate in Bamako in December 2019 organized by the Malian president and offering "truth, sincerity and conviviality," was well known by many respondents and seen as a useful instrument for change. See online: http://www.rfi.fr/fr/afrique/20191214-mali-ouverture-dialogue-national-inclusif-dni-ibk-ibrahim-boubacar-keita, accessed 31 October 2021.

51   See online: https://www.bbc.com/news/world-africa-57290761, accessed 31 October 2021.

and Chad), moreover, are fighting against migration in the name of counter-ter-rorism.[52] Consequently, migration control has been increasingly militarized (see also Müller, 2018).

The European "refugee crisis" and its political aftermath have since reshaped the border, migration, and deportation regimes fundamentally. As part of a second wave of externalization, Mali was chosen as "priority country" together with Niger, Nigeria, Senegal, and Ethiopia to establish a Migration Partnership Framework with the EU (European Commission, 2016). The Valetta Summit, which inaugurated this process to find "solutions" with African partner countries in November 2015, was a turning point in the management of irregular migrants and of "official" development assistance in sub-Saharan Africa (cf. Kipp & Koch, 2018; Dedieu, 2018). It is accompanied by an Emergency Trust Fund (EUTF) of 5 billion Euros (as of September 2021) of which more than 200 million Euros are specifically intended for projects in Mali; while migration management has a dedicated section, it is above all a cross-cutting issue.[53] Moreover, Mali is part of several regional projects on migration management and border control.[54] The logic of the narrative of "root causes" assumes that, if migrants' home territories were developed and able to provide opportunities for potential candidates for irregular migration, the latter would not risk their lives in tragic and deadly migratory adventures. Not only is this questionable because migration cannot be addressed by economic or development scenarios only; but social, cultural, political, climatic, gendered, and other factors make migration a very complex phenomenon.

While the Valetta approach thus does not stand up to a critical analysis of the causes of migration, return has become the paramount paradigm in the cooperation with African states within the European partnership framework (cf. Castillejo,

---

52   See online: https://www.diplomatie.gouv.fr/en/french-foreign-policy/defence-security/crisis-and-conflicts/g5-sahel-joint-force-and-the-sahel-alliance/; https://www.deutschlandfunk.de /anti-terror-operation-barkhane-umstrittene-mission-in-der.795.de.html?dram:arti-cle_id=395933;   https://www.foreignaffairs.com/articles/niger/2017-08-31/europes-migran t-hunters, accessed 31 October 2021.

53   The fund allocated to migration in Mali has a threefold objective: (1) to help immigrants to stay on the spot; (2) to compel the state to regulate the flow of migrants and welcome citizens considered "undesirable" in Europe; (3) and finally to put in place measures of deterrence for potential candidates for emigration. Among others, Mali received roughly 80 million euros for resolving the conflict in the north of the country to be dedicated, among other things, to border control and roughly 18 million euros for migration management in particular, see online: https://ec.europa.eu/trustfundforafrica/region/sahel-lake-chad/mali_e n, accessed, 31 October 2021.

54   See online: https://ec.europa.eu/trustfundforafrica/content/trust-fund-financials_en and h ttps://ec.europa.eu/trustfundforafrica/region/sahel-lake-chad/regional, accessed 31 October 2021.

2017), thereby potentially also linking deportations and development. In accordance with that framework, migrants forced from Europe or on the way there are preferably to be returned through "assisted voluntary returns" (AVRs),[55] which are easier for collaborating African governments to accept as they promise a more dignified return, even if they are potentially still unwanted (cf. also Adam et al., 2019). Within this context, the IOM expanded its role becoming determinant in the assistance of "illegal" migrants in transit in Algeria, Libya or released from Libyan detention centers (Trauner et al., 2019; European Commission, 2011). Together with European or African development agencies (e.g., Bartels, 2019), IOM's work consisted above all of facilitating return and supporting economic and social reintegration, not least to prevent people from re-emigrating. By retaining deportees and repatriates as well as would-be migrants on the spot, they are also made development actors in their region or country of origin. In Mali this is done in collaboration with the EU and the Malian Government.[56]

More than that, deportations from European and mainly North African countries rose to a new and massive peak in the last few years: thousands of migrants were set down in the desert and pushed over borders.[57] This added to the rising numbers of so-called "voluntary humanitarian returns" and AVRs, which came as consequence of the images of slavery-like conditions broadcast during the AU-EU summit in November 2017, Alpes (2020) speaks of "emergency returns." Effectively,

---

55   Built on the self-initiative and participation of returnees in the (post) return process, this political-administrative measure is most often carried out after an expulsion order or where there is no perceived alternative. Others therefore speak of self-deportation (cf. Collyer, 2018), "neoliberal deportations" (Andrijasevic, 2010; see also Bartels, 2019; Plambech, 2018) or "soft deportations" (Kalir, 2017). There is a considerable difference observable between the large number of repatriations and, lately, emergency returns from Libya, which are not necessarily voluntary, and those "assisted returns" accompanied before, during, and after return by the IOM or through the program of the Office Français de l'Immigration et de l'Intégration (OFII). The latter are single cases, however. Whether they remain after their return is another question.

56   Recent Malian repatriates from Niger and Algeria are embedded in health care and housing services, and returnees are eligible for individual and collective reintegration projects. So called "reintegration kits" may include tricycles to undertake an income-generating activity and management training for small and medium-sized enterprises.

57   According to the European Council on Refugees and Exiles (ECRE), News, and Algerian official counts, Algeria deported 25,000 Sub-Saharans in the course of 2018 alone and about 27,000 Sub-Saharans were deported between 2015 and early 2018: https://www.ecre.org/?s=Algeria+Deports+25%2C000+Migrants+to+Niger, accessed 31 October 2021. Also see the ongoing documentations by Alarme Phone Sahara, an international and local civil society initiative to support those in distress in the desert: https://alarmephonesahara.info/reports, accessed 31 October 2021.

a considerable number of those returning from Libyan prisons emerged out of desperate situations. However, returnees who did not come through IOM channels or were not "on their way" to Europe were not eligible for reintegration funding (Sylla, 2019), thus differentiating between desirable and undesirable ("irregular") migrants. Even so, this new orientation of the European agenda is more humane and development-oriented, in making more flexible measures available to reintegrate returnees. These IOM reintegration activities with their collaborating NGOs-structures have developed into a literal industry of a kind in rural areas. In 2020 alone, IOM assisted 9,995 people with voluntary returns in Mali.[58] In the course of this, the organization was furthermore assigned to start returning transit migrants from Mali to their countries of origin as well (cf. Alpes, 2020).

In this context, deportations and returns have become an ever more publicly contested phenomenon in Mali: civil society organizations in particular, which were established in the context of "assisted involuntary return," have become louder in denouncing these new measures for all-encompassing return, migratory control, and development, and have fostered a public debate on the subject. Some of them have increasingly become involved in implementing safe migration campaigns and also EU-funded reintegration. This multiplicity of actors and interwoven issues has created new challenges for migrant associations and other organizations around the EUTF, which legitimizes their presence on the one hand, while influencing their agenda on the other. On the way, deportations have become a market for official development assistance, integrating development agencies where "non-deportees" act in respect of deportation often disadvantaging "real" deportees. At the same time, former deportees and potential migrants are made development actors themselves through EUTF-programs, marking a clear nexus of deportation and development. Simultaneously, all this has given space to efforts to Africanize and develop new forms of activism and civil society engagement about migrations, deaths, and deportations (cf. also Sylla & Schultz, 2020).

The case of Kita, reversed migrations and deteriorated developments

The Kita Cercle in southwestern Mali, where I conducted a substantial part of my field research "beyond Bamako," is considered to be an area of international emigration par excellence, (Konaté & Gonin, 2016, p. 25). It is located administratively and culturally in the region of Kayes, where the nexus between migration and development is most pronounced with 70% of its migration being said to leave for destinations outside of Mali (to Africa, Europe, America, Asia). Bordering Senegal, Mauritania and Guinea Conakry, it has been marked by trade and mobility

---

58   See online: https://mali.iom.int/en/facts-and-figures, 31 October 2021.

(Choplin & Lombard, 2014), emigration as well as immigration, especially to mining regions, but also to agricultural and rural sites as well as cities (Dwell, 2013). The region of Kayes, moreover, is the mainland of the Soninké ethnicity, as explained above, and builds on histories of mobility and migration. For 50 years, migrant associations from the region have been involved in development schemes for their communities of origin, building schools, health centers, and roads (Galatowitsch, 2009; Lima, 2005).

The town of Kita is an urban commune on the Bamako–Kayes (and previously Dakar) railway. The rural hinterland of Kita always had a cosmopolitan orientation toward migrants (Koenig, 2005a, p. 80). There are municipalities where emigrants from abroad developed models of public, political, economic investment as well as connectivity by positioning themselves as the true agents of development. The area is mostly inhabited by Malinke, Kakolo, and Fulani. Its economy is based on the high production and processing of peanuts (with two factories built in 1962 and 1976) and commercial transactions along the railway. Export revenues from peanuts fell in Mali, Senegal, and Gambia by between 50% and 80% from 1960 to 1980 (Badiane & Kinteh, 1994, p. 6). Post-colonial international emigration from Kita was spurred by the "rail crisis" and the closure of the state-owned oil mills between 1986 and 1995 due to a more liberal state economic policy (Lachenmann, 1986). A transfer to the production of cotton, even though supported by the state, created a new pioneering migration front towards Senegal and Côte d'Ivoire (Falconnier, 2016; Mamadou, 2015).

Colonization caused the first displacements of the population, while the great droughts (1972–74, 1984, 2002) fostered the idea among Kita's population of increasing their agricultural incomes by migrating within the subregion as well as to Europe (Konate & Gonin, 2016, pp. 104f). As elsewhere in Mali, due to the possibilities of globalization on the one hand and the political unrest in the 1990s in Côte d'Ivoire on the other, many of Kita's emigrants moved further north (Libya, Mauritania, Morocco, Spain, and Italy). Between 2004 and 2008, among Kita's young migrants, Libya outplayed other destinations (Konaté & Gonin, 2016, pp. 117ff; Koenig, 2005a). This coincided with the EU experimenting with its rigorous border management policies there, as described. Lately it has been shipwrecks that have dominated the debate here, in addition to a new rise in deportations: there are villages where the majority of their young men died all at once. In 2015, for instance, about 360 of a total of 372 shipwrecked persons originated from the region of Kayes, where Kita is located.

Individual female migration is less developed in this area, and involves shorter distances, mostly to urban areas as described above (e.g., Konaté, 2012). This is related not least to the role of women, who only rarely serve as heads of household (Koenig, 2005a, pp. 80f; see next subchapter). Marie Rodet (2009), on the other hand, deduces from archival sources, the often overlooked, but economically important role of women actively migrating to neighboring countries in the first half of the 20th century, but eventually disappearing from statistical sources.

Migration and mobility, furthermore, have contributed to rural social stratification (Koenig 2005a, p. 83; cf. Faist et al., 2021; van der Land, 2015). Mobility usually served those who were already well-off and had substantial transnational networks (Koenig, 2005a, pp. 95ff). In this sense, remittances can better function as investments for affluent households than to supply the basic needs of less affluent ones. In terms of return, migrants from more affluent families are better able to invest as they have often obtained better jobs or education (see further Chapter 5). Usually those with a longer migration history have more powerful transnational social networks and can enable more migration as well. Today this is clearly visible in some areas, particularly in southwestern Mali in the region of Kayes. Sometimes houses change from one village to the next as a consequence of, and thus "showcasing," the impacts of their migratory history and networks, along with their supposed successes or "failures."

Today, many migrants and people in Kita are forced into forms of involuntary immobility. A "successful" return is no longer guaranteed, as it was before. Against this background, migration has also become more permanent in terms of urban–rural mobility, but also intra-regionally and continentally. Schooling and waged jobs have been concentrated in particular zones, often bigger cities, and have kept families or individuals staying there (Konaté & Gonin, 2016; Koenig, 2005a). Although deportations have been known here since the first expulsions of Malian workers from African states, the great numbers built up from the 2000s until today are unprecedented, and seem to have substantially reshaped the entire social composition, particularly of the rural hinterland of Kita. The Libyan crisis of 2011 had a notable impact there. The return assistance programs, which were tested in some villages of Kita by the IOM and the Kita branch of the Association of Repatriates of Mali between 2006 and 2010, were short-lived (field investigations, January 2016), although they received a new push through the activities financed by the EUTF and reintegrating the latest "emergency" and "voluntary humanitarian returns" (Alpes, 2020). At the same time, migrant networks and the roles and functions of emigrants in the development of their villages remained steady in these communities of origin.

Kita research sites

Two villages in Kita Cercle serve as embedding context in the following study. Here, the situation has changed considerably due to the effects of externalized borders and increasing deportations. There are at least two generations of deportees in addition to a considerable number of repatriates and returnees in both villages. In the larger of the two villages they come mostly from the Côte d'Ivoire, but also from several North African countries and even Europe; in the smaller one, they come mostly from Libya.

The small village has about 500 inhabitants but no separate primary school. Most houses here are built close together, constructed mainly on a simple, rectangular plan and made of mud and straw, which is typical for this region; there are also concrete houses, which indicate some degree of wealth, mostly from migrants' investments (see further Chapter 5). The village is densely surrounded by agricultural fields, where people seasonally grow peanuts, maize, and sorghum, chiefly, and some are involved in cotton production; there are vast garden spaces with large fruit and nut trees as well as vegetables growing. The next small village lies 10 minutes' walking distance, and the district capital is close by. The village has a particularly intense and varied history of mobility, predominantly to Libya, particularly since the 1980s (with some migrants also going on further to Europe). When the conflict in Libya escalated in 2011, almost the entire youth of the village and the older males abroad, returned or were repatriated or deported. It became a real social and public issue here and the presence of former deportees has been an everyday phenomenon since, as I will elaborate later (see above all Chapter 6).

The larger village is a community center at the same time, housing about 2,000 inhabitants. The houses are scattered over a wide space, the sandy roads that cross it are broad. It has both a primary and a secondary school, a marketplace, several little shops, a mosque, and a health center, plus a gardening project for the women set up by a Spanish NGO. The fields around the village are vast, but often dry and used for growing peanuts, maize, and sorghum; some are given over to cotton as well. There are some scattered gardened spaces around. After the rainy season, the village is greener for a short time. This village has a long tradition of circular migration to Côte d'Ivoire and, increasingly, to North Africa since the 1990s and to Europe later on. Several of its inhabitants live in Spain, in Italy, some in Libya. This is visible also in the improvements made to some houses, which have fancy paintings and wall elements, for instance, and roofs made of corrugated iron sheets. People who work in the administration, of whom there are several in this village, usually show some more signs of wealth on their houses (for further information see Chapter 5). Other houses are built of mud and straw. According to the community's administrative assistant, the number of migrants has tripled within the last 20 years, from 1–2% to 5% today.[59] This is more than half of the young (male) population that is able to migrate. It may be related to the size of the village as well as the large spaces it provides, that the villagers do not talk as publicly about migration and deportations they would in the small village. I will provide further detail about these interrelations as well as expanding on the specific socio-economic contexts

___

59   Conversation with community representative, 1-25-2016.

that embed these situations and post-deportation cases throughout the following chapters.

Bamako – hub of migration, return, and transit

The capital Bamako, where I stayed for a long time during my field research and accompanied many deportees, counts about 2.7 million inhabitants today and is one of the fastest growing cities in the world (in 1950, it had a population of 89,000).[60] This increase is due to rapid population growth and, above all, to rising rural-to-urban internal migration over the last few decades. However, the majority of the Malian population still continues to live in rural areas (about 56%).[61] At the same time, urbanization is not a recent phenomenon in this region, as some of the oldest African cities flourished here from the 9th century CE (cf. Meillassoux, 1968).[62] Bamako has been known since ancient times as a thriving market on the trade route between the Sahara desert in the north and the rainforests in the south.[63] This has created a place characterized by a wide variety of often controversial influences, cultural heterogeneity, and diversity (Steuer, 2013).

The French colonizers introduced a system of wage earning and taxation which centralized the monetized economy in Bamako. By 1987 80% of industrial and commercial enterprises were located in the capital, 75% of the institutions of secondary and higher education and 55% of the salaried workers (Gaudio, 1988, p. 178).[64] Following the severe droughts of the 1970s, people fled for the first time in large numbers to the capital. This rural exodus constituted a new wave of immigration in Bamako. The population almost doubled in the six years between 1968 and 1974 from 182,000 to 317,000 (cf. Van Westen, 1995, p. 88).

In the course of the Structural Adjustment Programs (SAPs) from 1981, many people lost their jobs in the capital, above all in the public sector; salaries were

---

60   See online: https://worldpopulationreview.com/world-cities/bamako-population, accessed 31 October 2021.

61   See online: https://www.macrotrends.net/countries/MLI/mali/rural-population, accessed 31 October 2021.

62   Such as Kumbi Saleh, the capital of the Ghana Empire, or later Niani, the center of the old Mali empire (Steuer, 2013, p. 77)

63   After the salt caravans at the end of the 18th century, the French colonizers, who occupied Bamako in 1883, built the railway line to Dakar ten years later and expanded shipping on the Niger. The city then became a hub for trade not only from north to south, but also from west to east.

64   Particularly since the 1980s decentralization programs have been implemented, however, creating legal and administrative difficulties between central and local governments as well as community institutions, e.g., over natural resources and land tenure (see Idelman, 2009; Benjamin, 2008).

frozen and public spending cut to reduce the government deficit. Since then, the majority have been employed in the informal sector. After some economic recovery during the transition to democracy, in 1994 the introduction of the FCFA (*Franc de la Coopération Financière en Afrique*)[65] caused the Malian currency to lose 50% of its value (as decided by France for the entire currency zone). Since then, a sense of economic crisis and deterioration has gripped large parts of the Malian urban population (cf. Schulz, 2012, pp. 47ff; see Chapter 5 in particular). Since Bamako was no longer so attractive for incoming migrants, people left for the sub-region and increasingly for Europe, facilitated by the beginnings of globalization.

Since the 1970s and increasingly in the 1980s, rural–urban and also female migration has been directed to Bamako (Brand, 2001, pp. 40ff). The latter, unlike male migration, was oriented toward earning enough to pay for a trousseau (Hertrich & Lesclingand, 2017, pp. 63f) though girls' incomes may have contributed to the household, too. Bamako's neighborhoods still represent patterns of urban–rural mobility and migration, grouping people from certain villages together.[66] Returnees also assemble in particular areas. The city mirrors parts of the country's and region's migratory histories.

Migration and mobility largely continue to characterize the city today. People keep moving between the urban and the rural, and a strong connection to one's village of origin forms people's lifeworld and contributes to a pronounced sense of flexibility (typical of many other post-colonial cities as well; cf. Steuer, 2013, pp. 77f). Furthermore, Bamako is a major immigration hub for migrants from other West and Central African countries, having served for a long time as a transit place for those coming from the villages and moving on towards the north and also to other West and Central African countries (e.g., Dünnwald, 2012, 2011). This, not least, was the reason why the EU selected Mali as the first country to set up the CIGEM. As mentioned above (and further explained below), Bamako is a transit hub for returnees too – Malians who do not want to return to their villages, as well as returnees from West and Central African countries. During the Malian crisis, the number of transit migrants stuck in Bamako doubled temporarily (interview, ARACEM, 10-16-2014). Also, those who were internally displaced largely found refuge with their families or in municipal housing in Bamako. The city is an entire microcosm of migration, immobility, and deportations in particular. As I followed returnees, I did my research in several districts of Bamako in places frequented by deportees and the people socially close to them, as to be detailed in the next chapter.

---

65   The common currency of several ECOWAS members, which is linked to the French national bank (*Banque de France*).

66   For more detail see above all the works of Meillassoux.

Concluding remarks

This chapter has provided a contextual sketch of the Malian setting as a particular example of the conditions and experiences of migration, mobility, and deportations and their social, economic, and political impacts. Moreover, Mali represents a remarkable case of reactions to forced returns throughout the last decades, starting with the independence and formation of the Malian state and the first African deportations. It has been shown that EU externalization measures add to European deportations and build on the established deportation national practices of African states. Even if lately the situation has become more securitized and complicated, the Malian state follows an ambivalent policy towards European and international actors. At the same time, it has developed very specific regimes and institutions for the return and reintegration of returnees. Civil society actors have been pioneering this arena. The migrant associations, set up both abroad and, in particular, by different returnees and deportees in Bamako and in Kita, in the region of Kayes, can be seen as outposts of externalization and protest against deportations and forced return today. Individual deportees and their social surroundings are thrown into this setting, highly charged by the legacy of migration. It is in this ambivalent setting that the analysis that follows develops. In the next chapter, I will sketch out the methodological approach it takes.

Chapter 3
Methodology in context

This chapter will give an overview of the methodological steps I took to operationalize my research question. At its center is an account of how I constituted my field – "a crucial step in an empirical study" (Gupta & Ferguson, 1997), given that field work is at the heart of anthropology. First I had to define and limit my group of respondents in a context where refoulés, as introduced in Chapter 1, seemed to be "everywhere," as a consequence of the extensive, diverse, and long-lasting effects and experiences of deportations in Mali.

As a first step, therefore, I will describe how I gained access to the field, which constituted a distinct dialogical and rhetorical process (Lassiter, 2005, p. 15), in chronological order; as a second, I will outline the collection of data and the specific limitations to which this was subject, briefly sketching the places and cases that I researched during two field trips to Mali between 2014 and 2016 that lasted a total of eight months.[1] In addition, I will reveal the methods I used and the analytical steps I implemented to generate my results. This will involve showing how specific questions and main themes emerged. I chose to follow the general lines of grounded theory (Strauss & Corbin, 1990), which allowed me to openly generate knowledge from the ground. This I combined with an ethnography of conditions post deportation in Mali, including elements of participatory and action research. Ethnography, as an "undisciplined" approach (Breidenstein et al., 2013), gave me the freedom necessary to explore and develop deportees' narratives and (life) stories and to observe the practices that constituted their social worlds (cf. Lachenmann, 2010).

In all this, reflecting my own and others' positionality was vital, as "researchers and their subjects influence each other" (Strecker & La Tosky, 2013, p. 17) in such a way that there is no "beyond positionality." A certain immersion in people's life-worlds turned out to be key for this research: I temporarily lived with deportees

---

1   Given this time frame, it is again necessary to highlight that the field and data presented date from before the last "wave" of humanitarian returns and *refoulements* from Libya, Algeria, and Morocco described in the previous chapter.

and their families and accompanied them during their daily lives. This went along with very specific power discrepancies, sometimes impossible to eliminate, which influenced how I did my research, which events, places, and cases I selected, how I did my analysis, and not least what I did not do. Critical reflection on how my positionality impacted my findings will thus figure prominently throughout this methodology chapter. I will conclude with the question of how conditions after deportation in a given time and place should be studied and describe the specific kind of ethnography that developed in the course of this research. In the end, however, this is an ethnography of a young white woman in southern Mali.

In the field: associations, activists, and deportations "everywhere"

This first phase of my field work, which took place between October and December 2014 mainly in Bamako, constituted an early stage in my project to research deportees' narratives, lifeworlds, and practices in Mali. It was supposed to provide me with an overview of the relevant actors and topics, to establish a contact network, and to start me off on data collection – mainly with deported migrant actors, but also with relevant institutions and NGOs. My aim was to enter the field by way of the AME and the ARACEM (*Association des Refoulés d'Afrique Central au Mali*), a self-organized group of Central African deportees, mostly from Cameroon. I set up my base in a transnational research center, where I could meet and talk with a number of Malian doctoral students. From there, still at some distance from the field, I started to reach out.

My primary aim was to conduct a multi-sited study,[2] my intention being to explore and capture the (social) field of post deportation in Mali in its varieties and forms in different localities. However, the protracted crisis in Mali and the issue of security impeded field work in northern areas, where deportees were reported to have been pushed back over borders or were stuck in transit (e.g., cf. Lecadet, 2013; Trauner & Deimel, 2013), thus fundamentally reshaping my field and my own capacity for mobility: the German Ministry of Foreign Affairs warned against "non-

---

2   The "multi-sited" approach emerged in the 1990s as a new way of doing ethnography. "This strategically situated ethnography [...] attempts to understand something broadly about the system in ethnographic terms as much as it does its local subjects: It is only local circumstantially, thus situating itself in a context or field quite differently than does other single-site ethnography" (Marcus, 1995, pp. 110f). Ghassan Hage, on the other hand, demonstrated the exhaustion that can result from multi-sited research. For him, following the global transnational Lebanese community all around the world was simply physically unbearable (Hage, 2005, p. 466f).

urgent travel,"[3] including to Bamako, specifically prohibiting access to certain areas. Eventually, I conducted an ethnography that included several localities in rural as well as urban Mali (see the map below). In so doing, I first wanted to find out the potential differences between places in the rural hinterland and the city; and, second, to center on individuals' stories and their specific social embedding. As I have said, rural places of return in particular had barely been researched so far. In the end, what I wanted to do was to grasp the phenomenon through a heuristic case-by-case approach. This kind of development of my field created what Ruben Andersson (2014) would call an "extended field site" of situations post deportation in Mali, produced by transnational and global political interventions and constituted through the activities of associations and NGOs and, above all, by the presence, actions, mobility, and immobility of former deportees, (re-)emigrants and their close social contacts. The "Extended Case Method" of the Manchester School (cf. Gluckman, 1963) that this approach builds on thus allowed groups that previously had been considered separate to be brought together in an analytical conversation that reached well beyond the confines of the geographically bounded villages, which were the main object of anthropology back then.[4] Meanwhile, the security aspect kept impacting my field work.[5]

I first set foot in the post-deportation world through the AME's office, after sending emails from Germany (which remained unanswered) and eventually talking with their spokesperson on the phone a couple of days after my arrival. Everybody was preparing to travel to the African social forum in Dakar the next day. The small rooms were crowded and packed with pictures and posters for international and local events, the *"théâtre des expulsés"* (Canut & Sow, 2014; Lecadet, 2011), the Bamako–Dakar caravan taking people to the world social forum, and visits to France and Germany, as well as pictures of funding partners and other researchers. Toumani, the person responsible for receiving and assisting deportees, welcomed me cordially. I was soon taken to the Association's meeting room and introduced

---

3   Travel to the North would have been possible in UN company only, constraining an open ethnographic approach (that did not have the UN mission itself as its subject). Another trip to the Mauritanian border never became a reality either, as it as was simply too dangerous for me, as a white person, to be exposed to the traffic of every imaginable kind passing along this swath of land.

4   Ruben Andersson builds, among others, on the "extended case method" in defining his research into the European border industry (2014, pp. 283ff). In its original sense, the method was all about selecting a single conflictive event in a small social environment to observe over a long period of time.

5   With the attack on the Radisson hotel in Bamako in November 2015 in reaction to the Paris bombings, white people became an obvious target, which was also reflected in the anxieties of my Malian companions on my behalf. See online: https://www.theguardian.com/world/201 5/nov/20/mali-attack-highlights-global-spread-extremist-violence, accessed 31 October 2021.

like one of their usual stagiaires (interns); a balcony led out onto an animated street in the neighborhood. The organization had a vast number of shelves full of deportee dossiers. My recording device was running almost constantly; I sat and listened, asked questions, and took notes. The former deportees had become "professional" in various senses (cf. Andersson, 2014, p. 258), and routinized in receiving international guests. The spokesperson even claimed to know me. This built some common ground: I was instantly involved in the organization's wide network.

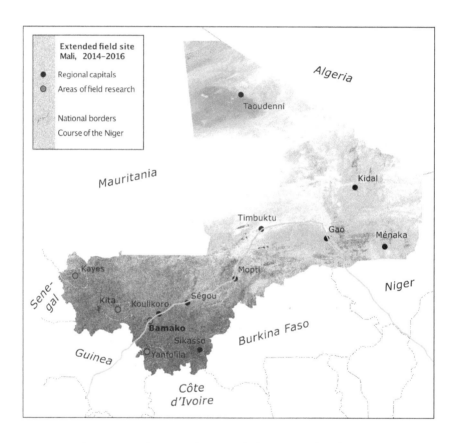

Toumani soon agreed to provide me with the contact details of individual deportees. "Yes, yes, yes, of course! There are always people like that here." And, indeed, after a very short time a young man, Lamine, was standing in the doorway, timid, but friendly. Deported from France two days before, he had been referred to the organization at the airport needing support with his "false" *laisser-passer*. It was his second visit to the NGO. He appeared disturbed and confused. We were introduced and were able to sit next door and talk. He wanted to go back "right away!" While we were still in conversation, another young man entered the organization's office space. A staff member had called him in to have a chat with me. This man had been deported from Spain and Libya previously, and from a multiplicity of other places at other times, as I shortly learned. Now, he had been back for two years. In no time I found myself in the middle of my research topic; it was going almost too fast for me to follow. There was a "restless" pulse, I could sense, accompanied and contrasted by a kind of stasis. It would become constitutive of my field work.

Similar things had been reported by studies on migrants in transit (for more on this subject, see Chapter 4). When two days later the organization presented me with a "selection of representative deportees" – people with characteristic as well as salient trajectories, as they described them – as potential interviewees, I became hesitant. I was not after a ready-made post deportation reality or the image that the NGO wanted to present of itself; nor did I want to replicate what others had been doing. I had used the same entry points as others, but apparently, I had to go beyond the organization's realms in order to gain a less filtered view.

ARACEM, mentioned above, was my second point of entry to the field in Bamako. Unlike the AME, their working world was quiet; the spacious patio of the organization's building was almost empty. A broken, upside down chair in the corner, and a set of slightly faded housing regulations marked the change from busier times in the past, a reminiscence of former deportees from the days when the routes to the north were open.[6] One of the ARACEM's Cameroonian coworkers, Dave, a recent deportee from Morocco, was an excellent guide to the world of Cameroonian transit migrants and those dumped back in Mali from the routes to Algeria, Morocco, or Libya. Many of them lived in an empty garage, which they called their "*ghetto*," located in a run-down market "*Halle de Bamako*," just next to the ARACEM office and the central bus station "*Auto Gare de Sogoniko*" (with buses to and from the north – cf. also Lecadet, 2013): most of them were somehow trying to eke out a living through little daily jobs. They were strangers, much more so than Malian dportees (see also Chapter 4), who needed to survive and were trying to continue on their way north as soon as possible. Entering their transit space in Bamako allowed me to better shape the field by delimiting the lifeworlds of the Malian deportees from theirs. From this base, still in October 2014, I started my data collection process.

Shifting positionalities in action research among associations and activists

The participatory research I started from within the organizations, contained elements of action research. All of the organizations' staff had previously been de-

---

6   Rooms were located around the patio: one dormitory for men, one for women. The other entrance led to the office spaces of the association, consisting of two rooms and a small bathroom.

ported and were now engaged in caring for others arriving in a similarly miserable situation, providing orientation and support and engaging with them politically as well. As far as I was concerned, getting involved with the organizations implied acknowledging, and up to a certain point going along with, their reality as the "what was there" in terms of representing and shaping conditions post deportation in Mali.[7] At the same time, it meant being a researcher, activist, and "*stagière*" – being able in the latter capacity to pass my time on the organizations' premises and take notes, but also to report on my activities, when I was out in the field, and, above all, to conduct interviews with state and international officials.

My supposed belonging to several associations was a sensitive issue. On the one hand, taking different positionalities and building relations with a variety of actors and organizations meant gaining different access to and different perspectives on my subject matter; on the other, it required juggling my loyalties. Collaborating with a white European researcher implied potential benefits and advantages – in the civil society sector funds and donor relations provided legitimacy and enabled survival at the same time (cf. Sylla & Schultz, 2020).[8] Critically, the AME and ARACEM were partially funded by the same donor. After causing some irritation to the organizations by belonging to both, I increasingly came to exchange information between them or pass on greetings from the one to the other. Throughout my entire fieldwork I reported on my activities when I entered their premises. This was, not least, about building trust relations. While the AME was nationally and transnationally quite well established (cf. Lecadet, 2011), it remained a small association with a handful of staff and a three-room office.[9] Since then, the situation has changed substantially in the aftermath of the "refugee crisis," creating another form of competition and reshaping these organizations as described in the previous chapter.[10]

More than that, I participated in organizing events in a network among various African, mainly Malian, and European activists. There were significant overlaps and interrelations among the self-organized groups, which aroused internal conflict and competition, accompanied by gossip and mistrust – it seemed a bit of

---

7   For a recent discussion of using a "returnee identity" for political recognition in Benin City, Nigeria, see Shaidrova (forthcoming).

8   Lack of funds and an often existential dependency on donors from the global North have created uneven relationships and major dilemmas that have been thoroughly discussed as the pitfalls and downsides of development aid (see, e.g., Macamo & Neubert, 2012).

9   In 2016 the organizations were in a phase of strategic reorientation. Central points were: "want[ing] to be ourselves…," but nevertheless following a "strategy of moving together" (field notes, 03-1-2016).

10   ARACEM has become much more involved in humanizing the external borders of the EU since the "refugee crisis," being confronted with a massive new increase in deportations, above all in the form of transit and humanitarian returns.

a snake pit sometimes. In particular, the craving for funds and for relations with promising prospects created serious ruptures and embezzlement on a large scale. Outrageous rumors were circulated, and nasty speculations aired in order to belittle other parties or to create new or reinforce old loyalties. I tried to stay out of these conflicts and later withdrew from my activist engagements, as things became complicated. Moreover, my focus was on the *refoulés* themselves.

It was essential to differentiate between the points of view of activists and organizations and my own. Susann Huschke's term, "activist's blinders" (2015, pp. 61f) fits this well: it points to a certain unavoidability, or at least the danger, of seeing things from an activist perspective when intensely engaging in such circles. At the same time, this kind of immersion – one could describe it as "going native" up to a point – is part of a "usual" ethnographic approach of "cultural inclination, adaptation, transformation" as well (cf. Lachenmann, 2010, p. 10, transl. S.U.S.), and has to be constantly counterbalanced by a sufficient degree of alienation. More than that, actively engaging in one's field and doing ethnography for purposes beyond those of publishing has become self-evidently part of activist or action research (e.g., Reason & Bradbury-Huang, 2012). In meetings with (Malian) administrative bodies, for instance, remarkable scenes occurred as well. Different groups of people, either directly or in more subtle ways, expressed their need for and expectations of additional funds and projects from Germany or contacts with people there. In the end, all of us – the organizations, the *stagiaires*, the researchers, the deportees, the politicians, the journalists, and the activists – formed part of the absurd "bordering Europe" industry that Ruben Andersson (2014) aptly describes, and of the deportations industry in particular. Nevertheless, we took different roles and perspectives, which I had to differentiate and thoroughly reflect in order to document and later analyze my data in as balanced a way as possible. Thus, my involvement required caution in specific areas, which led to a quasi-never-ending negotiation that at the same time defined my field (cf. also Breidenstein et al., 2013).

Accessing and researching with former deportees

To encounter deportees' lifeworlds in a more unfiltered way and to understand how they coped with and were impacted by having been forcefully returned, I had to take more independent steps. Increasingly, I kept looking – sometimes proactively, sometimes passively – for relevant contacts and "potential deportees," broadly following the idea of a snowball system (Atkinson & Flint, 2001). In Mali (post-)deportations seemed to be everywhere, pace Collyer (2018, p. 111), who states that research on deportations faces major issues as returnees are hard to identify among the larger population. Beyond the organizations and arranged meetings with institutional contacts and others, my entry points were random conversations with other researchers, friends of friends, the security guard and the shop owner next door, taxi drivers, and more and more with people in the streets.

Brahima, for instance, one of the main respondents of this study, I met accidentally at Bamako's *Grand Marché* in 2014 when buying credit for my mobile phone at a tiny, lopsided stand. The vendor, responding to a request from me about my research, spoke up loudly enough to drown out the high-volume activity of a busy road crammed with cars and people: "Ah, we have a Spaniard here! – Brahima!!" A somewhat shy, but friendly-looking young man appeared. Quickly, Brahima and I made contact, exchanged a few words, and I came back for an in-depth interview a couple of days later. Several visits and conversations followed over the next one and a half years and after that occasionally via telephone. Others showed me their passports on similar occasions; some told me about their brothers, friends, or acquaintances who had been deported or had potentially left again: "I have been deported too! I've been in Spain/France/Morocco ..." was frequently the starting point for such random encounters.

Most of them were doing little jobs in the market or at the side of a street, like selling mattresses, dates, or telephone cards – getting by as best they could. Some had returned a long time ago and were now doing better – or doing even worse; others had returned recently. The latter seemed as if they were in an immense tension between restless "hyper mobility and waiting" (Streiff-Fénart & Poutignat, 2006, p. 137; transl. S.U.S.). Some expressed a craving to leave again, come hell or high water, and accompanied this with a gesture of pointing to their forehead – "you know I have something in my head, I have to go on" was an emblematic expression that I will further develop in the next chapter.

Following returnees, I did my "urban" research in several districts of Bamako frequented by deportees and the people socially close to them. Besides the premises of institutions, these were the offices of the self-organized groups of former deportees, the *"Halle de Bamako"* market, the *Grand Marché* in the city center, the youth center (*Maison des Jeunes*), a number of returnees' workplaces, restaurants and cafés, as well as the private houses of deportees' families, often their uncles or cousins as their parents were still in the village.

The following box provides a summary of the characteristics of my interviewees and a first overview of their backgrounds and the main patterns of their lives. (Differences between the urban and the rural contexts will be further detailed throughout the book.)

> The large majority of interviewees were male. Their ages ranged between 20 and about 50. In Bamako the majority of them were aged between 25 and 40, though in some villages there were also quite a number of older deportees in their fifties. Those I interviewed in Bamako had mostly been deported from European countries,

but some from Morocco and Libya as well. All of them originally came from rural areas, from North, South, or mostly Southwest Mali.

Those I met in rural villages (see below) had mostly been deported from Libya, Mauritania, Morocco, or Algeria, but some from European countries too. (Furthermore, there were deportees from Gabon, Guinea Conakry, the Central African Republic, the Congos, etc., whom I engaged with as additional respondents mostly.)

The level of education of the people I spoke with varied from illiterate to holding a high school diploma, with a tendency toward the lower levels of education. Particularly among those who had returned to village sites, the level of education was relatively low. Most respondents were, or felt, constrained in their capacity for mobility. Differences considered significant related to migratory and deportation experiences, whether one had earned money or not, and most notably to one's age and generation. Still, all of them considered themselves to be refoulés, even if they had experienced different journeys and deportations or repatriations (by land, sea, air, or even via humanitarian evacuation from Libya 2011–2014, as covered in the introductory chapter).

Those living in the village were mainly married – most, though by no means all, since their (last) deportation. Among those living in the city, there was more diversity in terms of family status as well: some were married, but the wife usually lived in their father in law's village; others were not (yet) married.

Certainly, there were considerable structural inequalities and asymmetries, since I came from a very different position, being white, young, highly educated and thus supposedly privileged, mobile, European and a woman. Susan Coutin speaks of "irreconcilable incompatibilities" in studying deportations from a "white" researcher's point of view.[11] Even if I principally agree with that, being a young white woman at the same time spurred me on to discover former deportees and relevant contacts. More than that, I met a lot of openness. It seemed that encounters between deportees and myself provided them with a certain relief. Contrary to what one might assume, people often had difficulty in speaking about a traumatic or shameful past. While some reported their nagging memories very frankly to me, they also indicated their social alienation and estrangement through comments such as: "I've not forgotten. Often, thinking about it makes me want to stay by myself. I stay away from the others." Accounts might remain indirect; things were kept silent about, or took longer to come out, in order to retain face and some respect.[12]

---

11   Ines Hasselberg even warns of a "pornography of suffering" (2018, p. 32) in researching excluded, abject, traumatized subjects, which is what deportees may be.

12   I will discuss the role of silence after deportations in Chapter 5.

In other cases, ironical or bitter laughter about arbitrary deportation practices, for example, that randomly distribute deportees throughout West Africa, could alleviate stress by incorporating deportation experiences into everyday life. Some shouted their anger and frustration about experiences of exclusion and administrative abuse, embodying a feeling of unjust treatment and betrayal. Others presented themselves as isolated or victimized but saved their most vehement objections for experiences of criminalization. For me, it was sometimes difficult to stay calm and "endure" in such conversations, to accept people's lamenting and suffering without interfering and reminding them of the structural effects of their situation. Such interventions could, however, clearly influence the course of our conversation and my findings. At the same time, our conversational interactions need to be seen in terms of the narrative styles and self-construction of the deportees, without discrediting the suffering they experienced (see Chapter 4). There were moments when I wondered if people made up their stories. How could deportations be literally "everywhere"? People repeatedly telling me that they would prefer to travel and live in Germany were an obvious indicator of discursive, somehow opportunistic adaptations of content and narrative strategy.

The openness and the reserve equally possible in research encounters need to be seen in relation to the "common ground" (cf. Drotbohm, 2012) that emerges between the researcher and deportee through a connecting international experience: my interlocutors "had been there" or at least had been "on the way," while I came "from there" and was with them "here" now. My co-researcher Birama Bagayogo (2019)[13] reasoned that, as I was an outsider, there was nothing to hide. Engaging with a European woman and a Malian man from the capital – as was the case in our collaborative research – seemed to diminish an often-widespread competition between people. There was less danger of the gossiping and mistrust which often occurs in narrow social spaces like village sites, or in city neighborhoods, or among self-organized groups and activists of the kind described above. Moreover, this feeds into what has been discussed as the positive effect of being a researcher from outside the field (Diawara, 1985), and the researcher's (the anthropologist's) position as a "stranger," uninhibited by social convention and commitment (Simmel, [1908] 1958); cf. Jónsson, 2007, p. 16). It might, moreover, lend weight to the observation that former deportees want to share their stories (Lecadet, 2011, p. 17ff).

Despite being a woman, I rarely met female deportees – only in rare cases through the organizations. I was also told about some. Most deportee women had been returned together with their husbands, particularly from Libya. In addition

---

13   Birama Bagayogo was a 33-year-old Malian anthropologist, with whom I collaborated starting in summer 2015, and who assisted me on numerous occasions during my second field phase, October 2015 until March 2016. I will detail this collaboration in the next section.

to the fact that there is less (independent) international female migration, women seem to be deported less often than men and female deportees are less publicly visible. That may relate to the fact that female migration has long been viewed ambiguously. Women's international migration in particular may still be suspected of having a possible connection to sex work or the development of new sexual attitudes, both of which are easily stigmatized (Lesclingand & Hertrich, 2017, p. 66).

I will briefly describe one incident, as it demonstrates how positionality imbalances can intersect in research with deportees, influencing people's lifeworlds to some degree and research findings most of all. A former deportee from Belgium, whom I had known from the beginning of my field work, became firmly convinced that he and I were going to marry. We paid a visit to his village in the region of Kayes after spending some time making plans to do so. The respondent wanted to show me the place, and I was curious and grateful for this research opportunity to accompany somebody "back to the village." We went there together taking Birama's cousin with us for co-research. During our stay I had mixed feelings, which turned out to be well-founded: back in Bamako, the respondent confronted me with his ideas about getting married. It turned out that during our visit that he had told the entire family about his/our marriage, even about plans to migrate to Germany.

Obviously, the respondent and I had been in frequent contact in the course of my ethnographic research; I was interested in him and cared about him – but as a researcher, not as a woman. With the help of Birama's cousin, I tried painfully to clear up this enormous misunderstanding between the respondent and myself. His family was deeply disappointed and his aunt in Bamako demanded extra clarification. She was irritated about this "unexpected development." It seemed that our encounter had converted a long-cherished desire to leave into a supposedly attainable reality for them, making all of them fall for the idea. The respondent was deeply sorry when he realized his mistake. At the same time, this incident can be read as another arbitrary outcome of the political and moral economy of conditions post deportation, another result of the global social inequalities and injustices manifested in the deportation regime (cf. Khosravi, 2018, p. 6). It proved the existence of asymmetries in our research situation and, importantly, of differing gender conceptions as well. The respondent's aspiration to leave again was revived and he continued to talk about leaving again, but now he was focusing on other means.

Extending the site to the village. Researching post deportation in the rural hinterland

The major aim of my second stay in the field, from October 2015 to March 2016, was to continue following the cases and people I had met in 2014. I planned to concentrate on the themes developed from the data I had acquired so far (see further analysis, pp. 91ff). More than that, though, I saw it as of central importance to explore rural Mali further, the places of origin of the deportees and the places to which they would potentially return after their forced removal, thus substantially extending my field beyond Bamako and deepening it.[14] It was also an opportunity to shed light on the little researched post-deportation context in rural areas. I continued to be fascinated by the tension between stasis and the urge to leave again, as well as by the "issue in the head" that it embodied, which seemed to originate from and be condensed in the designation "migratory adventurer" and, most notably, "failed migratory adventurer." However, the intention to focus on deportees "on the move," those who had recently returned and were about to leave again, altered substantially as I continued my research. Increasingly, I realized that conditions post deportation were often characterized by physical immobilization and imagined mobility, or rather by some kind of a continuum between different forms of internal and external mobility and immobility, not, as had often been suggested, by the predominance of a desire for re-emigration (cf. e.g., Schuster & Madji, 2013). Even if all the respondents, Malian former deportees as well as the Cameroonians stuck in "the Ghetto," had previously announced that they were leaving again, all of them were still there one year later.[15] They engaged where they were, bit by bit, continuing their lives and doing their best to support their families or get along by themselves.[16] This impression of immobility and permanence (cf. Gaibazzi, 2015a) became even more remarkable when I extended my stays in the rural areas of Kita and Yanfolila, where many young men seemed to stay on and live after their last deportation, sometimes after several deportations.

During ten months of absence from the field, a lot seemed to have changed. Migratory routes to the north had been opened up again and so the associations became more active in their daily assistance work. The period from 2015 on, furthermore, was the time of the large-scale shipwrecks. Among the 800 people ship-

---

14   As described in the last chapter, Mali remains very much centralized in and around Bamako, notwithstanding the fact that it contains a number of medium-sized cities (of about 100,000 to 225,000 (Sikasso) inhabitants), these being, in most cases, the capitals of the different administrative areas. For that reason, I speak about rural Mali and beyond Bamako, even though some of my research was also conducted in the cities of Kita, Kayes and Yanfolila, for instance. The great majority of my field research outside Bamako took place in the rural hinterland.

15   A young man I had met earlier shortly after his deportation from France was an exception, as were three young Cameroonians encountered in the *"Halle de Bamako."* All of them, however, had already moved on while I was still in Bamako in 2014 – either to gold mining sites to the southwest or northward, with a first stop in Algeria. The young man from France had suddenly gone off the radar (see further Chapter 4). In fact, being "highly mobile" they had re-emigrated.

16   Since 2016 two more of my main respondents in Bamako have left – one went to the gold mining sites in southwest Mali; the other one returned to France.

wrecked in April 2015, a catastrophe that sparked off the European "refugee crisis," as described above, were almost 200 Malians (Sylla & Schultz, 2020). This brought a new dimension to the migratory phenomenon in the country. In some villages vast groups of youngsters were leaving: "there are so many young people who are leaving currently" one former deportee told me, though he himself remained in Bamako, facilitating the migratory activities of the young of his community. Curiously, the German chancellor Angela Merkel became a repeated theme in my daily conversations as everybody wanted to know more about how she had contributed to a "summer of migration" (Schwiertz & Ratfisch, 2016).

I quickly put the plan to extend the site and become multi-local into practice. It was all about exploring *refoulé* hotspots in the rural hinterland, in other words, places that many deportees had returned to. Moreover, I wanted to accompany those I had met in Bamako back to their families' village sites. Meticulously, we negotiated with the representatives or associated partners of the self-organized deportee groups in the different localities. The AME had only recently appointed an associated representative in Kita, some 190 km west of Bamako, as the organization had become more aware of the large presence of deportees and repatriates in this area, many having come from Libya, and of their significance for the political dimension of post-deportation experiences in Mali as well. Boubakar had been an active migrant and retail dealer in the sub-region and also been deported from Libya about 15 years ago.

A first exploration with a coworker of the AME from Bamako to Kita built the base where I met (disappeared) migrants' parents, returnees, and local government and association representatives: an intense debate around a large table in the city hall revealed the obviously burning issues relating to migration and its current corollary effects. Several villages had been devastatingly affected by the shipwrecks, with sometimes 10–15 or more young men dying at the same time. This had led to bewilderment and despair in the face of an unprecedented situation; moreover, new voices repeating "the youth need to stay" were making themselves heard (as touched on in the introductory chapter and to be further explored in Chapter 6).

In addition, there was already a large presence, many hundreds in total, of deportees and repatriates in the surrounding villages, though a new "wave" of deportees and repatriates from Libya and Algeria would increase the numbers again in 2017, reshaping rural landscapes through the presence of returnees and their organizations and the setting-up of reintegration projects in the context of the EU-IOM-Joint-Initiative (see Chapter 2). Boubakar, the new AME representative in Kita, had not only announced our arrival on the radio,[17] but had also paid personal visits to a number of villages informing them of my envisaged fieldwork. He was

---

17   It is a common practice to announce different kinds of activities, news and occurrences on the radio as radio is the most widespread and established medium in Mali.

well-known and respected in the city and many surrounding communities. He was engaged in a variety of development and migration projects, but notoriously lacked money: donors had often promised to pay but their promises had rarely been kept.

It took some explanation of what I was after in my research (ethnographic basics such as staying in relevant places, speaking with relevant people, living with a deportee's family, etc.). The major criteria we agreed upon eventually were: the presence and number of deportees in a certain village; deportees who for the most part had been on their way to Europe or North Africa; and places that were accessible. The selection of extended field sites necessarily depended on Boubakar's personal contacts and relations. Eventually, I made repeated prolonged stays in two villages in particular. Intense negotiations continued about being part of this field.

In these "selected" villages, we each stayed with a family of former deportees. Each beginning was meaningful in itself. It was clear that we had to follow the "official" and hierarchical procedure for paying visits in this region: through the mayor, if he was based in this specific locality, the chief of the village, and the local notables. Extended introductory meetings, presentations of one's role and research interest as well as exchanges of gifts were essential steps in any first encounter in order to build a dignified foundation and the trust required to enable collaboration. It was indispensable, therefore, that I came with some more or less local counterparts, Boubakar and Birama Bagayogo in this case. Often we would sit together with a group of former deportees and drink tea in the village center or on the patio of a former deportee's house. It was mostly deportees themselves or other key people in the villages who brought together former migrants, deportees, and repatriates by spreading the word that a German researcher was there and wanted to speak with them. This seemed to be a great attraction and maybe a welcome diversion particularly in moments of boredom during the dry season. At the same time, my presence seemed to spark a multiplicity of experiences, expectations, and hopes, or maybe mere curiosity. Certainly, a certain degree of self-selection among respondents needs to be taken into account as well. Overall, however, the high number of people attending underlined the omnipresence of deportees and repatriates.

In one small village near Kita, which eventually became one of my research sites (as contextualized in the previous chapter), it was young men, former deportees themselves, who contacted Boubakar following the first radio announcement. They paid him a visit aiming to get organized to raise funds for little projects for the *refoulés* in their village and to speak up for them. One of them, who had been sent back on a vessel from the Mediterranean close to the Libyan coast several years before, knew Boubakar from a joint project. When I returned to the area for a longer stay some weeks later, I met these committed young men and became installed in their village. It was during longer stays in their village as well as in the larger village with a community center that I was able to go into greater depth in my research into the rural, social embedding of post-deportation experience.

Collaborating with a co-researcher – considerations of give and take

Through my collaboration with Birama Bagayogo as a co-researcher, my project received a particularly substantive character. Not all former deportees spoke French. Particularly beyond Bamako conversations were mostly held in Bambara, the most widespread local language. My own attempts to learn it by taking classes had only taken me as far as being able to speak in a rudimentary fashion, though my proficiency was enhanced through engaging with people on the spot. Still, having somebody to provide assistance, translation and collaboration, became indispensable for solid research. Birama was a 33-year-old Malian anthropologist, consultant on health issues, and an acquaintance of a Malian doctoral student I knew, who recommended him. From October 2015 to March 2016, he accompanied my fieldwork on numerous occasions as a linguistic and cultural translator, and increasingly as an appreciated interlocutor, advisor, and friend.[18]

While we obviously had to find a modus operandi, our collaboration became smoother and smoother over time. We shared intense days, thoughts, and work during the weeks in a village, but also in Bamako, where I partially worked from his office. Birama supported me as much as he could. I tried to do the same for him, introducing him to the self-organized deportee groups and activist circles as well as other researchers. It turned out to be a very fruitful and productive research collaboration. Mostly received positively by people who were curious and welcoming, we were both strangers in the villages, one more than the other, of course, and in different ways. In these positions, we also represented "money," "foreign knowledge," and a supposed "power." I was often confronted with stories of experts who had visited and, for example, promised a large project, but had never come back. This created mistrust, which needed to be overcome. Otherwise, our supposed expertise was requested for consultations on alternative earnings, discussing small projects like installing a garden, or organizing animal breeding. As foreign researchers, this seemed to be an unavoidable role, and came despite constant clarifications of our reason for being here.

Generally, collaborations such as the one between Birama and myself have raised multiple concerns regarding power imbalances or loss of accuracy through translations (Englert & Dannecker, 2014). However, this research constellation brought essential benefits. Since deportees in the village sites were almost exclusively men of little education and from a rural background, having a male counterpart created more commonality. Birama, for instance, could hang out with the young men, when I was somewhere else in the village or talking to somebody. They would tell him about "male" intimacies, such as hooking up with women in

---

18   On two occasions, I was accompanied by Birama's cousin Madiba Malé, also a young anthropologist, as Birama had other commitments.

the nearby city while their wives and children stayed at home. These things would hardly have reached my ears otherwise. On the other hand, Birama received a good salary; we had negotiated according to his standards (which I considered high and demanding at first). Even if he had had little connection with the topic of migration so far, he was intrigued to explore this new angle, and applied it in subsequent projects, for instance on informal gold mining.

Birama and the others who provided access to the field, notably the deportee organizations, were of tremendous assistance in handling the complex requirements of giving and taking in the field. Importantly, I had to learn about the social meaning of money and the complexities of a widespread generalized reciprocity (see Chapter 5). I had to literally pay some of the respondents, although many textbooks would suggest the opposite. "It's your business!" one deportee in Bamako said quite frankly, when discussing the issue of how I could compensate them for their time and sharing their (life) stories, suggesting that I give a little money when we met next time. Not only did the run-down economic situation in Mali create existential needs for many,[19] most importantly, those in the city without a social net were suffering: sometimes, it was hard for me to overcome a sensation of wanting "to give support" and being hounded by the awareness that I was unable to do much. Obviously, these historically grown and reinforced inherent inequalities were impossible to overcome simply.[20]

My conversations, collaborations, and relationships with the Malian field have continued until now, in different forms and at different intensities, with a number of respondents, with my gatekeepers, the organizations, with Malian researchers and with Birama – on Facebook, via WhatsApp or email, and sometimes over the phone. They consist in exchanges regarding information and money, or in simple courtesies and keeping up friendships. Despite evident "irreconcilable incompatibilities," particularly with some, being indebted (to one's field) is a condition and characteristic of social relationships. It is not only that the field "never stops," it is rather that the field and my experiences have become part of me and I have become part of this field.

---

19   Before, he had been doing little trips with and services for tourists, who were absent now.

20   Others have developed approaches to balance such imbalances (e.g., Giebeler & Meneses, 2012), toward more "equal" and reciprocal giving and taking. However, this requires extensive preconditioning and cannot always be put into practice. I had had an excellent start, beginning my research embedded in a Malian academic institute. I presented my first field results in a small colloquium there and organized an event with the German embassy about educational opportunities in Europe. One scholar was following a similar topic to mine. We started a fruitful and frequent exchange, sharing contacts, thoughts, and arguments, and even conducted joint field research activities; in fact, we have been engaged in academic projects together up to the present. This latter combined effort might meet most expectations of collaborative research and a thorough give and take.

Methods, sampling and data gathering in polyphony

The corpus of data material for this study is very extensive and diverse in form and quality, as is typical for most ethnographies.[21] Even though I followed a snowball process in the main, the idea behind the sampling (Corbin & Strauss, 1990) was to collect the narratives and observe practices of former deportees and their social surroundings. To be considered deportees, subjects had to have been forcefully returned or obliged to return, which included having been repatriated or undergone a transit return. Most such people were defining themselves as *refoulés* (see Chapter 1; cf. also Table 2). In the course of the research the aim became more specific: to collect contrasting samples of urban and rural cases, with central respondents and people who had presumably stayed on after (their last) return and including younger as well as older males. In the following, I will briefly summarize the methods I used, the data I obtained, and the results I analyzed.

I applied a reflexive ethnographic approach (cf. Davies, 1999) including a variety of methods, types of persons, documents, and institutions. To approximate deportees' experiences in accordance with their personal stories, their practices, and everyday observed behavior, I used different forms of qualitative interview (in-depth and semi-structured[22]), informal conversations, and (group) discussions, (participant) observations as well as field notes (cf. Bryman, 2012, p. 213; cf. also Rubin & Rubin, 1995). I used ethnography as an overall approach since it allows going beyond "methodological constraints" ("*Methodenzwang*"; Feyerabend, 1976), thus allowing the researcher to draw on a complex of methods applied according to the needs of the field. Breidenstein et al. (2013, pp. 31ff) describe the methodological "trademarks of ethnography" as fourfold: its subject-matter is social practices; it conducts field work through "continuing immediate experience"; it allows for methodological opportunism through an "integrated research approach"; and, finally, it ends in "writing and verbalization of the social."

---

21   Bryman (2012) calls the sampling of respondents in an ethnographic research project "sometimes a combination of opportunistic sampling and snowball sampling" (p. 424). Accordingly, much of the time ethnographers are forced to gather information from whatever sources are available to them. Very often they face opposition or at least indifference to their research and are relieved to glean information or views from anyone who is prepared to divulge such details (ibid.).

22   The term "qualitative interview" (in-depth interview) sometimes refers to an unstructured interview but more often refers to both semi-structured and unstructured interviewing. The use of this term seems to be increasing. And the term "semi-structured" typically refers to "a context in which the interviewer has a series of [somewhat more general] questions that are in the general form of an interview schedule but is able to vary the sequence of questions" (Bryman, 2012, p. 212).

Conducting ethnographic field work is based on the experience of the ethnographer as well as that of the respondents. Memorized experiences in my research were retrospectively recounted and gifted with meaning and sense in narrations and stories. As a matter of course, it needs to be acknowledged that there is a large gap between experience and expression (Bruner, 1986, pp. 6f) and we have to take into account respondents' narrative reconstructions as well. Rosenthal, building on the narrative interview after Schütze (1976), highlights the need to differentiate between experience, memory, and narration as researchers. She refers to the "narrated personal life as related in conversation or written in the present time" and the "lived-through-life" (2006), and the need to differentiate between narrated and experienced life history. Narratives of experienced events, consequently, refer both to current life and to past experience.[23] It is essential to take this into account when interviewing and analyzing. One has to familiarize oneself with the given context, not least in order to define the field and one's research topic. In my case, the local language constituted a particular issue. On the other hand, coming too close or, as it were, "going too native" might lead to a loss of oversight and analytical clarity. I had to beware of what I termed, with Susann Huschke, "activist's blinders," so as not to obscure my research capacities. Coming too close might lead to losing this position of neutrality (cf. Jónsson, 2007). The ethnographic challenge lies in a constant shifting of roles, in negotiating, exchanging, balancing, and reflecting over and over again in all possible constellations.

I first of all followed a relatively open interview structure to generate topics and set the scene for understanding deportees' general interpretative patterns of situations post involuntary and forced returns. To do so, I often started with an open question such as "I would like to hear your story of leaving and return: Why and how did you leave your place? Where did you go to? How and why did you return? I will just listen and ask questions afterwards..." Such openings frequently resulted in an interaction made up of questions and shorter or longer answers, which had the character of a conversation rather than a consecutive narration. Some people started talking and talked for a long time. In other cases, it felt as if I was getting bits and pieces, which certainly had to be accepted as respondents' boundaries as well.[24] So, I adapted to each specific situation (cf. also Hasselberg, 2018) over the time of my research.

---

23   In this way, "even in the case of a spontaneous memory-based narrative of experienced events we have to assume that there is a difference in general between the experienced event in the past, the recollection thereof and the narrative" (Rosenthal, 2006, p. 3).

24   It is important to note that my interview partners had been thoroughly informed and had agreed to participate in the specific setting and purpose of the research. Moreover, they knew, they could withdraw at any point. I tried to be as careful as possible not to dig deeper when issues appeared to become sensitive.

For the second phase of my field work, I built substantially on the analysis results of that first round of interviews, conversations, and observations. My interest was predominantly in the aspects of failure and shame, suffering, the migratory adventure and *la chance* – let's call it a broader spiritual and cosmological embedding; in addition, I was interested in the complex of family, social, and kin relations and in the complex of hard work, everyday life, going on and "real chances" as well. Questions in conversations with former deportees circulated mainly around their everyday and economic activities, experiences before, during, and after deportation, and their social relations and reactions to the migration and return. Accompanying questions (without spelling them out) were: what did this supposed failure of expectations imply exactly? What role did the families and social surroundings play? What did the unwanted return mean in socio-economic terms as well as in the long run? I developed a semi-structured interview guideline that I discussed and shared with Birama. Eventually, our conversations left a lot of unstructured space, where we ended up talking openly in each conversation.

I conducted repeat interviews during both field phases (cf. Fauser, 2009). This enabled selective points to be researched more concretely, and contradictions and conflictive statements to be carved out (cf. Schultz, 2014). Several of the people I was able to accompany, meet and speak to over the course of the two field phases, became key respondents allowing a specific depth of research. More than that, the twofold sampling over the two research phases, even if primarily implemented as snowballing, also served as a triangulation strategy.

Table 2 (see page 95) gives a rough overview of the methods used and the data obtained.[25]

Besides the framing through the organizations that I had started my field research with, I aimed at getting a grasp of the views of the social environment – the former deportees' brothers, sisters and cousins, their fathers and mothers, their friends, neighbors, colleagues and other acquaintances – to better capture their social embedding. Again this was done through qualitative interviews and informal conversations, as well as group discussions – in Bamako, but mostly in the village

---

25 Instead of differentiating according to the destinations of deportations, repatriations, and transit returns, the table divides respondents by the research sites in Bamako and rural areas. The large majority of deportees consider themselves as falling into the category of *refoulés* (see Chapter 1). Self-induced return without external help refers to those who describe themselves as having returned involuntarily, constrained by the external conditions, mostly unplanned, particularly in the context of the Libyan crisis 2011–2014; "voluntary" self-induced return refers to those people who describe themselves as having decided and planned to return, for instance, from Spain, but also from Morocco or Libya. In the latter cases, it may still have been a general worsening of conditions that provoked a return decision, such as increasing unemployment or racism.

sites – oftentimes with the entire extended family. Moreover, I observed the institutional context at different levels: administrative representatives in the village, municipality, and at the regional and national level. Additionally, interviews with Malian government officials, and representatives of NGOs, international organizations, embassies (those of France, Switzerland, Spain, and Germany), and civil society, as well as with other academics, allowed an understanding of the political and economic embedding of post-deportation experiences in Mali.[26]

Furthermore, we had a variety of group discussions with former deportees (see e.g., Bryman, 2012, pp. 501ff), more formally organized or spontaneously emerging, sitting together, drinking tea and passing time chatting or in rather more "serious" conversation. Such group gatherings contributed to grasping the individuals' embedding as well as their situations after deportation more broadly; furthermore, they served as a means to cross-check dates and background information. Sometimes there were illuminating discussions on terms introduced by me or Birama, such as the different meanings of "suffering," and the meaning and practice of "the migratory adventure," but they also covered people's everyday lives and general perceptions. In these "gatherings," the social situation and specific interactions were often the most interesting aspects as they arose out of dealing with the issue of (post) deportations in a semi-public space, which allowed me to grasp the views of the others. Laughter or sudden silence, for instance, could be indicators of issues considered shameful. Still, it was not all about finding out what had "actually" happened; it also involved taking into account the way that the participants presented their stories and how this was related to the intervention created by the interview situation, here taking place in a group (Rosenthal, 1993). Even if this this kind of intervention may come across as rather informal in an ethnographic approach (Breidenstein et al. 2013, p. 80), it allowed us to get an idea of the specific ways in which deportees related their doings and activities post deportation in a group setting. At the same time, accounts given in such groups could replicate what I had heard from other respondents during more intimate sessions.

---

26   Here, I was mostly interested in the roles and responsibilities of the institutions, their mandates, their evaluation of the current situation with regard to migration / migration and development / involuntary return migration, their perception of the developments in current migration policy and their potential involvement, their take on voluntary return vs. involuntary return and reinsertion, in general and in policy development, their collaborations (with government, NGOs, embassies, the EU), and how they saw the future of migration (policy), in Mali in particular, with regard to (involuntary) return.

Respondent / Data Group	Method	Quantity Persons / Groups
Representatives of Malian governmental organizations, embassies of EU member states, the EU, Malian and international NGOs in Bamako, Kita, Kayes, and Yanfolila	Qualitative interviews (partially repeated in both field phases)	45
Deportee self-organized groups in Bamako, Kayes, and Yanfolila	Qualitative interviews (repeated)	16
	Informal conversations and (participant) observation (repeated)	
	Contacts via Facebook, WhatsApp, email, or telephone (continues)	6
Transit migrants (mostly from Cameroon, also from Liberia and Sierra Leone)	Qualitative interviews	5
	Informal conversations and (participant) observation (repeated, mainly in 1st field phase)	
	Group discussions	2
	Contacts via Facebook, email, WhatsApp or telephone	2
Malian deportees in rural sites	Qualitative interviews	48
	Informal conversations and (participant) observation (repeated during several longer stays in the village)	
	Group discussions	17
Social surroundings of deportees in rural sites (family members, friends, neighbors)	Qualitative interviews	24
	Informal conversations and (participant) observation	
	Group discussions	19
Malian deportees in Bamako	Qualitative interviews	28
	Informal conversations and (participant) observation	
	Group discussions	2
	Contacts over Facebook, email, WhatsApp or telephone	5
Social surrounding of deportees in Bamako (family members, friends, neighbors)	Qualitative interviews	9
	Informal conversations and (participant) observation	
	Group discussions	3
"Assisted voluntary returnees" with the support of the IOM in Bamako	Qualitative interviews	2
Self-induced voluntary returnees	Qualitative interviews	2
	Informal conversations	10
Self-induced involuntary returnees	Qualitative interviews	5
	Informal conversations	18
Random encounters and informal conversations with people in the streets, taxi drivers, etc.		
Conversations with Malian academics at the transnational research center, the University of Bamako and other research institutes in Bamako		
Field diaries Electronic notes	Fieldnotes Fieldnotes, reflections	13 numerous
Policy and project documents, reports, and statistical data from the deportee and other organizations or political institutions	Collection, lecture and partial content-analysis	numerous
Newspaper articles	Collection, lecture and partial content-analysis	numerous
Materials from academic and national archives	Collection, lecture and partial content-analysis	numerous

I wrote up as much as possible in field diaries, as well as electronically "writing and verbalizing the social," often sitting to one side, observing, reflecting, listening, and also asking questions. On other occasions, note taking was hard. Judith Okely (2008) coined the term "knowing without notes," which implies the idea of an embodied field: in this sense, many things that I experienced contributed to understanding and deepening my work and later my analysis, even if they were not meticulously written down.[27] I complemented my note taking with an audio recorder and sometimes a video camera to generate a more "focused ethnography" (Knoblauch, 2001)[28], especially in light of my "extending the field site." I also took many pictures. While respondents, particularly those I knew better, would take a video themselves, on other occasions this observing external eye caused serious uneasiness and suspicion of errant publicity and lack of privacy. In the end, though, the visualizations and recorded interactions provided more atmospheric and enriching impressions to support my analysis.

Throughout, I appreciated random encounters with people in the street, the shop owner next door, and, importantly, taxi drivers, "classic" informal respondents (cf. Lachenmann, 2010). In addition, I collected policy and project documents, reports, and statistical data from deportee and other organizations or from political institutions, as well as newspaper articles and relevant academic literature, paying particular attention to material from from Malian researchers and others in the region. Not least, I went to Malian academic and national archives. I never did a formal analysis of these materials, but they served to supplement my understanding of the broader context and the embedding of my data. Even so, if pertinent lectures and reading were indispensable, some aspects or specific expressions could only be understood with the assistance of people from the field. Eventually, I clarified questions and local terminologies through "going back virtually" to the field by talking over the phone, skype, or exchanging messages by email.[29]

In the end, the polyphony of my research, the different types of people interviewed, the institutions and sites selected, the positions taken as well as documents included, served to triangulate my data and perspectives. Triangulation of interview and ethnographic materials is an important quality criterion for justifying and

---

27   Breidenstein et al. (2013) describe a central intuition, which has led to criticism of the method as it cannot be "objectively" measured as other qualitative approaches would be assumed to be.

28   The idea of a "focused ethnography," which in sociology is mostly about doing research in one's "own" society (Knoblauch, 2001), seemed to constitute a sociological ethnography beyond the "ethnos" of another society (which still requires an "estranging" of the familiar; cf. ibid).

29   After I left Mali in 2016, Birama also remained in contact with some of the respondents. Moreover, he conducted an additional fieldwork exercise in 2018 in the village where I had spent most time and verified some issues.

assuring results (Englert & Dannecker, 2014). More than that, this polyphony was an indispensable research strategy when it came to answering my research question. Understanding (post-)deportation experiences, their social embedding and life after deportation back in the Malian south, could not have been adequately done by speaking to deportees only.

Analyzing along the general lines of grounded theory

I quickly got an inkling of the essence of what I later termed the supposed "failed migratory adventure." It lay in the recurring motifs of money loss, "*la honte*" (shame), social expectations in light of the observed "issue in the head," and restlessness, that came out of my first round of analysis and was built on my immediate observations in the field. As described in the introductory chapter, talking about failure, in terms of "*j'ai échoué*" or *maloya*, was an emic conception; but one that was also used in the political setting and, importantly, by the deportee organizations and other political actors. Furthermore, it was a media and academic discourse that I felt needed to be explored in more depth and with more differentiation.

A "thinking about data" (Schultz, 2014; transl. S.U.S.), i.e., a going back and forth from the data to theoretical reflection, started early on. I took my first steps in the field guided by the parameters of grounded theory: from an entry into the organizations to a snowballing of my respondents, to developing broader and more specific questions and extending my field site. From the enormous corpus of audio and video data, and the notes I had collected, I selected what was to be processed, transcribed, and analyzed further on the basis of places and cases – those I had known best and for the longest time, in Bamako and in the countryside, as well as those that were most contrasting, in order to best explore and describe the range of the phenomenon. Contrasting, in this instance, meant selecting those with the largest differences in outcome, so long as I had sufficient validation of the type in question (in terms of theoretical saturation, see below). Data from the rural hinterland mainly derives from the two villages in the area of Kita where I stayed longest.[30] I transcribed parts of the data in French myself; while Birama carried out the majority of the transcriptions from the second field phase. Parts of this

---

30   Even though I also spent several weeks in the area of Yanfolila, where large numbers of deportees returned in the first decade of the 2000s, I had to leave the data out of fine-grained analysis and, above all, when writing this study. It would not have been possible to present it here in a sufficiently contextualized way. Nonetheless, the insights gained from this tranche of research and first analysis contributed substantially to my understanding of my overall topic and to better shaping my argument.

audio material were in Bambara, which he translated simultaneously. In this process we talked intensely about central emic terms and conceptions; still, I am aware that aspects must have been lost in translation. Transcribing serves as a first, more in-depth round of analysis. I revised the transcriptions I made with Birama thoroughly and supplemented them. This was an essential step in becoming familiar with the data and starting the analysis. Some sections needed to be listened to over and over again before I could grasp their subtle, emotional meanings.

The issue of theoretical sensitivity and prior knowledge is the central conflict between Strauss and Corbin, on the one hand, and Glaser, on the other, the founders of grounded theory.[31] Clearly, the selection of my general research topic, the social dimensions of post-deportation in Mali, was driven by knowledge of the political setting and academic literature in deportation studies. I set out to do my first field work early during my research project in order to preserve some of my own openness. I conducted a first analysis through open coding of interview data and field notes orientating myself on the descriptions of Corbin and Strauss (1990) after both field phases. Instead of generating full-fledged theoretically saturated categories at first, I formed code groups indicating three thematic blocks and tensions, which served for continuing my field research.[32] From all of this I selected a number of terms to be more systematically researched in their emic meaning and local embedding back in the field.[33]

A first impression of "theoretical saturation" (Strauss & Corbin, [1990] 1998, p. 212, cf. Bryman, 2012, p. 421) was gained through people giving me similar accounts. I thought at first that this meant that they were providing me with superficial stories and I would need to go deeper; however, I soon realized that it was much more to do with their stories, how they perceived and told them and the kind of

---

31   While Anselm Strauss and Juliet Corbin suggested that prior knowledge would exist in any research and contribute to theoretical sensitivity towards the research topic, Barney Glaser was convinced this prior knowledge would hinder openness towards grasping the research phenomenon in the field. In line with Strauss and Corbin (1990), Schultz (2014) recommends writing up one's knowledge in order to visualize and be conscious of potentially hindering presumptions. This can be done, for instance, by making situational maps (cf. Clarke, 2005).

32   The first tension was inherent in the term "the migratory adventure," the shifting between leaving and staying related to hardships and sufferings and simultaneously chances and opportunities. The second tension emerged from the complex of sociality, responsibility, and obligations towards the family, in close or more distant social relations, and from embedding after deportations. Third, I found a tension between being hard working yet having nothing to do, which could again be a form of suffering. In fact, these already closely resembled my final analysis and argumentation.

33   These circulated around three complexes: 1) stigma, shame, failing ("la honte"; maloya); 2) migration, mobility and adventure and related terms such as tounkan, clandestin or voyager; 3) the meaning of la chance, of suffering (la souffrance), expressions such as "ce n'est pas facile," "il n'y a rien," succeeding (réussir), and money (le moyen; wari).

reconstructed narrative that came out of that. Of course, in some cases there could be even more subtle layers of meaning that I came to, as well as differing theoretical angles. Not least, my polyphonic and at the same time in-depth research approach was driven by the need for theoretical saturation. Even if cases sometimes seemed to be erratically different and dispersed, I was able to analyze comparable and similar patterns and commonalities clearly in accordance with the specific deportation trajectories, origins and destinations of former deportees, their time spent abroad and, after their return, the money they had earned or lost, and their age, gender, and education. These aspects will be developed throughout this study.

From the open coding of the material after the second field trip, I again formed summarizing codes and code groups in order to come to categorizations, comparing them with the codes and code groups from the first field trip. While axially and selectively coding, I started to write up, beginning by constructing and following my cases – again starting with those that were closest and best "known" to me. From there, the topics emerged again through writing. They centered more and more on the issues of the adventure, (im)mobility, suffering, money, kinship, hard work, courage, and *la chance*. I went back to axial coding again, and even more to axial wording – that is to say that I worked with the word cloud function in my MAXQDA analysis tool as I was not fully satisfied with the results of my open coding and grouping, it seemed far too broad still. What came out again were the complexes family/kin, money/*moyens*, migration/adventure/(im)mobility/journey, hardship/suffering, and failure. So I went back to the transcriptions and searched for the embedding of the terms "money/*moyen*/wealth," "suffering," and "adventures/(im)mobilities," and how these were interlinked. I started reading and theorizing further, while continuing to think about my data. Recapitulating what I had analyzed through earlier categorizing, I was able to develop more full-fledged categories and theoretical concepts. Overall, it worked out like a circular process. In the end, the recurring topics and theoretically saturated[34], undergirded main themes were "failures, success," "suffering and courage," "masculinities," "social navigating," "*la chance*," "money, social surroundings," "mobility, immobility," "youth and becoming," "rural–urban," "narrating, talking, not talking."

I selected the supposed failed migratory adventure as core category for this work as it best captures and combines all relevant phenomena in one guiding

---

34   In the language of grounded theory, a category operates at a somewhat higher level of abstraction than a concept in that it may group together several concepts that have common features denoted by the category. Saturation does not mean, as is sometimes suggested, that the researcher develops a sense of déjà vu when listening to what people say in interviews but that new data no longer suggest new insights into an emergent theory or no longer suggest new dimensions of theoretical categories (Bryman, 2012, p. 421).

theme.[35] It allows me to shed light on how the political and economic dimensions of deportations are socially reflected in deportees' narrations and lifeworlds, and how the explicit political effects, emotional and material losses of the global deportation regime translate into embodied and ambivalent individual and social dimensions. I will develop the chapters that follow along the lines selected.

How to study conditions post deportation? Concluding reflections

This chapter has provided a methodological account of how I researched the multi-locality and omnipresence of deportations over an extended field site in Mali within a relatively short time. To conclude, I will briefly summarize my response to the question of what kind of ethnography I carried out in order to eventually come up with fully developed and satisfactory results.

Deportations need to be analyzed in all their complexities and dynamics. The multi-sited approach is quasi tailor-made for researching people on the move, and allows one the best standpoint from which to grapple with the rupture and other effects of the administrative practice of deportation in its transnational dimension and all aspects of the migration cycle, as research in deportation studies has increasingly shown (e.g., Hasselberg 2018; Plambech, 2018, 2017; Alpes, 2017; Drotbohm, 2016, 2015, 2012, 2011; Khosravi, 2016; Golash-Boza, 2015). I did not, as originally and theoretically intended, follow the "highly mobile" deportees and *refoulés*, but more and more applied myself to and embraced the topic of immobilization after deportation as it emerged from the field. My research was still multi-sited in a sense, though, in that I started to explore and capture the post-deportation field in Mali in its different varieties and forms in different localities. Against this background, my field work was characterized by a tension between being called by the field and staying focused, following "the local cultural grain," but also conducting research in as "polyphonic" a fashion as possible (Meyer, 2013, p. 312), thereby collaboratively developing the field and fulfilling the respondents' and gatekeepers' expectations as well as my own research demands. This had to be balanced and renegotiated over and again.

I developed a combination of a "go along" (Kusenbach, 2003) and, what might be called, a "hang out" ethnography. I followed individual deportees over a longer period and increasingly focused on the everyday life of Malian deportees in rural and urban places as well as their social embedding. I thus eventually used some of what

---

35   Even if it can be hard, or even impossible, to find one all-explanatory core category (cf. Corbin & Strauss, 1990, p. 14). In the end writing a study of this kind is a matter of making decisions – where to start, what empirical data to select and what not – there may eventually be different stories to tell from the data.

Hahn suggests are the benefits of a place-based approach, to observe the translocal, global, and transnational (social, cultural, political, economic) dimensions in their connections with and disruptions of what I would call the effects and embedding of the (post-)deportation regime. The extended site gave me both a particular view and a broad understanding and allowed me to go beyond potential localized/place-based limits, enabling me to gain an in-depth view of a broader phenomenon in one analytical frame, in one single site – the post-deportation situation in Mali in its different facets, the various actors, places, discourses and deportation practices it involves.

As a white European woman, I need to acknowledge that there are specific re-sults and shades of narrative presentation I collected, which others would have come to differently. Against this background, my research collaboration with Bi-rama Bagayogo turned out to be particularly beneficial as we fruitfully combined a Malian, academic and urban (though rural in origin) with a German research view and positionality. Moreover, my research strategy to set up a polyphonic and in-depth approach at the same time allowed the operationalization of my research question in finding out about deportees' lifeworlds, conceptions and social em-bedding after deportation. In all this, our encounters, interactions, and observa-tions represented in themselves a current effect of restricted mobilities, external-ized borders and the deportation regime in a society characterized by longstanding "cultures of migration" and migratory adventures.

In the chapters that follow, I will analyze conditions post deportation as effects of the global deportation regime, reproduced by deported actors on a local site. I will develop grounded descriptions of these conditions by presenting my argu-ments on the basis of the data I collected in Bamako and in the two villages near Kita where I did most research during eight months over the course of two years, supplemented by telephone calls, email, Facebook and WhatsApp conversations, from the end of my field work until the time of publication.

Chapter 4
"The adventure is not easy." – Narrating forms of suffering in deportation experiences[1]

"The adventure is not easy" is a mantra for many former migrants who have become deportees, likewise for potential migrants and those stuck in transit. Suffering, in fact, is omnipresent in their narratives, in phrases such as "it's always the same suffering" or "it's hard to forget the suffering." To summarize the experiences of their migratory journey and eventual deportation, they link different forms of suffering in evoking the specific ambivalence of the entire "migratory adventure," which was the starting point for this book. This chapter is now set to dive into situations after deportation, but it focuses first of all on deportees' experiences of actual deportation processes and deportation regimes to aid our understanding of what happens to them as a result. What does deportation do to them? How do they change (physically, emotionally, and socially) as it impacts their situation and the situation of their social surroundings afterwards? From a theoretical point of view, the chapter centers on specific patterns in the accounts of suffering that emerge from the experiences depicted in deportees' narratives. As an intensely rich emic and theoretical concept, suffering can be seen as culturally, socially, and historically contingent, and, as a theme, it will accompany the analytical discussion throughout the book. This chapter provides a conceptual and empirical basis for deportees' narrative accounts and reconstructions of suffering.[2] The experiences and memories of migration and deportation have often left literal marks on deportees' bodies, and this damage may continue to be part of their everyday experience. Suffering also represents how people deal with the situation after deportations.

The forms of suffering that appear in deportees' narrative presentations of deportation can, in the terminology of Kleinman and Kleinman (1991), be deemed to be both "suffering resulting from extreme conditions" and a "routinized form of

---

1   Parts of this chapter have been previously published in Schultz, S. U. (2021b).
2   The richness of local perceptions of and allusions to suffering found in Mali will be revisited in Chapters 5 and 6.

suffering."[3] Suffering and hardship are most often discussed with respect to structure and agency (Bruijn et al., 2007)[4], subjectivity (Jackson, 2005a; Foucault et al., 2005; Boskovic, 2001) and concepts such as social navigating (Vigh, 2006) – defined as a "motion within motion" (p. 14), building on De Certeau's work on strategies and tactics as "the art of the weak" – and future-making (e.g., Kleist & Jansen, 2016; Chabal, 2009). Both these latter concepts are to be further discussed in subsequent chapters. Here, suffering is understood as both structural and agentic: structural in being inflicted by EU-driven deportation regimes and externalized border controls, which are extreme yet routinized at the same time; agentic in being part of the subjectivities that people develop within their local spaces to make sense of expressions and experiences of suffering.

This interrelation is well captured in the concept of social suffering, which focuses on the group dimension of suffering across contexts. Individuals are generally always social, but the Malian and West African context is particularly characterized by a dense web of social relations, as previously described. Social suffering "results from what political, economic, and institutional power does to people and, reciprocally, from how these forms of power themselves influence responses to social problems" (Kleinman et al., 1997, p. ix). In this sense, social suffering is caused by the impersonal forces inherent in deportations and bordering practices, as people suffer from the implementation of deportation as a political, legal, and administrative instrument of state power (cf. Drotbohm & Hasselberg, 2015, p. 559). At the same time, the social, political and institutional nature of deportation influences the agentic responses to it, which range from silence and endurance to social navigating (cf. also Kleinman et al., 1997, pp. xiiif). As products of constraints, these agentic responses may be highly ambivalent. Kleinman et al. (1997, p. x) claim that social suffering may even ruin the collective and intersubjective

---

3   Kleinman and Kleinman distinguish *routinized forms of suffering* that are either shared aspects of human conditions – chronic illness or death – or experiences of deprivation and exploitation and of degradation and oppression that certain categories of individuals (the poor, the vulnerable, the defeated) are specially exposed to and others relatively protected from," and *suffering resulting from extreme conditions*, such as survivorship of the Holocaust or the Atom Bomb or the Cambodian genocide or China's Cultural Revolution" (1991, p. 280; emphasis added by the authors). They also define as a third category suffering due to *"contingent misfortunes* such as serious acute illness."

4   Without claiming to enter any further into in-depth discussion of the wide topic of structure and agency, it is important to emphasize that agency is not equal to action, but rather the "self-reflective beliefs we have about our abilities and capacities (our self-efficacy) to act" (van Houte et al., 2016, p. 4). In the case of Malian deportees, I prefer to speak of imaginations and aspirations rather than beliefs. Van Houte et al.'s discussion of agency in the context of return migration is helpful as it places desires and capacities as "intermediate factors" between structure and agency. An actor's agency is then "determined by these desires and capacities, and is both shaped by and shapes structure" (2016, p. 4).

connections of experience and gravely damage subjectivity. From the point of view of sequential analysis (see, e.g., Rosenthal, 2006), suffering also needs to be seen as a narrative style or even strategy, given the position and power discrepancies inherent in our particular interactions with Malian respondents. Finally, too, it has to be acknowledged that suffering is barely graspable by researchers in an adequate way (cf. Jackson, 2005a).

After deportation, forms of social suffering may continue or even intensify over time through negative administrative or social treatment in the country of return. Deportation not only constrains deportees' agency but may create or even "enforce" new ways of thinking about and going on with their lives after it has happened.[5] In some senses, social suffering may even be a motor for change and new activities, not least since suffering needs to be overcome so that life can go on, as the saying goes; a correlation to be discussed in Chapter 6.

In what follows I will first carefully reflect on deportees' narratives of their interactions with state, legal, and bureaucratic practices and their emotional and embodied outcomes in terms of social suffering. I will show what this suffering constitutes for them. Experiences of violence, shock, alienation, fear, and stress, traumatic accounts, and anger are to be shown, as well as spatial and temporal disorders. This helps shed light on the social organizations supporting former deportees and on reactions among the wider Malian public. The last subsection reflects on the powerful symbolism surrounding the states (those of the EU and North Africa, and Mali itself) that initiated or go along with the deportation and externalization regime. Thus the chapter goes beyond the embedding context previously outlined to revisit the specific social suffering and deportee experiences caused by the deportation regimes that run from Europe through North Africa, and the localized and more agentic forms of narrative created around social suffering in bringing the deported actors of this study in focus.

---

5   Like others, Henrik E. Vigh considers the role of agency to be key in (social) suffering but pleads for a more flexible conceptualization of structure and agency in order to be able to focus on social processes. He highlights the fact that even if there is "a close correlation between impairment of agency and suffering" (Vigh, 2006, p. 113, n.9), suffering should not be confused with constraint, but agency and suffering can be analyzed carefully in their complexity and relationality [of structural coexistences and simultaneities.

Experiencing North African deportation regimes

The deportation regimes of North African countries, facilitated and progressively reinforced by the externalization of EU borders, constitute a particular case of creating hazards and suffering in deportation experiences. In our field conversations, deportees describe being spat at in the street, harassed and persecuted (cf. also Tyszler, 2019). This built on the widespread racism of the populations in Maghreb countries, culminating, for instance, in raids on sub-Saharan migrants and their mass deportation on the occasion of the Libyan national holiday in order to please the local population ?.

Dave, a humanitarian worker from a deportee organization, who speaks self-confidently about "the migrants" and deportees he provides assistance to, hesitates to go into details about his own deportation and the distress he survived: "It's not so easy to tell this, Susanne," he admits in a restrained manner. In rough sentences, he describes his withdrawal from Ceuta, the Spanish enclave in Morocco, in fear of death if apprehended by the police:

> When I saw these guys jump, it's really horrible. This barrier is made of wire. It cuts. I could not do Ceuta, because I told myself that I had not gone out to die because this is a sentence of death. So I went back to Morocco to Casa. That's where I was taken by the immigration services and thrown out in the desert. [..] So yes, it was I who decided to return – after having been thrown into the desert. (Dave, 10-21-2014)

"Throwing out in the desert" is a standard procedure for the authorities deporting migrants from Morocco and very similar to practices reported from other Maghreb countries, especially Libya (cf. Lemberg-Pedersen, 2017; Lecadet, 2013, Trauner & Deimel, 2013). People, including many women and children, are apprehended, taken away and detained, forcibly crowded into a truck, driven to the Algerian border for days without food and water, and dumped in the desert. Literature on the United States and Latin America in particular talks of deportees as disposable "human rubbish," undergoing "waste removal" (De Genova, 2018, p. 253) or as "trash" (Nyberg-Soerensen, 2010) in the context of mass deportations on a literally industrial scale, above all under the Obama administration (cf. e.g. Kanstroom, 2011). What the externalized borders of Europe are increasingly producing is comparable. Dave would have preferred an IOM-assisted return program, which was not available at that moment: "Now I am a *refoulé*." Importantly, however, Dave describes himself as having decided to step back from a new attempt to cross the Algerian–Moroccan border. He thereby demonstrated some agency, even if this agency was clearly provoked by EU policies and thus quite ambivalent.

In this respect, deportations from within the African continent are not reported by former deportees to be any less violent, unjust, or disturbing than those from

Europe. On the contrary, Libya in particular has become known for its rigorous attitude and policies and developed into a "demon" with regard to the treatment of sub-Saharan migrants in its territory. Since the Libyan civil war, conditions have become anarchic, as described in Chapter 2. Deportees' accounts, having left this "hell," are shocking. Salif, for instance, two years after leaving and earning a living and making a failed attempt to reach Italy, spent a total of six months in three Libyan prisons. As if haunted, he recalled the unbearable conditions in words that burst out under pressure like a stream of tears:

> Last, I was in Sabha. It was the worst and most dangerous of the prisons. There were hundreds there. There was almost no food. Every morning, one loaf of bread for 6–8 persons, no tap water, no clothes. Nothing else. Telephones, everything had been taken from us. And every morning the Libyans came in and beat us. Just like this.... There was no communication between the Arabs and the Blacks. Like animals. That's also what they called us. Between ourselves, the black among "us," there were no problems. Everyone was afraid. That was just the feeling against the Libyans. And there were little bugs everywhere, which bit: in the clothes, which were so dirty because of the salt, in the bed sheets, which were on the mattresses, where we lay. Many people died there. Only someone who had a mobile phone number in his head could call to get help, to get someone to send money to buy something at the small kiosk: drinks, small things, cigarettes. You did not really know what was going on, how long you had to stay in there. Then, the transfer from one to the next prison. Just like that. Without notice. We were packed into a truck – like a black barrel, you did not see anything – and transported somewhere else. Then all you saw was prison again. (Salif, 11-29-2015)

Salif's references were very graphic, literally evoking the physical abuse they underwent. He touched his body, lowered his head, sighed and stared at me alternately while speaking, underlining this horrendous depiction. In the end, he was repatriated with 150 other Malians by airplane. Still, he spoke about his returning with "empty hands" as the central impression of his return, the symbolic meaning of which I will explore further in the next chapter:

> It is disturbing, because when you leave, it was the joy, and upon return it's a shame (honte) because you return with empty hands, as if one entered Bamako without clothes or shoes. In the prison you do not wear any shoes or anything and they deport you like that. (Salif, 11-1-2015)

Besides having lost money and suffered from emotional and physical destitution, Salif describes himself as debased as it is possible to be. He had to arrive without clothes, dishonored, stripped of human dignity by this anarchic administrative treatment. These deportees seem literally to be reduced to "bare life" (Agamben, 1998) and "naked" (Arendt, [1943] 2018). Many, particularly those who left during the Libyan civil war, arrived wounded, shot, with broken arms, or sick. In such cases, recovery after deportation is not only emotional and moral in nature, but may require weeks or months of medical treatment, causing additional insecurity and trouble for the family and sometimes the payment of large sums of money. Some returnees remain physically impaired. This is particularly visible in some villages where the majority of the men, young and old, returned from Libya (before, during, or after the civil war in 2011). One former deportee could not use his hand for more than a year before being able to help again on the family farm. Another still had a bullet in his back when we met in 2016. It restricted his ability to engage in heavy physical work. His family was unable to pay for the required surgery. All these injuries became bodily inscribed memories of migratory control and war. We can speak too of the "language of the body" (cf. Sayad, 2004, pp. 210ff). The body speaks and remembers. It puts experiences of continued social, physical, and emotional suffering and destitution on display.

Among the Malian population, these violent practices and the large numbers of deportees from Libya were met with widespread irritation and anger, even riots from the 2000s on when Libyan deportations increased (see Sylla, 2019, 2014): "The people were upset that this could happen and compatriots were treated like this," Salif said. This needs to be considered against the background of previous close Libyan–Malian (migration) relations and guest worker agreements as described above. It constitutes a collective, though desperate, agentive act against the constraints caused by deportations.

Within the externalized transit corridor

Many deportees never get beyond the vast transit corridor through North Africa to the Mediterranean and the Atlantic, fragmented and shaped by the EU's externalized borders. The accounts of their turbulent journeys – journeys that in many cases are reversed – express a spectrum of aspects and forms of suffering. The trajectories of many are arbitrarily shaped; they pass through long phases of waiting, standstill, and mobility in many countries, undergoing multiple deportations and re-emigrations. At the same time, this is what people describe as being captured by the notion of the migratory adventure.

"Having something in the head." – Stress, violence, and pain after deportations

As recounted in the previous chapter, one of the most striking impressions from the beginning of my field work was of a certain restlessness I encountered in deportees, generally shortly after their deportation (though sometimes even many years after).

These people seemed anxious, delusional, and urgently searching for something in a rather desperate state of "stress, between hyper mobility and waiting" as Streiff-Fénart and Poutignat (2006, p. 137) aptly describe situations of transit – a mixture of pressure, bewilderment, resignation, commitment, conviction, consciousness of any horrors one may have seen and expectations that remain unfulfilled. Either directly after being deported or in retrospective narration, such "insanity" became visible as embodied memory, when former deportees like Salif stopped talking, and stared into space in the middle of a conversation, or touched their heads. "There is something in my head"; I heard that said many times – for instance, by Madou, who left for Mauritania from his village near Kita, describing his feelings after his ship was wrecked crossing the Atlantic: "At that moment, the idea of a journey had taken over my mind. Either, I went on an adventure or I would die, because there is so much poverty in Mali." Flown back to Bamako, he re-emigrated directly from his uncle's house with some money he had received from his brother. He did not care that the uncle was against it. The mission had to be accomplished, and he did not see any immediate alternative to doing just that.

Souleymane very much embodied a combination of recklessness and serious-ness that might be called quite "adventurous." He was deported, sent back, stuck on the way, imprisoned, then re-emigrated many times on literally "fragmented journeys" (Collyer, 2007), "turbulent trajectories" (Schapendonk, 2012) and "frag-mented stays" (Stock, 2019) between Mali, the Maghreb states, and Spain. With €50 received from the Spanish authorities on one deportation, Souleymane imme-diately made his way north again, leaving from Bamako airport in the direction of Libya. Like Madou, describing his restless commitment, he recalled: "It was not my idea to return home at this stage .... I wanted to go to Europe to make a living there!"

One of the ARACEM workers said: "The migrants are people that I don't know how to describe, how to characterize them, it's a bit like they tell me their ... part of their way, some of their way, then it stops there, and from there they don't tell you anything else" (field notes, 11-7-2014). Among all the sub-Saharan Africans passing through the organization, there are many Malians as well. They may return to their villages, but they may instead go on right away. For many deportees in Mali and elsewhere, deportation is just a moment of transit, a rupture, and a stage in a (new) migration cycle (cf. Kleist, 2017a; Cassarino, 2014; see Chapter 1). Many say their first thought is to leave again directly, being unwilling to confront the people who are socially close to them. Others prefer to remain in transit, at the border or in a town on the way, such as Gao, Agadez, or Tamanrasset.[6] Lucht (2017) depicts deportees stranded in Niger as preferring to die rather than return empty-handed

---

6   For literature on this historical transit space, see, e.g., Brachet, 2018; Lecadet, 2013; McDougall & Scheele, 2012; Boesen & Marfaing, 2006.

and face potential social death. He frames it as an "eternal existential unrest" in the "human struggle that migration represents in the globalized world" (p. 155). Hence, as long as the adventurers keep going and try to make it, they see value in their lives for they can still achieve something better for themselves and their kin.[7] According to one of the AME staff, "if the people find something to do, they will stay; but if not, the deportee always wants to re-emigrate. That's the big problem."

Staring eyes and nervousness may accompany accounts of deportation experiences many years later. The post-deportation condition may be prolonged for individuals, their social circles, and entire communities. Not everything can be expressed in words (cf. Vium, 2014). To cite Michael Jackson (2005a, p. 152), "it may be more realistic to admit that suffering brings us to the limits of language." Particularly, the experiences of violence and hardship before, during, and after migratory adventures may become more graspable through gestures, sighs, and silences. From the perspective of trauma theory, silence is fundamentally important to enable the sufferer to recover again as a self. Afflicted by "deeply painful memories" (Eastmond & Mannergren Selimovic, 2012, p. 524), the shattered self needs to place the cover of silence over the painful and shameful past, all the humiliations experienced and difficulties seen. Hardships and violence obviously do not start with deportations ?; the journey itself is often depicted as an encounter with tremendous suffering, physical distress, and death, the opposite pole to learning, getting to know the world, and eventually becoming "a man."[8] All this is substantially shaped by administrative control through visa regulations, illegalization, detention practices, and the use of force.

"Having something in one's head" is thus like an emblematic winged word, recognizable among those who have experienced deportations and those who know such people and work with them. There is a specific "air" particularly around those who have just returned. Some take increased migratory controls and violations as reason enough to stay after their return, sometimes ending up in social isolation and precarity in the anonymity of the city, as I will shortly revisit. Through these violent, physical, and emotional interventions, deportations change people. Some report having been literally driven crazy. Such insanity may entail a split in personality that cannot be recovered from. But, despite all the different stories, there are patterns in the aspects of suffering, embodied and memorized, that characterize those who have come back.

---

7   Bredeloup depicts shame as "an extremely effective emotion driving migrants to take enormous risks, to cross deserts and the sea, to push their boundaries beyond previous limits in order to avoid social death" (2017, p. 145). These interrelations will be further explored in Chapters 5 and 6.

8   The latter will be particularly explored in Chapter 6.

Shock, alienation, and the luck of survival

Deportees' narratives explicitly describe it as a shock, when they are deported – the kind of shock and experience of violence that may eventually bring them to a halt, even if many continue oscillating in their minds between returning and leaving again, potentially alienated and estranged from their social circle, at least at first. In view of the manifold processes of violation and humiliation that may accompany situations during or after deportation, the grades of alienation from society experienced may differ widely.

Brahima, whom I met in the Bamako market place when buying credit for my mobile phone and described in the previous chapter, was only 18 when he was deported from Tenerife in the Canary Islands after only "40 days." "Honestly, the fact that I was deported shocked me very much. I did not imagine that somebody could deport me!" (Brahima, 12-5-2014). Deportation came unexpectedly, and as an instance of unjust administrative treatment with severe economic as well as social repercussions. All his money, he said, was "wasted [gaspillé]. This discouraged me a lot."

Since his parents sent him to Bamako to earn money at the age of ten, Brahima had spent many years saving for the journey by sewing shoes and doing other jobs. As one of a group of youngsters, he took a bus to Mauritania. By bush taxi and boat, after several stopovers, a lot of negotiation, intermediaries, hazards, and exhaustion, the group headed for the Canary Islands. Brahima recalled the voyage, which took an entire week to cross the 200 km strait[9]: "During this week, honestly, we were very exhausted." "You've endured some suffering!," Birama, my co-researcher, exclaimed. "Too much," said Brahima with conviction, "I do not want to live through that again. Really!" The 70 passengers arrived alive, but several were sick when they reached Tenerife. Having just escaped death at sea, they were immediately arrested, held for three days at a *Guardia Civil*[10] police station, then detained for another 40 days in a reception and deportation center. While some were allowed to continue "to Madrid or even Malaga," others had to return. He did not have family members in Europe to be "reunited with."[11] A charter flight brought

---

9   From Tripoli, Libya, to Sicily, Italy, is about double the distance.

10   The Guardia Civil is the oldest law enforcement entity in Spain organized as a military force charged with police duties under the authority of the Ministries of the Interior and of Defense. In collaboration with FRONTEX, the Guardia Civil is charged with the protection and security of the external Spanish and EU borders.

11   Family reunification is one of the major reasons for immigration to the EU and also a widespread migratory strategy, particularly for minors. It is one of the few and most frequently used legal pathways possible, besides seeking asylum, notably for persons from the African continent; see online: https://ec.europa.eu/home-affairs/what-we-do/policies/legal-migration/family-reunification_en, accessed 31 October 2021.

them back to Bamako airport. He called his family upon arrival: "They were not happy at all. They cried on the telephone" (Brahima, 12-5-2014). While others, like Souleymane or Madou, hid away or left again the next day, Brahima could be seen as courageous in reporting his supposed migratory "failure" (cf. also Bredeloup, 2017, p. 147). But he was deeply demoralized: his objective had not been attained.

Souleymane's "hyper mobility" (Streiff-Fénart & Poutignat, 2006, p. 137), traveling back and forth and waiting in the vast externalized European border space, as described above, was eventually stopped by another deportation. He worked in Libya on a construction site where he was detected during a raid, detained in dire conditions and deported to Mali. This time, he decided to stay there. He described his appearance upon return: "Everything was flapping around. I was barely recognizable." And he had been "SUFFERING!" in the prison, he exclaimed. He returned, with the help of a patron, partly on his own resources, through the Sahara, southern Libya, Niger, and Gao to Bamako. He remained in the capital afterwards, refusing to return to his village close to Kita. Through the network of the same patron, he soon found a job as a security guard, a relatively recognized and safe occupation. His turbulent journey was interrupted and, at least for a time, stopped. The memories of the suffering remained, however, or became revitalized by our conversation.

After arrival, Malian deportees, in most cases that we found, sought shelter with a relative in the capital or in a bigger city to take a first breath before either continuing to their family's village or making a new attempt. Brahima used the €50 from the Spanish authorities, which Souleymane took to leave again immediately – "it was the European Union who financed this" – to pay for some food and water. But he spent an "uneasy time," as all his money was *gaspillé*. Moreover, he was met with general mistrust: "The people are afraid of deportees"; "they don't know you at all." He appeared like a stranger, alien to them. Upon arrival, deportees often need to become recognizable. They may look different. Academic literature speaks of deportees as "estranged," a "deportspora" (Nyers, 2003)[12], "unclassifiable" (Douglas, 1966), and "ghostlike" (cf. Coutin, 2013); in extreme cases they may behave like the returning son described in Kafka's "Homecoming," mentioned in Chapter 1, who shies away to verify his estrangement, the alienation he feels. (Long) periods of absence, the world abroad, potentially hazardous and violent experiences and treatment shatter, impact, and can alienate returnees from those who stayed. In addition, they may be suspected of wrongdoing. While the previous practice of detaining deportees in Bamako after arrival based on accusations of illegal migration (see Chapter 2), may have encouraged people to consider deportees as criminals, the AME's and others' activities opposing this practice and its abolition after 1997 have substantially changed the public discourse in this respect, even though deportees

12   According to Nyers (2003, p. 1070) a "deportspora" is an "abject diaspora," "oscillating between re-departure and re-deportation," in a "global circuit of deportation" (Khosravi, 2016, p. 178).

may still be received ambivalently. In other countries similar detention practices continue today (cf., e.g., Alpes, 2018). Deportation literature in this regard speaks of multiple forms of "punishment" (Bosworth et al., 2016) – the administrative act of deportation and a potential stigmatization and exclusion afterwards – or "double abandonment" (Lecadet, 2013), as deportees may be "expelled from one country and outcast in another" (Khosravi, 2018, p. 2). In cases of (post) deportation affecting mostly Latin Americans from the United States, stigmatization and potential exclusion mechanisms take an even more extreme form. There it is not the country of reception that criminalizes the deportees, but the country that deports them. In the US, migrants without papers from countries such as El Salvador, the Dominican Republic, or Cape Verde in particular have been often convicted for, mostly minor, criminal offences, and subsequently deported (e.g., Radziwinowiczówna, 2019; Golash-Boza, 2015; Coutin, 2013, 2004; Drotbohm, 2012; Nyberg-Soerensen, 2010; Brotherton & Barrios, 2009; Peutz, 2007; Zilberg, 2004). The stigma of being criminal may be reactivated, (re)produced and deeply inscribed after arrival and often over time (e.g., Golash-Boza & Navarro, 2020). Eventually, this underlines a specific symbolism with respect to the deporting country, which I will briefly detail further.

Brahima's experience of alienation was increased by the fact that he was "the only one to remain." Many of his traveling companions left again during the following months. Their parents paid. Brahima stayed behind with his uncle in Bamako, unwilling to go to his village. The different economic and social backgrounds, financial resources, and the influence of their family networks divided the young men on arrival in Tenerife and after their deportation back to Bamako; their trajectories were deeply shaped by these differences, which offered them unequal chances. What started as a – as I term it – "collectivity of travel," enduring the hazards of the adventure together, was lost at that moment. Belonging to a group of adventurers is a centrally important reference in the accounts of former deportees, enabling survival and keeping them grounded. Souleymane smiled somehow proudly, when he reported: "We've done Libya together." These are emblematic expressions acknowledging memories of joint journeys and belonging. Brahima felt alone, once back. Detached from his collectivity of travel, he was particularly alienated, "estranged," and moreover economically deprived through his deportation.

In this way, deportations often constitute a literal existential rupture in a migrant's life and his social lifeworld in multiple respects and at multiple scales. Many deportees are "thrown" into the situation post deportation, involuntarily, without the envisaged objective having been attained, thus completely unprepared (cf. Cassarino, 2004) to face their socially nearest whose expectations are unfulfilled. From the perspective of existential philosophy, this corresponds to the initial position of any human being: "we find ourselves thrown into the midst of a world where things often seem strange or confusing, and where we need to get a handle on what is going on around us, if we are to be able to function" (Guignon & Pereboom, 2001, p. 184; cf. Kleinhans, 2007, pp. 11f). In a similar sense, the deportee can be seen as being existentially and involuntarily forced into making sense of this situation, despite all the irritation, violence, and constraints he or she has lived through. Like, to use another literary reference, Samuel Beckett's "L'expulsé/The Expelled" (1984), who is unexpectedly thrown out of his house into an unknown street in an unknown town, Brahima was existentially thrown into a space of "cultural in-betweenness" (Collinge-Germain, 2009), even though he knew the society he was thrown back into. Others were able to make it, but, for him, there was a dichotomy between the in- and the outside, rather in the sense of the stranger described by Alfred Schütz (1944, p. 502), who has to reorient from his "relatively natural conception of the world."[13] Left to his own devices, he needs to recover and overcome humiliations in order to be accepted again and eventually "reinitiated."[14] Such experiences of alienation and estrangement are specific forms of suffering brought about by the ruptures of deportation, which one has to cope with.

Even though, it appears, risk, death, and deportations may not deter people from re-emigrating, as the cases of Madou and Souleymane show (cf. also Alpes, 2017; Dougnon, 2012; Hernández-Carretero & Carling, 2012), others prefer to stay, even if in the capital, sometimes after several attempted crossings. Abdoul, for instance, was quite outspoken about the hazards of the trip. He was repelled by the clandestine journey and his deportation from France. It was not only the violent administrative treatment but the physical and psychological distress that terrified him and convinced him to stay, refusing to live in constant fear again. He provided an emotional plea for staying:

> I've seen people that just died like that. Often I see their images when I sit like this. Yeah. That's quite sad. But I, I don't wish anybody to do adventures like this. Even if you gain a 100.000, here you can do something. You can do a little business, and if God wills you can make it, you can go [incomprehensible]. Just stay at home. That's better! That's why I prefer never to go on an adventure again. (Abdoul, 11-21-2014)

---

13   Schütz follows the idea of Max Scheler's "relativ natürliche Weltanschauung" (1926; cf. Schütz, 1944, p. 502).

14   "Reinitiation" links in the concept of the migratory adventure as a *rite de passage* building on former rituals of initiation: the returnee needs to be reinitiated and re-incorporated into the community. Victor Turner (1969) built his theory of *"rite de passage"* on Van Gennep's ([1909] 1981) three phases: separation, liminality, and incorporation. Accordingly, "liminae personae are no longer/not yet [...] neither here nor there; they are betwixt and between the positions assigned and arrayed by law, custom, convention" from a marginal position in society (Turner, 1969, p. 95). Rather than a phase of transition, Khosravi (2018) sees liminality as a being stuck in the case of deportees (2018, pp. 7f). In line with my argumentation, I would dispute this point as a "failed" migratory adventure might function as transition and transformation too. This will be discussed in the following chapters.

Abdoul even considered himself lucky: "The adventure is over. I've had luck. All my friends with whom I went away, they are all dead" (ibid.). Such existential memories were present in all his accounts. He had been interviewed for an anti-migration awareness-raising campaign for the youth on television, as he mentioned by the way. This presentation may have had a substantial influence on the way he presented himself in our interview. Most importantly, though, Abdoul had survived, which gave him strength, enabling him to go on. But he still has difficulties getting through. Due to the Malian crisis, he cannot work at his job as tourist guide anymore as the country gets barely any tourists. He occasionally works as a guide for the UN mission or sells wooden Dogon statues at his cousin's boutique.

Even though some hesitate and stay away, many former deportees eventually do return to their villages (often in the absence of any alternative). This has been increasingly the case in recent years. Others, such as Souleymane, Brahima, and Abdoul, prefer the geographical distance, anonymity, and potential autonomy of a bigger city. Often people continue to oscillate, torn between leaving and staying in light of their supposed "failed" adventures, representing the dilemma of migratory cultures in a world of constrained mobilities. This is how the young men agentically go about dealing with being thrown in. A similarly restless continuance has been described with regard to many young men in Africa more generally in light of the overall crisis: a lack of prospects, coupled with the pressure to do something, become someone, and take care of things (cf., e.g., Weiss, 2004). I will say more about these everyday patterns of being thrown in and going on in the chapters that follow.

"Legal violence" in European deportation regimes

Deportations from Europe seem to constitute a very particular case, causing severe social suffering, principally in the form of incomprehension, loss of control, and anger. This could be called legally produced violence, the term that Menjívar and Abrego (2012, p. 1380) used to capture the "normalized but cumulatively injurious effects of the [immigration and criminal] law" as experienced by migrants with precarious legal status.[15]

Lamine, whom I met for the first time two days after his deportation from France in the rooms of the AME, appeared clearly disoriented and lost (see Chapter 3); speaking as if hunted, fast and nervously in excellent French, searching for help and repeating "I don't know what's going on" ("*Je ne suis pas au courant*") – apparently unable to grasp what had hit him. In fact, the entire process of his re-

---

15   Coutin (2013, p. 334) applies the concept to the case of deportations, which reproduce the "legal violence" of emigration "generationally."

turn appears to have been deeply unfortunate, frustrating, and disturbing: he had been picked up by a street control in France, detained ("*c'était dur, c'était dur là-bas, franchement*") and deported despite the Malian embassy's refusal of consent, and the support of a lawyer, an NGO in France, and many friends of the family.[16] He was returned without any official order – just "something that the police had written." The Malian officials at the airport were irritated; so were the representatives of the AME, which was where they sent him. Lamine had been about to sign a contract for an apprenticeship, which would have eventually regularized his status. His entire family was in France. After all that, the "unjust" deportation appeared to him to be "incomprehensible" and "bizarre." He described his deportation flight, during which he barely talked to the police officers:

> At Charles de Gaulle airport already they put me in handcuffs and I said "I am not a criminal!" I said, Susanne, "I am not a criminal… I never hit anybody I never stole, I just don't have an identity card … I am not a criminal … You don't have the right to keep me like this." He said, "But we are obliged to, we don't have any choice, we are obliged." (Lamine, 10-14-2014)

The deportation regime became materialized in the handcuffs he was forced to wear, his being treated like a criminal. Lamine vehemently protested against this condemnation, affirming his innocence to me, as if I might have considered him a criminal, too; obviously feeling the need to demonstrate this confirmation in our interaction. Others in the detention center in France had committed "real crimes" and were released. Face to face with the policemen, he claimed the justice that was due to him. They did not have the right to put him in handcuffs and treat him like this. But when the policemen alluded to a higher state authority that obliged them to carry out the deportation: "Well ok, it's not a problem," he eventually said resignedly. "It's for that reason that I was not happy" (Lamine, 11-3-2014).

Lamine's approach provides an example of what deportees report as blatant legal injustices in deportations – from European countries in particular, as people expect to be treated more justly there. Anger, anxiety, and outrage resurface when the events are recounted. The legal processes may not have been fully understood, or people may not have been informed about them. This lack of knowledge creates additional anxiety and sometimes deep uncertainty (cf. Hasselberg, 2016; Coutin,

---

16   The refusal of the Malian embassy in such cases needs to be seen as collaboration with the potential deportee, and the Malian diaspora more broadly, in order to prevent his deportation, in contrast to the phenomenon that has been discussed as "estranged citizenship" referring to a "disrecognition" of deportees' citizenship (cf., e.g., Khosravi, 2018, p. 2f).

2015; Boehm, 2009).[17] These too are forms of the social suffering caused by deportation presented in deportees' narrative accounts.

The violent destruction of deportees' individual and social lives through the bureaucratic execution and standard administrative routine of the act of deportation might, moreover, be covered by Hannah Arendt's concept of the "banality of the evil" (1963), which Nicholas De Genova aptly applies to challenge "such otherwise routine 'administrative' punishments." Individuals are dehumanized and reduced to "functionaries and mere cogs in the administrative machinery" (De Genova, 2018, p. 255).[18]

In the end, however, instead of opposing the perceived injustice he suffered at the hands of the police, Lamine sees himself forced to back down, eventually consenting to the exercise of force. He is "not happy," and in saying so sounds quite reserved in the way he characterizes his reaction to this violent act. Though he refused to collaborate in his return at first, he eventually gave in to avoid being imprisoned and banned from French national territory for years.[19] Yet, after all that, he was so full of anger and hatred that he thought of murdering a person just because they were French.

> I was hogtied all the time ... Yes, all the time hogtied ... My hands were tied like this, and even my feet ... This was ... hard, you know ... That's why I say, when I find a Frenchman, I will kill him, I will not regret it. That's it. (Lamine, 10-14-2014)

This expression of hatred was in other respects a deeply agentic act, one might say, produced by and in reaction to the post-colonial deportation regime (cf. De Genova, 2018, p. 256): an instance not of giving in, but of existentially protesting.

Accounts of trauma and self-organized groups as intermediaries

Within this setting, talking about trauma time and again plays an ascriptive role as well as a narrative one. The self-organized groups of former deportees, such as the AME, ARACEM and others, serve as intermediaries between the structures that produce violence and suffering and those who experience and narrate deportations.

---

17   I will explore the concept of uncertainty after deportations more generally in relation to future-making in Chapter 7.

18   "As well as the reduction of others into the mere objects of its power – that Arendt deemed to be not only 'the essence of totalitarian government' but also, remarkably, 'perhaps the nature of every bureaucracy' (Arendt [1963] 2006)" (cf. Genova, 2018, p. 289; cf. idem, 2014).

19   European countries usually issue a re-entry ban, denying return to the country after a deportation: https://www.service-public.fr/particuliers/vosdroits/F2782, accessed 31 October 2021. In France this period is usually three years after a deportation, while the UK requires up to ten years. This does not necessarily stop people from re-emigrating as this book underlines.

Being themselves products of existing deportation regimes, the organizations have developed an approach and procedure to ease the hardships and suffering experienced, and to facilitate arrivals post deportation. Dave, the worker with another assistance organization whose deportation experiences I reported on earlier, described the situation:

> At such a moment, I have to go quickly to see him [the returnee I am dealing with] so that he can wash himself and eat under good conditions to regain confidence. Otherwise, the next day you cannot tell him anything. All of this is done so that he can forget the suffering he has experienced on the road. (Dave, 10-21-2014)

The AME has two rooms to receive deportees, which were used increasingly often from 2015 on after the silence and emptiness caused by the Malian crisis at first. It provides a space of orientation.[20] Its representatives' own deportation experiences help build connections. "Even if one has no money, one can help them morally" (Dave, 21-10-2014). Some of the professional migrants maintain a certain distance from the deportees they care for, adopting a rather paternalistic approach. This may be necessary to enable them to do their job in the first place:

> Sometimes I call this a trauma; because they come traumatized because of all that they have lived through on the road. That's why we have to leave them time when they arrive before we welcome them. There are some who come without clothes and for these it is necessary to find clean clothes, to set them up and to give them something to drink and to eat. People are DIRTY! That's it... (Dave, 10-21-2014)

"Traumatism" is not a term one would necessarily hear from the *refoulés* themselves – only if they consciously aim at placing themselves in a political context. It is a common marker and ascription in organizational speech, not least because some organizations have received funding for deportees' psychological counselling.[21] The number of such programs has increased through the renewed assistance approach financed by the more "humanizing" EUTF for Africa, described in Chapter 2.

Abdoulaye was one of the few cases to receive psychological treatment within a limited program run by the AME. He had been living in Paris for two years, in uncertain conditions of "migrant illegality and deportability" (De Genova, 2002), without papers doing "undignified" little jobs in a restaurant. One day, he had a motorcycle accident. Whiplashed, he needed medical treatment, and his arm was

---

20   According to AME, ARACEM and other organizations, three days is the length of time recommended by the World Health Organization (WHO) for those in mental distress to recover after a traumatic situation of shock and disorientation.

21   There is a large body of literature on trauma and post-traumatic stress syndrome in relation to flight, migration, and beyond, which needs to be discussed elsewhere. For some groundwork literature see, e.g., Fassin & Rechtman, 2009.

badly injured. He received a three-month residence card, but his request for an extension was denied, although the treatment needed to continue. One day, a police control did not release him, as it had repeatedly done before: he was detained and deported to Bamako immediately. Apparently, he was lucky: the AME received him at Bamako airport. The retrospective report by their staff sounds dramatic. It reveals deep shock and irritation that left Abdoulaye apathetic and disturbed. The diagnosis: "acute post traumatic syndrome" (AME, internal report). After two years, he was presented as a "complete success." The psychiatrist released him as able to deal with his life on his own.

In Abdoulaye's own account no psychological treatment was mentioned. He spoke in a matter of fact tone. His arm was injured and treated, though it was never completely cured. It was the "unexpected betrayal" and rupture in a situation where he had managed to live well by his own account – even without papers – in the Promised Land of France that was the most important thing. He returned to this incident over and over again when speaking. Even if he did not explicitly accuse the French state or European migration policies for being deported, he named its administrative implementers, the prefecture and the police, as responsible and was very upset about them. In this sense, Abdoulaye's "illegal" situation became existential and pathological as it not only determined his state of health but brought it into relation with the administration of the immigration state that controlled and eventually excluded him by deporting him to Mali, – it turned him into a deportable commodity, no longer worth providing for. His body was only partially cured. He kept talking about Paris, but was in Mali for the time being doing little day-to-day jobs: "*je me débrouille*" ("I'm getting by"), he repeated. Still, he continued to be unable to do any "hard" work. The deportation left a physical imprint; an embodied memory of the sufferings of the migratory journey, his stay abroad, and of being deported.

Spatial and temporal disorders over time

The deep anger and violation caused by perceived unjust administrative treatment and the feeling of powerlessness may endure after deportations. In many instances the actual deportation experiences dated back a long time, but quickly became current when deportees renarrated their stories in our conversations. Some experiences seemed to cut particularly deep. In European countries, it appeared to be very unfortunate incidents that provoked deportations just before a person was regularized, as demonstrated in the cases of Lamine and Abdoulaye: the police not recognizing one's papers or acting arbitrarily. Many people were apprehended in the street and deported straight away. People were often furious, when they described their deportation to me and the conditions that occasioned it – their voices were frantic and quivery. At the same time, I represented a supposedly powerful addressee potentially able to influence the situations that formed the subject of the conversation and thus the content of their narrative as well. Susan Coutin (2013) describes deportees' narratives of linear time resulting in "spatial disorder" if they are divorced through deportation (p. 334). A spatial and temporal disorder is the more disturbing the longer one has been abroad, most importantly if deportees emigrated as (little) children.[22] Not even able to take one's belongings with one after all the years of transnational life, one may have arrived in Bamako with entirely empty hands. Such incidents can fundamentally disrupt someone who is being "disappeared from [his own] life" (Turnbull, 2018, p. 48) and "dispossessed of the time, [they] had before removal" (Martin, 2015; cf. Khosravi, 2018, p. 7). These people are indeed deeply "estranged." Being unexpectedly thrown back, as described above, constitutes a disconnect (Alpes, 2014) at multiple levels for those who aspired to and moved towards global connectedness (Geschiere & Nyamnjoh, 2000).

Lamine, back in Bamako, lived with some acquaintances of his mother's (from France). He reported feeling very uncomfortable at being thrown into something entirely unknown. Unlike his family, who had been legally living in France for years, Lamine had grown up with his grandmother in Mali. She died when he was 15, and he immediately left the village for Bamako "to feed himself." By chance, he met a friend of his father's, who set up contact with the family in France. Through their support and a tourist visa for Spain, he was eventually able to join them. Lamine's subsequent deportation cut a deep hole in his family's daily life: "My little brother is always crying on the phone. He does not understand, what has happened." His narratives kept up this presence far away (cf. Coutin, 2013, p. 334), and illustrated the spatial as well as a temporal rupture in his life in Bamako.

Maher speaks of a "third space of forced return" (2015, p. 37) in which people are obliged to live. Another "spatial disorder" phenomenon may come about when deportees are arbitrarily flown to the "wrong" place such as Ouagadougou or Abidjan instead of Bamako, where I met some people who had had this experience. Such treatment is likely to increase insecurity, disorientation, and distress post deportation even more.

Even so, Lamine appeared calmer, when we met three weeks after his deportation from France. The AME tried to support him in appealing his case at the French embassy, demanding a new visa and family reunification. The process was said to be going to take two to three months. We met a couple of times during these weeks and also talked over the phone. We planned a visit to where he lived. Nothing moved. One day, I was unable to reach him anymore. Eventually, and after talking to a representative of the AME, I realized that he might have re-emigrated, either

---

22   Drotbohm, for instance, develops an analysis of cases of deportation to Cape Verde (2016), Coutin for deportations to El Salvador (2013) and Peutz for forced returns to Somalia (2006).

clandestinely via the dangerous and deadly desert route, or suddenly through a forged visa obtained by the family. Clearly, he was unwilling and unable to continue waiting "powerlessly," being restless to go on. Re-emigration is an agentic reaction, besides potentially influencing the restriction of restrictive policies as well.

Symbolism of the state

Despite the apparent ingrained symbolism of the state exercising its sovereignty through deportations, in some of the deportees' narratives, the state's role remains interestingly undefined or only broadly addressed, while others accuse it quite aggressively. The state is mostly represented by the police officers responsible for carrying out the deportation or the reception afterward, as in Abdoulaye's and Lamine's accounts – but may also be personified in the staff of a prefecture, lawyers, social workers, or employers. Allusions to representatives of the deporting state are often pejorative, ranging from accusatory to hate-filled – like Lamine's, who wanted to kill the next French person he met. Anger can sometimes be the only possible form of revolt against the experience of subjection to unjust treatment, violation and criminalization. State bordering practices are seldom criticized as structural injustices but rather referred to as instances of individual suffering or individualized in some state's personnel. The social nature of suffering originating from politico-institutional interventions is not identified.

At the same time, for the respondents in Mali, especially potential (re-)emigrants, European states served as broad screens on which to project a safe haven of security, justice, and economic potentials. "Europe is much better than Africa," I was told in a multiplicity of ways. Through the media, transnational (migratory) contacts, and networks, people are well informed about the world abroad; consequently, harsh conditions are also well-known. At the same time, "it was the European Union, which financed" the €50 return assistance for Brahima and Souleymane. Against this background, deportations may be experienced as particularly arbitrary and incomprehensible.

In the case of deportations on the African continent, such as from the Maghreb countries, human rights violations take place out of official and often mediatized European or international sight, even though, or perhaps because, they occur within the framework of the EU's externalized mandate outside European territory. Legal standards seem to count for less there. Indeed, deportations from North African countries seem to be valued less by deportees themselves, considered less drastic in terms of global social inequalities and unjust treatment, even if some of the accounts, as in the case of Salif, report extreme violence. Moreover, although African nation-states have been deporting people in large numbers since their independence and are now increasingly being "paid" by the EU for deporting

African citizens to keep them away (as developed in Chapter 2), the externalization of deportation practices from European shores to North and West Africa has resulted in a new collectivity of return, which seems to play a role in social and symbolic terms as well, making a return potentially less severe and shameful for the individual. Involuntary return from a European country, by contrast, is usually a lonesome experience. Deportations, even in cases involving a charter from Spain, or previously France, seldom reach numbers comparable with those for intra-African deportations and repatriations. Moreover, deporting European states do not return entire villages or city districts, as people are usually caught randomly and individually.

Brahima, Abdoulaye, Souleymane, and many others, who were deported from European countries, France, Spain, and increasingly Italy, were outspoken about preferring to stay in Bamako when they got back to Mali. From many accounts, a return to the village is more difficult after a deportation from Europe. The "estrangement" between life in a European city and in the Malian hinterland can be particularly enormous – the more so, the longer one has been away. And, several of these men had been living in Bamako before they left. More importantly, in small villages, the unfulfilled expectations relating to travel to Europe are impossible to hide (see Chapter 5). Brahima, Abdoulaye, and others reported on contacts with other adventurers, who had been deported recently by the same charter or whom they met on their reception by the *protection civile*[23] or at the AME. Some met with fellow returnees randomly in the streets, as I met them. With increasing numbers of deportees since the refugee crisis, these experiences have become ever more collective.

The differences in the perceived gravity of deportation from Europe as opposed to North Africa hint at a critical symbolism regarding which state deports. It makes a fundamental difference whether people reached a European country before being deported or if they were forcibly returned en route. In the former case, re-emigrating was not a simple matter, but a costly, hazardous, and potentially impossible endeavor in a time of constrained mobilities. Spatial and temporal disorders caused by deportations contribute an added symbolic charge to migration to, and likewise deportation from, the European continent in comparison to migrations within Africa.

---

23   The General Directorate of Civil Protection of Mali (Direction Générale de la Protection Civile, DGPC), created by order n°98-026/P-RM of August 25, 1998' is a central Directorate attached to the Ministry of Security and Civil Protection. The DGPC, among many other things, oversees welcoming the groups of deportees upon their arrival at Bamako airport. This institutional assistance structure consists, however, in a very minimal reception in the premises of the civil protection (cf. Lecadet, 2011).

The symbolic potency of Europe can also become a value for someone who has already been "there." Brahima, who stayed "only 40 days" in Tenerife, was called "the Spaniard" and used to greet me with "Hola, ¿como estas?" It gave him an air of sophistication and, what I term, "adventure-hood," a combination of the terms adventure and adulthood, related to the particular experience of the migratory adventure (see further Chapter 6). Beyond the specific experiences of the migration and deportation themselves, the symbolic meaning of the destination from which one was deported seems to impact on a person's return and conditions post deportation to a considerable extent as well. The means of transportation used by the specific deportation regime are of importance too: whether it is a deportation by air or over land, by plane, bus, or truck. Former deportees somehow proudly emphasize that they have been deported by plane. Being deported by airplane from Europe appears to carry a particular value in many deportees' eyes.

Interestingly, (Malian) nationality serves for many as an identity anchor during turbulent migratory journeys. Depicting places of transit, for instance, former deportees may compare themselves with migrants from other countries, who may not have the same qualities, particularly as courageous adventurers.[24] This underlines the meaning of the collectivity of travel, which becomes a collectivity both of transit and potential return. The group of adventurers may be a source of security, protection, and confidence in all these hazards and sufferings. Although earlier deportees were detained upon arrival, in respondents' narratives the Malian administrative forces, such as police officers, airport staff, and the civil protection service are depicted as neutral or positive in their reception and facilitation activities. One's citizenship may keep one grounded to some degree amid the insecurity of being thrown into conditions post deportation. Clara Lecadet (2013) has analyzed the interrelations within deportations in transit, such as through the organization of collective groups in "ghettos" according to citizenship, and also after their return, when "citizenship can be used as a temporary response to the politics of rejection by foreign states." It "offers a form of opposition to the state's practices and politics which may seem minimal, but is nonetheless symbolically powerful in this context" (p. 145). In this same vein, citizenship serves as a positive anchor for individual and collective agency in light of rejection and abandonment by the state (p. 157).[25] From

---

24   A related phenomenon is the organization of one's group in the form of a national "ghetto," as with the Cameroonians in the Bamako market hall (see Chapter 3) or the Congolese, Ivorian or Nigerian ghettos at the Mali–Algerian border analyzed by Lecadet (2013). This established practice has become mediatized with the so-called ghettos on the route to the Mediterranean, most notably in Oujda or Maghnia, Algeria and Morocco (cf. also Andersson, 2014).

25   Lecadet (2013, p. 157) follows "the idea of Abdelmalek Sayad that, if the issue of citizenship has had different meanings and had been subject to changes over the past century, it was still the only means of affirmation and recognition of a political and civil existence."

this point of view, involuntary and forced return to one's place of citizenship may have aspects of being taken to a safe haven as well, and be a fundamental source of individual and collective agency.

Concluding remarks

This first analytical chapter has shown how deportations rupture the sociopolitical realities of migrants' lives and illustrates the damage inflicted by European as well as North African deportation regimes that are reinforced by externalized controls – controls that condition substantial aid payments to countries like Mali and enforce cross-border expulsions there. It has done so by describing what such deportation experiences do to deportees, personally and through broader societal responses, based on narratives of deportation experiences detailing violent, traumatic, and unexpected returns. Repeated *refoulements*, living long years in transit situations, or hiding undocumented in Europe have impacted peoples' bodies, their very appearance, and their sense of self. These embodied memories of various forms of social suffering eventually become part of the notion of the (failed) migratory adventure. Many live through numerous deportations and phases of hyper mobility and waiting before they can return to their own country and, potentially, to their village at last. For quite a number of them, deportation constitutes only one moment in their migration cycle. The destinations of deportations, and the specific migratory journeys and back-and-forth experiences produced by the violent structures of North African and European deportation regimes, may differ, but, as the chapter shows, there are similar patterns in almost all accounts of deportation, and the social suffering that results is both collective and individual. Specific emotions noted include alienation, stress, disorientation, fear, and anger, and a deep sense of social injustice. Many former deportees appear restless, disillusioned, and distressed, especially shortly after the deportation experience; they sense that they have "failed" in their "existential quest" (Hage, 2005; cf. Stock, 2019). People may be "doubly abandoned," "estranged," and stigmatized, facing even more difficulties "at home" upon their return than they faced before – mental, physical, economic, and social. And many are immobilized afterwards. Suffering is the expression of how people experience and deal with these situations. This chapter has shown the spectrum of suffering undergone by deportees depicted in their narrative accounts, shedding light on this macro-, meso-, and microcosm of deportation experiences and thus what impacts conditions post deportations. It has, moreover, served to further introduce the people whom this whole study is about.

Using Kleinman & Kleinman's terminology, forms of suffering "caused by extreme conditions," which are at the same time, or may become, "routinized forms" of suffering through and after deportation as they continue impacting on deportees' memories and their representations, are what is at issue here. The concept of social suffering was introduced to best capture these entanglements. Throughout this chapter, I have highlighted expressions of agency by former deportees, self-organized groups of deportees and other actors as well as the broader population. Former deportees express different forms of agency despite their subjection to deportation practices. Even in the most destitute and desperate situations agency and subjectivity are possible. Nicholas De Genova (2018) speaks of the "autonomy of deportations" (p. 262), for example, and I have shown that mere survival can express agency, in the shape of a restless going on, as can the decision to leave again. Even a decision to stay expresses agency – likewise collective forms of travel, transit, return, and protest and demands for more social justice above all. Organizations of former deportees help – or at least try – to bridge the space between structures and agency, capacities and desires (cf. van Houte et al., 2016). While the Kleinmans define agency in terms of suffering from the marginalized positions of individual people, the chapter has indicated, how all these experiences and memories of deportations have become increasingly collective. I will draw this point out further in the last analytical chapter of the book, Chapter 7. The central question being whether, in the longer run, people consider themselves as suffering (cf. Bruijn et al., 2007) after deportations or not, will be one major aspect to be discussed in Chapter 6. A potentially "failed," ambivalent adventure and the suffering related to it may, in the end, become part of suffering as a condition of life.

Chapter 5
"It's [not] all about money." – About returning with empty hands and relational (re)negotiations in the adventurer's drama of return

In the context of southern Mali, money and wealth play a central though ambivalent role socially, particularly in post-deportation conditions. The central narrative of suffering and potential failure in deportees' accounts revolves around "returning with empty hands" (*"les mains vides"; bololankoloun* or *tègèlàkoloun*[1]) after having left "to look for money" (*"chercher de l'argent"; ka taaga wari gnini; warignini*). Salif, the father of eight children and husband of two wives whose story I told in the introductory chapter, returned with nothing in his hands, in other words destitute. Brahima in the previous chapter felt demoralized most of all because all his money had been "wasted" – a thing to be avoided by any possible means, people say, because it can lead to rejection and a deep sense of shame at not having made it. Kleist calls it "the epitome of failure" (2017a, p. 184). This chapter, most importantly it is about the meaning of contributing, reproduction, and the management of social relations.

"Family," "leaving," and "money" are the words I find mentioned most often in all my fieldwork documents – transcribed interviews, conversations and notes – when I word-filter them through the MAXQDA analysis tool.[2] This assigns the discursive level, giving evidence not only of established narratives, but also of the practices of family/kinship, livelihood, and mobility, which are intrinsically interconnected in West Africa. The particular meanings of money on the one hand and wealth more generally on the other have to be differentiated and analyzed more carefully, however, especially, again, in the post-deportation context. According to my respondents' narratives and practices, money is primarily needed to support one's kin and for use in the livelihood economy. One has to have it to marry, to

---

1   *"Retourner avec les mains vides"* is *ka segin bololankoloun* in Bambara.
2   Particularly in the second field phase as I conducted more research in the rural village(s) of return, where family connections were more explicit in everyday life and conversations.

build a house, for education and schooling, for leaving as well as staying, not least for participating in the consumption economy and, importantly, for acquisitions to be used in agriculture or in building up a small business. In the end, the aim is to become rich and bring wealth to the family. All that makes "a man." "Money helps to solve problems," as one deportee summarized it. In sum, money is needed for all the important matters in life, and wealth is considered to be what you can achieve by means of money. It is the ultimate goal, the end result of the whole process in terms of social status, becoming someone (*ka kè waritiguiyé*), and benefitting one's kin. Respondents consistently refer to money or means ("*moyens*"); this will be the term principally scrutinized here as well.

The meaning of going out to look for money and returning with empty hands can thus only be understood by regarding its broader social and symbolic dimensions, its "cultural matrix" (Parry & Bloch, 1989, p. 1). Narratively, money seems to be everything, but it is still not of capital importance. A common trope in Mali is "the highly ambiguous image of 'money,' both as epitome of what is aspired to yet cannot be achieved and as an almost personalized force responsible for the erosion of trust, love, and a sense of moral obligation" (Schulz, 2002, p. 813; see also Schulz, 2012, 2005; Weiss, 1996; Taussig, 1980). The monetization and commoditization of everyday life in African societies has been the subject of many debates (e.g., Jackson, 2017; Wooten, 2005; Guyer, 2004, 1995; Parry & Bloch, 1989; Hart, 1982)[3]: an obsession with possession is said to stand face to face with an increasing lack of financial means and prospects (cf. Mbembe, 2007).[4] Even so, money may have a fundamentally preserving function for social relations, as Parry & Bloch (1989) suggest in their standard work on the subject.

---

3   While money and monetization are not solely related to capitalist ideology (cf. Graeber, 2011; Parry & Bloch, 1989), commoditization refers to the introduction of market economies. According to Arhin (1995), monetization can be understood in two senses: "in the technical sense of a generally accepted medium of payment," and "in the substantive sense," which is applied for the purposes of this work, "of the extent to which the accepted medium of payment forms the basis of transactions or interactions in areas of the economy and in the social and political sectors" (Arhin, 1995, p. 97; cf. also Bohannan & Dalton, 1962, pp. 20ff; Wooten, 2005; Parry & Bloch, 1989, p. 12; Taussig 1980). Commoditization, as coined by Hart (1982), is used to define the unprecedented level of economic integration in human society and its evolution as an all-encompassing dialectic process, related to the growth of capitalism, the market economy, industrialism, and other aspects of life, centering on "a division of labor," and the production and exchange of commodities (p. 38). The term "commodification" further refers to the fact that consumption has taken over from production as the driving force structuring society (cf. Van Hear, 2014, p. 104; cf. Castoriadis, 1964).

4   Neoliberalism in particular has given rise to new forms of wealth and inequalities in economic production and social reproduction (cf. Meiu, 2017, p. 157; see also Comaroff & Comaroff, 2001).

West Africans have been using money for a very long time, but "the monetiza-tion of [their] economies accelerated and intensified in the nineteenth and twen-tieth centuries" (Berry, 1995, p. 299). The incorporation of West African economies into global markets in the 1980s made states as well as ordinary people "increas-ingly vulnerable" to fluctuations in those markets (Guyer, 1995, p. 17). Monetary transactions became ambiguous or unstable and people tried to maintain or create alliances and networks to negotiate successfully over goods and services. In turn, the ambiguity of social relations rendered the returns on social investments uncer-tain. Economic and political instabilities play into such bargaining and require a substantial multiplication of social networks and their management (Berry, 1995, p. 309). Accordingly, money is a contested issue relating to a whole complex of social dynamics, relations, and positions, particularly within the family. After deporta-tion, these are challenged and need to be (re)negotiated – not least the social order itself.

Migratory adventures have themselves become a versatile object of monetiza-tion and commodification, and the "ultimate act of consumption" (Newell, 2012, p. 186). As in other rites of passage, such as marriage and death, monetary pay-ments have replaced gifts in kind, or gifts of personal support and loyalty (cf. Arhin, 1995, pp. 97f), particularly with respect to earning money abroad and remitting it back home. Deportations disrupt this monetary endeavor. Intrinsically embedded in multiple social webs, they substantially impact upon social relations and the eco-nomic stability sometimes of an entire family, being bound to affect people's health and sense of themselves in fundamental ways.

Even though most consider themselves simply as *refoulés*, it does seem to make a difference how somebody has been deported, after how long a period of time, and from where, so that a socio-economic repositioning is usually necessary. Money and its loss are thus a useful starting point for fleshing out the social ambivalences of "failed" migratory adventures in order to better understand situations post de-portation and provide a more fine-grained analysis of them that goes beyond the restlessness, desperation, and suffering previously described. Consequently, I want to explore "leaving to look for money" and "returning with empty hands" as a set of material, social, moral, and symbolic processes, practices, and representations of value in order to understand what seeking wealth and experiencing loss reveal about the making of social worlds after a person has been deported (cf. Meiu, 2017, p. 143). To do so, I will empirically deepen the cases of Salif and Karim, contrast-ing them with Yakouba, who did return with some money. This principally relates to being embedded after deportation. Against this background, it is necessary to reflect further on the connection between searching for money and contributing (*ka gwa dème*) as a "good" member of society. In the second part of the chapter, I will further develop this theme with regard to the subjects' respective (re)negotia-tions and positioning of themselves within the family and neighborhood relations as well as to the social dynamics of shame, silence, and gossip over time and how they relate to contesting or confirming the social order. To conclude, I will briefly reflect on the ambivalent social and symbolic dimensions of money, wealth and debt vis-à-vis restricted mobilities and large-scale immobility post deportation in southern Mali.

Salif, Karim and returning to the village: *"tounga man ja"* [5]

Deportees describe returning empty-handed to one's family's village as demoralizing, deeply disturbing, and the primary source of their suffering after deportation. Salif returned, like many others, after a time of recovery with his brother in Bamako. Even though he was deported, like thousands more in the post-Gaddafi turmoil in 2011, he seemed to feel an individual responsibility for his loss. He was torn between resignation and relief, between having lost tremendous sums of money and the joy of being back healthy and alive: "It is a pity, but it is a pleasure, and also disturbing, the money that you've lost," (cf. Chapter 1) he sets the loss of money at the center of his narrative. Before leaving the village, Salif had been saving bit by bit. For 10 years he cultivated peanuts and bred animals. In addition, he sold his two draft oxen. Salif is a scrawny-looking fellow, thin, but strong. Like many of his age here, he is missing a number of teeth, which is clearly visible when he smiles. After his return to the village, he was unable to sleep, having difficulty believing what had happened to him. We should remember his traumatic accounts of living in Libyan prisons given in the previous chapter:

> I went for one week without sleep because this situation, in which I was deported, was very difficult for me, especially when you see the situation of the family. There are also some people with whom you went to the same class in school and when you see them, they have money; so if you think about all that, you get upset (*dérangé*), and many of my class mates work in administration, which is why I wanted to go and search [for money] abroad. So, if it's not possible, I'll come back, won't I? [*laughs*]
> It's lack of means that forces us to do the agriculture, if not, one does not earn anything you get less to eat and you have less wealth.
> (Salif, 11-1-2015)

Salif's economic situation when he got back was much worse than before, which obliged him to return to the village: "I had no other choice; all the money was lost." The comparison with the others' success – "they have money" – had originally pushed him to leave. In his village it is clear who has money and who does

---

not, and it is most visible in the investments (or lack of them) made in everyone's houses. Corrugated iron as the roof of the house is a sign of success in comparison to a roof made of straw; walls made of concrete are seen as a major advance on traditional walls made of mud, as the former withstand the rainy season, which is an existential advantage in this climatic region. Salif did not come from an over-all poor family, though. Dolores Koenig conducted research in the area of Salif's village, some ten kilometers south of the capital of the administrative area, investigating the connections between structural stratification and migration (Koenig, 2005a, 2005b, 1986). In terms of her findings, Salif came from a sufficiency household where potentially some, albeit small, investments in housing and schooling were possible.[6] Several graduate students lived in the family's village compound, searching and waiting for jobs: their elder brother, a small businessman in Bamako, was trying to find them something. Leaving to work abroad in order to support the family financially was meticulously planned. That it did not work out (*tounga man ja*) caused deep anxiety in view of the responsibility that Salif proved unable to take on. Still, he laughed. It was like a sign of desperation, but at the same time it somehow signaled acceptance – if he could not make it abroad, he would try here, even if it was generally more difficult.

Karim, Salif's childhood friend, gave similar reports about his deportation from Libya, which had taken place two years earlier. First, he refused to return to the village at all:

> I did not have so much money, that's why I went to Mamoutou [my brother]; also the aim was to rest down there. That was more comfortable for me than going to the village directly. In this moment, it was hard for me. My spirit was tumbled because, when you look at it, I went to school, it did not work out, and then I left on the adventure. They deported me to Mali. I did not like this. These two defeats marked me very much. That's why I took the initiative to go to Mamoutou. He and I, we could talk better and he could also provide me with some advice before I returned to the village. I could not go directly to the village, because I had left there to go and search for money. Well, the fact that the adventure did not work out, I did not know how to come to the village and explain this to my family (*laughs*). This was difficult. My father and my mother were old, and I returned from the adventure with empty hands. Oh, it was difficult for me to return to the village. (Karim, 10-31-2015)

---

6   Dolores Koenig differentiates "sufficiency" households from "more than sufficiency" and "in-sufficiency" ones. While more than sufficiency households are able to invest in various activities, insufficiency households often lacked the labor or capital to maintain adequate living standards (Koenig, 2005a, pp. 84f).

Karim impressively describes the difficulties of returning without money, empty-handed, unable to contribute and care for his aging parents. Penniless, he first of all took refuge with relatives for one month in Bamako. Then he went on to his brother, who was based in the community administration of another region. "My spirit was tumbled" and "my heart cried"[7] he graphically describes his deep emotions: first, his career as a teacher had not worked out, as he was sick for a long period; and the second try supported by his brother failed. He decided to leave his home village, go towards the Sahara and Libya and later continue to Europe. This is the processual, but at the same time ad hoc, development of migratory journeys that other respondents report. Leaving becomes an "exit option," as Aminata Dramane Traoré (2008, p. 34) calls it, when repeated failures – in school, education, and agriculture or within the family – add up. However, Karim's adventure did not work out either: without papers, he was caught in his "foyer"[8] in Tripoli, where he was working as a private gardener. Some were able to flee over the wall; Karim was imprisoned. After two weeks with little food and dirty water, he was flown out on a charter back to Bamako: "I did not earn any money. This was hard (*o ka gèlèn*)." He talks about his migratory "defeat." Karim was ashamed – though he did not say so explicitly. It was his brother who eventually encouraged him to return. At that time, Karim was one of the first deportees in the village.

Yakouba's return with some money

Once a migratory adventure does not work out, it means an economic setback and immediate decrease in life chances for the whole family (cf., e.g., Bredeloup, 2017; Drotbohm, 2015; Schuster & Madji, 2015) – it is irretrievable, as Salif said. To have sent remittances during one's absence would have been a better preparation for one's return (cf. Calenda, 2014b). Others who were able to send money seem to have had fewer difficulties, even if they returned unexpectedly and had been forced to do so. Yakouba, another young man in the village, seemed self-assured: "I did not have any difficulties with the family," he announced, "because when I was there [in Libya], I sent money and they [the family] did not wish me to find myself in difficulty when I returned. They helped me to do something." In Yakouba's eyes, the

---

7   My spirit was tumbled in Bambara: *né hakili koun fènan kodjoukou*; my heart cried: *o fila faralen gnongon kan; o yé ne dousou kasi*.

8   "Foyer" describes the communal accommodation of Malians abroad, often in very basic conditions. It has multiple functions such as social cohesion and security and, not least, allows one to maintain oneself cheaply over longer periods of stay. Often people live together in regional and ethnic networks, even ones that are specific to particular communities and villages of origin (cf., e.g., Cagnol, 2012; Calandre & Ribert, 2012), see online for instance https://montreuilonthemove.wordpress.com/2013/04/17/bamako-sur-seine-foyer-bara-montreuils-malian-village/, accessed 31 October 2021.

fact that he sent money was the reason for his smooth return. He came from a large family in the village. Most of his brothers and uncles were on site. "My father was old and I am the only son." Monetary support was needed, so he left his wife and little daughter "to search for money." He earned for his journey as a farm worker in the neighboring district and sold animals. Like Salif, he lost a fortune: for three years he worked as a gardener and transferred a sum to a facilitator to go by boat to Italy, but also sent some money home. He even financed his cousin to join him. After deportation, he stayed with family members in Bamako too, but worked on a construction site. Back in the village, Yakouba was able to buy some new animals to continue his livestock farming. In the event, he was able to share and contribute before leaving, during his absence, and after his return; he could thus somehow comply with the pre-eminent requirement, that of making a contribution.

In research on return migration, "preparedness" (e.g., Gerlach, 2018; Plambech, 2018; Turnbull, 2018; Hernández-Carretero, 2017; Cassarino, 2016, 2004; Flahaux, 2015; Sinatti, 2011) and "embeddedness" before and after the adventure are centrally discussed categories for ensuring a beneficial return, also in terms of development (e.g., Ruben et al. 2009; Davids & van Houte, 2008; Kloosterman, 2006). In a quantitative and qualitative investigation into return in Mali, Jean-Pierre Cassarino and colleagues' country comparison study (2014) found that the large majority of returns to Mali had been involuntary interruptions of migration cycles (cf. Chapter 1): being deprived of the possibility of deciding for oneself when, how, and whether to go back, was shown to be the most restricting factor with regard to a decent return and the returnee's ability to reintegrate sustainably, as it had the most degrading effect on his or her autonomy. Through deportation, any preparation for a return is violently cut off and rendered impossible, "non-existent" as Cassarino puts it (2014, p. 7; 2004, p. 20). Transnational connections can serve as source of social belonging while away, as well as for financial and social embeddedness after one's return (cf. Carling & Erdal, 2014; Ruben et al., 2009). The (social) embeddedness approach – with Kloosterman (2006) and Van Houte & Davids (2008) I understand embeddedness to consist in the relevant context and networks established before leaving and while away, and re-established after deportation – is particularly useful for analyzing situations after deportation as it allows one to capture conceptually the different contextual dimensions in which a person operates.[9] Khosravi (2018)

---

9   Kloosterman's approach of "mixed embeddedness" (2006) refers to economic, psychosocial, and social networks "and van Houte and Davids' "multidimensional and multilocal embeddedness" (2008) to different contexts, and spaces – in territorial (multi-local) and non-territorial terms. Van Houte & Davids highlight the importance of identity formation, which can be disturbed after deportations by being rejected by the closest family; it can also hinder the establishment of social networks, which are otherwise central for "re-embedding in all dimensions" (pp. 185f) after return.

furthermore sees the intersection of several factors, such as class, gender, age, and ethnicity as affecting one's embedding in society after deportation (p. 2). Preparation for one's return is thus of central importance (Flahaux et al., 2017, p. 1).[10] The lucky ones are those who are able to stay long enough to find a good job that enables them to remit money home and thus prepare the way for their return.

Salif and Karim had not been able to send or bring anything home in material terms. Committing themselves to work in agriculture was their last way out. However, their families enabled them to recover. Even though both had been unable to send gifts, they had kept up contact.[11] Kinship relations and the rural household served as their last refuge (Gaibazzi, 2015a, pp. 152f). The latter are put under particular pressure simultaneously, which forces them to "reconstruct" accordingly (cf. Carsten, 2004). Calenda illustrates how "half of the interviewees who did receive support [from their families] also experienced re-integration problems. Strong family expectations – e.g. of gifts, favors, financial support – constituted by far the major difficulty the returnees experienced" (Calenda, 2014b, p. 62). Accordingly, money is a central means both for leaving and for enabling a more dignified return, even if deported. Beyond the material aspect, it appears to be one's care for and presence among the family that count– something that I will analyze in more depth in the following section.

Searching for money, "success," and the meaning of contributing

Primarily people say they are leaving in order "to search for money" (*warignini*), and "to succeed" ("*il faut réussir*"), even if other factors are involved. First of all, this should be treated as a discursive framing of the migration: it is considered a legitimate reason for going, as opposed, for example, to leaving because of family conflicts. Most of the former deportees I spoke to then named the existential and social needs of their kin, their everyday hardship and perceived powerlessness ("*c'était la misère ici*"; *fatagna, geleya*). For many who come from a low- to middle-class rural background and have little formal education, a job in the administration as a teacher or functionary, such as Salif's former classmates obtained, is often desired but usually unattainable. Even those who go to live in Bamako have the larger

---

10   Cassarino defines "preparedness" in terms of "willingness" and "readiness" (2004, p. 17). Collyer (2018) identifies three central factors: returnees' work experience and skills, their social capital, and their ability to plan their return (p. 123); for more on this subject see the concluding chapter.

11   According to Cliggett's work with Zambian migrants, contact with the family is the most important thing while they are away (2003, p. 544).

part of their family back in the village, like Brahima or Abdoulaye, whom I described before. Everyday hardship and a certain powerlessness (*fatagna*), as referred to above, have been discussed as existential conditions, characteristic of everyday life in Africa (e.g., Féliz & Rosenberg, 2017; Mahkulu et al., 2010; Chabal, 2009, pp. 150ff; Bruijn et al., 2007; Jackson, 2005a).

The repercussions of economic liberalization cause feelings of "abjection" (Ferguson, 2006, 1999) and becoming part of a "global precariat" (Standing, 2011). Schulz (2012) has elaborated on the Bamana term *geleya* recurring in daily conversations in Malian urban contexts, particularly since the devaluation of the FCFA referred to in Chapter 2, indicating "the emotional and material dimensions of the daily struggle to make a living": "money affairs have become difficult" (*wari ko gèlèyara*), a shortage of money creates a general feeling of helplessness. Mbembe (cf. 2007; 2001) and Buggenhagen speak of a "moral crisis" (2012) even threatening the very basis of society.[12]

Eventually, all this leads back to a more general African discourse on "the fault of money," referred to in the previous paragraph, and its absence as a cause of poverty and suffering, as one side of the coin. In conversations with respondents, a narrative presentation of this kind may additionally be fostered by the power discrepancies in our research setting, which are impossible to bridge (see Chapter 3). Back in the 1930s, Meyer Fortes, one of the pioneers of the anthropological study of West Africa, identified the reference to poverty in people's self-representations as stereotypical (Fortes, 1936; cf. Ungruhe, 2010, p. 263); it was a practice that I found to be indeed widespread and conspicuous, and which could in itself suffice as a productive basis for analysis and insight. Clearly it cannot be denied that people live with, and leave as a result of, the existential and structurally induced need for a livelihood, as prominently discussed already. Obtaining money to care for one's kin usually plays a primordial role in this; furthermore, it is a way out of the moral crisis mentioned.

Adama, whom I call the modest philosopher and artist of life in Bamako and who came originally from a small village on the Malian border with the Ivory Coast, brought all these aspects together in an exemplary way. He recalled his intention to leave his mother's home when he was only 12 years old, back in 1984:

Adama: Everybody left because when there is no money, you have to leave.
Susanne: Was that the case for you too?

---

12   Mbembe and Roitman moreover figure that "the crisis is exiled to the domain of the inexplicable" as the enduring crisis and the transformations going along with it "are not necessarily correlated to precise factors and historical referents, even if one is aware" of them (1995, p. 338).

> Adama: Well I... I felt like leaving... It was also that I had to leave for elsewhere. Like my parents, everybody was in a terrible situation ("*étaient dans la galère*") (Adama, 1-7-2016).

Miserable poverty and a consequent need to contribute to the family were at the core. By that time, structural adjustment measures and privatizations were starting to have a negative effect. The downturn in agriculture that followed came after several droughts, in which the effects of climate change began to become slowly visible, while at the same time, the need for consumption started to rise and increased people's dependence on off-farm incomes (cf. Wooten, 2009).[13] Adama went on to describe his first years as an adventurer, mainly within the region:

> Yes, I was young. Because I started with Burkina... And a very new bike... At that time, this bike signified a success! (*laughs*)
> I did not even stay for two months before I left again ... I went off down there and stayed two or three years ... I returned. But since I have been leaving on adventures, I have barely stayed two, maximum three months in the village. When ... I come, I stay a little bit of time and I leave again. After I left for Senegal, I did not send any more news. In those days, there were no mobile phones. The people thought, maybe he is dead. It's embarrassing, when you don't have anything. Ah, it's not good if you don't have money, that's embarrassing. As if you didn't have a goal. (Adama, 1-7-2016)

Beyond the existential hardship of the family, which obviously required Adama's financial support, a new bike was the aim of his adventurous endeavor to *warig-nini*. Today it would be at least a motorbike, Adama laughs. These new signs of success and status go beyond the "traditional" aims of earning money for the bride price and contributing to the family livelihood (cf. Ungruhe, 2010). People want to buy, to construct and own the requirements for an increasingly modern life. Many simply state that there is no money where they are – particularly that income from agriculture can barely be monetized in light of low prices for surplus crops while the majority of the harvest serves for the subsistence of the family, without sufficing for the whole of the year.[14] In the city, people can run small businesses and do little jobs without much schooling (see further Chapter 6). "There is nothing here," was something I heard very often, and, more specifically, "there is no money in Mali." The latter reflected the then current feeling of increased uncertainty, crisis, and powerlessness caused by the Malian conflict. Mbembe speaks of an "incessant imperative to travel far away to earn money" (Mbembe, 2007, p. 305), even if money

---

13   Gaibazzi describes the differences between "for money" and "for life" production in a Gambian Soninké village (2015a, p. 143).

14   Usually additional grains need to be bought towards the end of the dry season; here for cash is needed.

itself has a "highly ambiguous image" (Schulz, 2002, p. 813). At the same time, schooling is seen by many as a mere delay.

The real economic conditions hardly enable anyone to make money in the village, but besides that according to local beliefs earning money on site is for strangers only and otherwise beneath one's dignity; to do it is thought to damage one's status as a person and impair one's honor (cf. Whitehouse, 2012; Jónsson, 2007). Jobs that are considered low-status and are assigned to strangers only can, however, be done elsewhere, in the city or abroad (Diawara, 2003a, p. 77). In fact, young men do engage in some economic activities on site, as many do not have the capacity or opportunity to leave, or the family may require them to stay, particularly in conditions post deportation (see further Chapter 6).

Even so, young men in particular have traditionally been expected to leave, not least in "functional" terms to learn how to become the head of a family, by knowing how to take decisions and lead and by being generally able to take care of things. For some, migration has also been a way to gain independence and escape from family pressure (de Haan & Rogaly, 2002, p. 7, cf. Koenig, 2005a, p. 80), to follow a certain lifestyle, to buy consumption goods, and eventually to achieve wealth for the family. In this sense, they learnt to remit from very early on (cf. Hertrich & Lesclingand, 2013, p. 181). Dolores Koenig observed: "While some elders ... showed concern about the timing of migration or the behavior of a particular migrant, they did not question the appropriateness of migration itself" (Koenig, 2005a, p. 80). Talking about his schoolfellows, Salif said that driving a motor to leave on an adventure is often said to be the mark of those "who have made it."[15] This kind of comparison with one's neighbors can also be discussed alongside the concept of "relative deprivation": proximity and perceived similarity are seen as key factors in the selection of a reference group for comparison of one's economic status (Stark & Taylor, 1989). When migration and mobility are seen as strategies to improve one's life chances, as long as social inequalities persist, relative deprivation may be a motor for expectations of migrating and achieving something. As a successful migrant, one can form part of the transnational exchange and remittance economy and build even more powerful networks of support. Meanwhile, the realization of a migratory adventure itself has become a highly expensive endeavor, often achievable only with the help of social networks and relations. Moreover, the probability of success has decreased substantially through externalized borders and migratory restrictions making migratory "failures" much more common.

Most people are webbed into a dense cluster of social relations and networks that require constant reciprocal exchanges. "If you have money, you can support everybody," Yakouba's uncle claims in the sense of Marshall Sahlin's concept of "gen-

---

15   The notions of envy and jealousy are at the heart of the migratory adventure and link to old
      notions of Mandé as I will show in the next section.

eralized reciprocity" (1965), a relation where everything circulates freely to eventually balance out all accounts, even if that may be particularly difficult between parents and children.[16] Money is part of everyday relations, not only in the villages in the south of Mali to ensure the intimate ties between a son and his mother, but also in the much more generalized reciprocity that is practiced between neighbors, friends, and also absent migrants. Relationships are constituted through exchanges of money and gifts, particularly in times of crisis (cf. Buggenhagen, 2012). Not only elder brothers, but also fathers and uncles or mothers and aunts may contribute to one's adventurous journey or to building up a business or funding any other activity, as much as they can. These contributions are sometimes mentioned by the way in the respondents' narrations, as if they formed part of an exchange that could be taken for granted. Otherwise, not taking over one's "care duties at certain life stages would be interpreted as an expression of disrespect or personal failure" (Alber & Drotbohm, 2015, p. 11).

Former deportees often claim that they decided to leave by themselves, after informing a hierarchically higher male relative. In fact, the family head may no longer be able to support their journeys as was previously the case. This renders the son's adventure economically even more important for the family, while imbuing it with more familial and potentially moral power. The intergenerational conflicts this may generate will be discussed in the next chapter. Given the idea that the individual serves the collective good, a person's wealth lies in his or her labor and capacity to contribute: wealth has, therefore, long been considered to consist in people (Meillassoux, 1981), and not in land, though access to land used to be easy (cf. Lentz, 2006).[17] In the end, people can obtain money, realize projects and become someone, which is what wealth is considered to be in current terms. This powerful institutionalization makes some even sneak out through "abrupt departures" (Koenig, 2005a, p. 89) without telling anybody. Usually, these endeavors have not created major constraints, at least not in the cases reported to me. The son's autonomous decision rather links in with the concept of an adventure as a project towards man- and adulthood. As a self-evident and necessary component of family livelihoods and embedded in the broader household strategy (cf. Massey et al., 1993, pp. 436ff; cf. Chapter 2), however, plans, to (re-)emigrate, can be refused by the family head as well (Koenig, 2005a, pp. 88f). Preferences for staying

---

16   Mauss realized earlier that some relationships never balance out, e.g., between a mother and a child. In the form of an "alternating reciprocity" one repays one's parents by having children oneself (cf. Graeber, 2011, p. 91; 405n.21).

17   Land is likewise attached through people and labor (Shipton, 2006, pp. 229f). This is admittedly a rather simplistic presentation, as access to and possession of land have been shaped by a multiplicity of historical and current processes and experiments since the colonialization of property rights and the colonists' local handling of complex symbolic, material, and spiritual meanings (Lentz, 2013; Shipton, 2009, 2006; cf. also Whitehouse, 2012).

or leaving, particularly within family contexts, are hard to disentangle: "individual agency ... remains a perplexing area" (Carling & Schewel, 2017, p. 14). Through deportations the reciprocity enabled by the migratory adventure is endangered. What this "shortage of money" eventually implies for familial and social relations will be developed in what follows.

Social and familial renegotiations and positioning post deportation

Even if the traumatic experiences of the journey hit hard and cause sensations of restlessness for both young and older deportees, it is the loss of money, expressed in the emblematic phrase "returning with empty hands" in its material, but more than that in its symbolic dimension, which substantially impacts the individual and his or her relatives. It further leads into the core of the social situation post deportation and its essential ambivalence.

On shame and *"fa den sago"*

All the deportees described so far demonstrated feelings and uttered expressions of shame and embarrassment as a result of, as they say, not having "found" money yet or, more importantly, having lost it. Many shy away from returning to their parents' village. Salif and Karim were unable to sleep. Others, restlessly again, took the hazardous route to the north, like Souleymane or Madou in the previous chapter, in order to achieve their objective. According to Scheff (2003), shame appears the moment one does not conform to an expected role, as when "seeing one's self negatively from the point of view of the other" (Scheff, 2003, p. 247, building on Cooley (1922) and Darwin (1872)). Deportees such as Karim or Salif were far from conforming to the obvious expectations of returning "successfully" and fulfilling the role of the adult son by taking care of the family. Worse than that, one may be left debased, traumatized, and with one's honor and dignity impaired. Deportees often use *maloya* to describe their sensation of shame to which I gave a prominent place in my introduction to this study and my discussion of potential "failure." Salif speaks of *"la honte"* (see Chapter 4), the French translation of *maloya*. The Bambara expression *maloya*, usually translated as "shame," but also as being shy or embarrassed (Adama used the French equivalent – *c'est gênant*), is one of the most important principles in Mandé societies to indicate correct behavior (cf. Brand, 2001, p. 16). First of all, it has a socially preserving function and also a positive connotation. Moreover, *maloya* is sign of nobility (*hòrònw*) and separates free people from slaves, who are said to have no shame (ibid.).[18] Thus feeling shame is considered as something positive and status-enhancing. The shame returnees talk about as a threat to their sense of self is thus of an ambivalent and very particular kind. As a sentiment central to keeping society together, shame may prevent one from returning home to save not only one's face, but also the reputation of the entire family. As "the master emotion of everyday life" (Scheff, 2003, p. 256), shame is key to understanding social life and relations, although it may be only a minor threat to the (social) bond. Most importantly, though, anticipated shame is continuously present in almost all social interactions (ibid.), and this conception of shame fits in well here as, in Mandé, relationships are of primordial relevance for human being and personhood:

> In Mandé, relations exist prior to the person: it is only by means of social ties that one can achieve personhood. An isolated individual does not have the slightest significance socially, and economically a life without social relations is not viable either: relations are important sources of information, resources and support (Brand, 2001, p. 14).

These norms and ideas of respectability and central relatedness in the conception of (masculine) personhood are hegemonic notions around which Mandé society is organized and to which it adheres. They imply a positive debt, in the sense of a "debt of life" (Latour, 2003, p. 186), or "family debt" (Mbembe, 2007, p. 28) toward one's close relations and the primordial and general reciprocity described before, not least as these norms help to constitute the social fabric and social cohesion. In the African context, one can speak of multiple forms of debt or "indebtedness" (Shipton, 2006) in social (as well as economic) relations, which signify something positive and productive, as will be shown.

Individual happiness and affluence, social harmony and the respect of others are thus only possible through compliance with socially prescribed roles (Brand, 2001, p. 134). Consequently, one can only be a respected and upright person in relation to and in the eyes of others (pp. 14f).[19] Ideals of masculinity are usually determined by respect (*bonya*) and commonly established modes of joking (*senankuya*) between different social and ethnic groups, built on the assumption of an unchallenged authority. Money allows one to be a respected son, friend, and father. Against this background, the loss of money puts one in danger of serious disgrace

---

18   According to this belief, slaves would not be able to distinguish, and thus apply, the social rules of correct behavior established for the nobility, who preserve respect and their honor accordingly. Among themselves, however, slaves are able to display shame, which enables them also to discuss issues that may not be confronted by noblemen (Brand, 2001, p. 16 n 13).
19   Even if there are fewer situations considered shameful for a man than for a woman in Mandé, "the consequences of disgrace are said to be more serious to men than to women" (Brand, 2001, p. 18).

particularly as "a man": "one has not made it" (*"on a pas réussi"*) refers to this hege-monic foil. In the end it was anxiety about not conforming to the expected role in others' eyes that drove Karim and others to stay away from their village in order to save face, a good name (*tògò nyuman*), and positive social recognition (cf. Steuer, 2012). Literature suggests this is tantamount to the fear of social death (Bredeloup, 2017; Lucht, 2017).[20] All these conceptions merge in the expression *fa den sago* that may be applied to people after deportation. It means "the capacity of one's will, desire or aspiration is suspended or has stopped." In its social dimension this may have dramatic consequences. Broulaye, Salif's neighbor, explained the meaning of money in supposed "failed" adventures as follows:

> If you return without money, you may be called lazy (*fa den sago*). The idea is that you are not someone who fights, as if you do not have any ambitions anymore, as if you are an individual without heart. That means that you don't want to go there (*"là-bas"*) that you don't want to succeed. And your mother gets criticized too, yeah, yeah... That's what may be being said among the half-brothers or cousins: you don't want to get on; you don't want to work. You can't cope with possible difficulties. (Broulaye, 11-7-2015)

Laziness is a summarizing term for *fa den sago*. Underlying it is the idea of an in-complete person without heart and soul. At its center, *fa den sago* refers to the social dimension and relatedness of the person, and thus to the expectations attaching to a person's actions for the common good. As in Mandé relatedness comes prior to the person, questioning one's will to be active is questioning one's integrity as a good member of society. *Fa den sago* is made up of the Bambara expressions *fa den*, which literally translates as "child of the same father," but also means "jealousy" (as in the sense of *fadenya*); and *sago*, which means will and desire. Consequently, *fa den sago* signifies that the will of the father's children or, better, of his family, is not fulfilled. This intrinsically relates to the social expectations of migratory success as far as the kin are concerned being literally left unfulfilled by one's monetary loss through deportation. In fact, *fa den sago* is a narrative depiction of social death. It is against this background that Adama preferred his parents to think he was dead rather than stopping to try to find money, being embarrassed and unable to allevi-ate his parents' poverty; at the same time, it is to guard one's respect and sense of self. While away, many did not call their families to avoid telling them about their complicated situation.

Broulaye was surprisingly open in commenting on others' situations and po-sitions after deportation. He had left for Libya to continue on to Europe, but had

---

20   Sylvie Bredeloup speaks of the "anguish of returning empty-handed," as the "anxiety of facing others and their views, of humiliating one's relatives because of one's failure" (Bredeloup, 2017, p. 147).

returned. Even if he could not prepare as he would have wished, he had been able to save some money. Most significantly, he decided to return of his own volition. The most important elements that contribute to a more successful reintegration seem to be retaining one's autonomy and dignity. So Broulaye seemed to speak from a place where he was not in danger of being accused of laziness or "failure." Karim, on the other hand, did not leave the family compound during one entire month: "I could not leave as I did not return with anything. ... I was anxious. The people could not ask me for money as they knew that I had come with empty hands." Beyond the family, he feared the villagers' malicious talk. Everybody knew that he had come back penniless. Some people are reported to have been rejected by their communities (cf. Tounkara, 2013), but these need to be seen as extreme cases as mentioned above (see Chapter 1).

Even if Yakouba was able to partially prepare for and embed his return socially and financially, he went to the family hamlet some kilometers outside the village immediately after his return. He wanted to engage in some agricultural work, which "needed to be done immediately." At the same time, hamlets in the countryside are spaces out of sight of the extended family and other villagers and far from their observing eyes and talk. They provide a certain kind of privacy and autonomy, and thus the possibility of recovering from a state of disturbance after a deportation. For Karim, it was the people who were close to him socially, who helped him out of his desperation: "My friends visited me to chat. It was they who made me, little by little, go outside the family compound. From time to time, we went for a walk. After that, it also worked with the others." There seem to be different social dynamics at stake in getting on with the situation after deportation. The questions of social distance or proximity as well as who to trust and to rely on, all relate to kinship relations, friendship and importantly the broader village population, literally the eyes of the others. I will do a breakdown of them in the next section.

Ambivalent (intimate) relations post deportation

Karim and his brother were our hosts in the village. We were accommodated in the ample courtyard, placed very prominently, sleeping in the most modern house that Mamoutou had constructed. Karim's brother had climbed up the social ladder and become mayor in his home community. He was oftentimes away taking care of his family in Bamako or participating in meetings. Karim, Birama, and I spent a lot of time together. Unlike his brother, Karim was calm and reserved. He warmed up and became more open, particularly as his elder brother was absent. After his deportation, Karim was the formal head of the family ("chef de la famille"; sòtigi). Mamoutou was living in another region. Karim's father wished him to stay and take care of them. "I would have left again otherwise," he says. "My brother cannot financially support his family [in Bamako] and back home." Karim signaled his responsibility and desire to contribute. By staying, he was able to guarantee the continuity of the family compound and farm. In the meantime, their father died, and Mamoutou became family head on his return as mayor. Importantly, Karim's deportation and financial loss apparently did not translate into a loss of status for the family. Both Karim and Salif became (interim) household heads. Still, Karim depended on others' financial support, including that of his elder brother.

Brothers are said to play a central role in hegemonic conceptions in Mandé. Through all the stages of migration and return, respondents reported that their brothers supported them by lending money, providing accommodation, and acting as a friend or a communicator with the rest of the family. Yet, as intimate family members, brothers may, in fact, have an ambivalent role. Salif's neighbor Broulaye explained this specific relationship:

> For example, certain elder brothers finance the journeys of their younger brothers. So, if the younger brothers don't succeed in entering [Europe], their elder brothers are upset. They can blame the little brothers for being lazy ("fainéant"). But that's not exactly it. Everybody has his destiny. Such accusations often make return migrants and refoulés see themselves as obliged to try to re-emigrate to be able to find the money to refund the money from the elder brother. On the other hand, others tell the refoulés that it's not that serious, and that the essential thing is to be in good health – so that they can still work to earn. (Broulaye, 11-7-2015)

Lack of success, again equated with laziness and justifying anger at the younger brother, who "failed" even though he had support, leaves the latter vulnerable to being pushed to set off again, financially indebted to the elder brother. Mamoutou, Karim's brother, may have been disappointed as well, but he received his brother openly and supported him while the latter recovered. According to Yakouba's mother's report and Salif, people are often simply relieved and grateful that the returnee has come back healthy and alive. Yakouba, though, was not very happy when the cousin he had funded to join him in Libya was also deported afterwards. This social space of negotiation is a good example of the difficulties inherent in "failed" adventures that potentially compromise the entire family. Still, the most important thing is that one survives as a person to go on and thereby contribute, the neighbor concludes. The returnee is obviously not socially dead in these cases. Moreover, in saying "that's not exactly it," Broulaye is referring to a widespread notion from cosmology and ultimate sense making: in the end, everything is part of one's destiny, which it is still possible to activate through one's commitment (see Chapter 7 for more on this topic).

Broulaye illustrated a specific relational ambivalence[21] caused by the situation of the forced return. It relates to more general constructions of social relations, and Mandé conceptions in particular. Despite all "defeats" there is a sort of self-evident solidarity and support in intimate kin relations. While the individual family is existentially and economically impaired by the brother's, son's, or nephew's unexpected loss, the supposed intimate kin relations are obliged, and privileged, to offer loyalty and internal support to a certain extent (cf., e.g., Jackson, 2017, pp. 103ff). The rupture through deportation puts these hegemonic conceptions and intimate relations particularly to the test. Literature underlines that close social relations, intimacy, and money are uncertain (cf., e.g., Geschiere, 2013; Graeber, 2011; Parry & Bloch, 1989) and fraught with ambivalence (Jackson, 2017). While kinship may carry an "axiom of amity," according to Meyer Fortes, a Tallensi proverb suggests "familiarity is better than kinship" (1949), even if both may overlap substantially (cf. Jackson, 2017, pp. 131ff). Keith Hart (1988) concludes that it is easier to trust friends in economic relations than one's kin ("as friends are free," p. 189).[22] In this uncertain terrain, "losing" money is in either case a tricky, and, above all, a morally loaded issue.

Brothers are constructed as playing antagonistic parts in polygynous families, in everyday life as well as in migration. This centers around the concepts of *fadenya* and *badenya* (cf., e.g., Bredeloup, 2017; Jackson, 2017; Gaibazzi, 2015a; Jónsson, 2007; Jansen, 1996; Bird & Kendall, 1980). *Fadenya*, literally translated as "rivalry, jealousy, and antagonism," is said to generate opposition among children with the same father but with different mothers, and particularly among brothers, driving young men to engage in heroic actions in order to stand out. The elder brother is usually placed higher in the family hierarchy. Jealousy is a strong tool of autonomy here. As already said, envy of others' successes and achievements is a primary motor for leaving. *Badenya*, by contrast, refers to children of the same mother (*ba*) and is a metaphor for harmony, more likely to stimulate people to accept their situation and the constraints imposed, for instance, by the authorities. These concepts are to be understood within the embedding context of the polygynous household, where co-wives have to compete for often scarce material resources and personal favors as well as specific blessings and care. These derive from the patrilineal line through the children and their father (cf. Jackson, 2017, pp. 146f). Thus, the social standing

---

21   According to Monika Palmberger (2019), the term "relational ambivalence" defines ambivalence "as a product of relationships individuals engage in" (p. 14). This fits well into the context under discussion, where people consider themselves not as having relationships but as being relationships. (See further Chapter 8).

22   Friends may not be directly affected, and reciprocity may be even more of an issue of negotiation. Marcel Mauss (1954) calls friends "the true locus of society" (Hart, 1986, p. 189). However, in a moment of crisis, friends may slip away more easily, while family members have a certain obligation to bond and belong (cf. Jackson, 2017, pp. 103f).

of the mother is intrinsically connected to the migratory success of the son, due to society's attachment to migration.[23]

From the perspective of *fadenya*, Karim left on an adventure in order to seek independence, manhood, and the capacity to contribute to the family vis-à-vis his elder brother. Mamoutou supported him to achieve this aim. Mandé discourse implies the younger brother has to leave the paternal compound in case of conflict and become autonomous. The younger brother is envisaged as returning successfully as a potentially violent stranger or hunter to replace the elder brother as the compound chief, when he needs support or replacement: the "hero is welcomed only on troubled days" (Jansen, 1996, p. 681, after Johnson, 1986, p. 42). Neither Karim nor Salif returned as a hero or successful adventurer. Contrariwise, it was again their elder brothers who had to help them out, thus reasserting the hierarchy between the brothers. Still, both were welcomed, not only as survivors of their adventures, but also economically for guaranteeing the continuity of the paternal compound. Formally, both had attained social adulthood many years before, but had to face up to their inability to participate in reciprocal exchange on every level. This created tensions within their financial and social expectations and relations. Both Salif and Karim complained about their economic constraints, and Karim led a humble life in comparison to his successful brother. Mamoutou took care of Karim and restored his morale even if the fact that they have different mothers, but the same father, would suggest they might compete according to *fadenya*. Even so, this may have added substantially to Karim's sensation of being left behind. Kinship seems to keep its promise of amity and care, by serving as refuge and savior (cf. also Wiedemann, 2018) – despite potential rivalries, the preservation of hierarchies as well as the ambivalence between obligations, (be)longing, and expectations (unfulfilled). Still, such situations remain precarious and need to be dealt with, particularly when it comes to the broader social and village context.

Revisiting the social order – talking or not talking

Everyday gossip and talking about other people is a constitutive part of everyday life in southern Mali, particularly in small-scale communities or defined groups (which may also include civil society, as described above). Many of the respondents spoke about having been mocked after their return, mockery being understood as some kind of by-product. Brahima faced substantial mistrust and alienation in the market place in Bamako (see Chapter 4). People did not know what he had been doing abroad, which gave them a reason for suspicion. "It is obvious who is a deportee,"

---

23   For example, if the son of one co-wife migrates, the other co-wife would do everything to enable her son to leave as well (cf. also Nyamnjoh, 2010, p. 134). An opposing discourse implies that the mother is left alone when the son departs.

said Salif's neighbor Broulaye describing the situation. "People may even call out *'refoulé, refoulé'* in broad daylight and point a finger at you." He laughed about the open shaming as he talked. "And then they denounce your mother," he says pointing out the probably most crucial connection. An open acknowledgement of one's supposed "failure" may even reinforce the shame of returning empty-handed (Vermont, 2015), which is "aggravated by the public ridicule" (Kleist, 2017b, p. 184). This has to do not only with the (intimate) family; whether the broader community talks – either openly or behind one's back – or does not talk is central as well. Mockery can sometimes be directed against one's close family as well oneself, though, besides shaming, it may at the same time have a correcting and preserving function.

Gossiping and mothers' roles in the adventurer's success

According to George Paul Meiu, talking about the others mainly serves to determine what it means to be a good member of society: "gossip, rumoring and scandal are central modes for the production and alteration of belonging" (Meiu, 2017, p. 149).[24] While on the one hand it is argued that gossip serves to preserve the "unity" of a group (cf. Gluckman, 1963) (which is in line with the preserving function of shame mentioned above), it is additionally "a way of dealing with emerging conflicts and contradictions and generating intimate alliances against oppressive political and economic hierarchy" (cf. Meiu, 2017, p. 149). Deportations, as we have already indicated, bring about substantial conflicts and contradictions in social worlds. Niko Besnier (2009) emphasizes that the real and substantial consequences of gossip for people should be considered as well as its power as a political tool. In this sense, gossip can actively reshape social worlds.[25] It works like an "indirect dialogue" about norms, values, and thus existing hierarchies in a kind of "semi-public sphere" beyond the usual "face-to-face situation" (Pietilä, 2007). Sooner or later, a person or group that is gossiped about usually learns what is being said about

---

24   In George Meiu's examples of young rural Kenyan men (Morans) seasonally working as beach boys to become "young big [rich] men" through transactional sexual relationships with white western women, it is not financial loss but so-called "shortcut money" that causes villagers' malicious talk about the "evil" and transient nature of immoral earnings. But rather than simply insulting the young Morans, young women also use gossip to express their fascination with and desire for them, which can eventually lead to secret love affairs; a similar ambivalence is expressed by other young men in search of income opportunities and upward mobility, for whom the young Morans represent aspirational idols. While the young men are in one way emasculated through gossip, they become masculine in other ways by this practice (Meiu, 2017, pp. 148ff).

25   Besnier's (2009) illuminating study based on 40 years of field work on a small Pacific island shows that gossip has not just the abstract function of social control of morality but real consequences for people: gossip is shaped by sociocultural processes that involve the community as a whole; it forms part of hegemonic discourses and the opposition to them.

them. Besides its preserving function, gossip can thus effect change of behavior and "review the order of things" (cf. also Drotbohm, 2010, p. 54).[26]

"People's mocking should not be taken too seriously," said Broulaye explaining his amusement at people's reaction to a *refoulé*'s return. His explanation comes as a surprise and might rather have indicated his own embarrassment vis-à-vis me with regard to such behavior: principally, joking relationships (*senankuya*) in Mandé allow mockery, accusations, and also harsh critique under the umbrella of mutual amusement and pre-established bonds. Such relationships can also consist in institutionalized social behavior to cope with forms of loss.[27] But, it would be difficult to characterize mocking *refoulés* and gossiping about them as features of joking relationships. The latter are a specific institution in multi-hierarchical Mandé societies, creating a field free from rivalry by assigning specific joking partners (cf. Brand, 2001, pp. 16ff). Mocking and gossiping on the other hand are fully power-loaded, rather enforcing old hierarchies or generating new ones.

The most important role played by mothers is in the gossip of the village population or social circle after a deportation: as Broulaye reported above, "and the mother gets criticized too, yeah, yeah." Such resigned and seemingly careless acknowledgement of this everyday reality hints at a connection which needs to be carefully analyzed, primarily in order to understand the specific dynamics of gossip, talk, and silence in this context. Eventually, it is the mother, who is in danger of being blamed for the adventurer's breakdown, which could potentially imply his social death (*fa den sago*). Broulaye explains:

> If a migrant returns with sufficient means, people say that his mother is a kind person, who respects her husband. But the migrants who have not brought anything back are criticized by certain villagers as if their mother had been malicious. That's a frequent criticism here in the village. (Broulaye, 11-7-2015)

The criticism that calls the mother into account is not expressed in front of the person concerned, but done secretly instead, Broulaye continues. Otherwise, it would engender conflict. In this way, social harmony can be preserved, he is convinced. Against this background, silence, non-communication, or limited communication appear strong tools to cope with the reactions to an unsuccessful return. "I did not say anything," "we did not talk about it" are frequently a part of narrations. Often,

---

26   Importantly, gossip is not only constitutive of the person who is gossiped about, but also of those who sit together and chat, as it creates a space of trust and "truthfulness" (Drotbohm, 2010, p. 54).

27   Michael Jackson depicts ritualized forms of mourning and grief, as having to do not only with the death of a person, but with losses of objects, homelands and ideals, enabling others to contemplate them together with the person immediately affected and thus to relieve them – through shared suffering – from the privatization of pain, and at the same time contribute to reconstituting the social order (Jackson, 2017, pp. 73ff).

there is one person of trust who can be spoken to intimately, a brother, as in the cases of Salif and Karim, an uncle, or a very close friend. While Karim was eventually led back into village life by his trusting friends, Salif remained silent: "Here? … No…." Salif never said anything about the difficulties of the journey, prison, deaths at sea, and his deportation:

> Here it's difficult because you cannot tell it with your own mouth because the people know quite well that you've done six months in prison and that you went in the Zodiac[28], but they want you to tell them yourself; otherwise, you'll be a liar and they will announce it everywhere. They will also say that the difficulties you had on your adventure or when you were deported, were the fault of your mother, because she did not obey her husband. That's why one does not talk about the difficulties of the journey. So, if you succeed you tell people, and if you don't succeed you say nothing. Our life is difficult, because everything depends on your mother; everything you have will be owing to your mother (*bè bi ba bolo*). (Salif, 11-1-2015)

Even if the people around him knew something of the trouble he had had, he would not spell it out openly. The moment Salif started to lament the difficulties he had experienced, he would be accused of being a liar, he reasoned – as if admitting "failure" would destroy the collective image of success and adventure. Instead of entering the quagmire of the village rumors, potentially damaging not only his own reputation, but, more importantly, that of his mother, Salif preferred to remain silent, if only to deprive them of any reason for calling him a liar. This was a measure taken to save face and maintain respect for himself and his mother. One AME staff member similarly admitted, "This suffering that you have been through, you cannot talk about it" (field notes, 10-28-2015). Salif never said anything to his mother himself. It was his brother who passed on some bits and pieces of information. The same applied to his first wife with whom he had already had five children before setting out on his journey. Both mother and wife had been greatly in favor of Salif's quest for money. Fatoumata, his wife, smiles: "Yes, I was very happy, when he got back. But when I heard people speaking about the deaths at sea and that he suffered in prison, I did not like this at all." The villagers' gossip, based on hearsay, informed her about the circumstances of her husband's suffering abroad.

The background for such gossip is the primordial relevance of the relationship between mothers and children in Mandé. Not only do mothers evoke the profoundest feelings of respect, but a certain complicity is assumed between children and their mothers. Once grown-up, sons in a patrilocal and polygynous household are expected to take care of their mothers (Brand, 2001, p. 17), who brought them into the world and took care of them through every essential step in their lives. One's

---

28   Small rubber boat, see Chapter 1.

mother's social standing and blessing are considered the keys to personal success – in the adventure too, as revealed above. Similarly, in terms of *badenya*, they are relevant to the success of the community as well (p. 21). All this is condensed in the Bambara expression *bè bi ba bolo* that Salif referred to and that translates as "everyone is in the hands of their mother (*ba*)."[29] It reflects the Mandé belief that gains as well as losses are related to and explained by one's mother's behavior, good or bad. The supposed strong bond between mother and son can have very negative repercussions on the outcome of a son's bid for success. According to Salif:

> The moment you return, people say bad words about your mother. When anyone gets to Libya or Spain, people say that their mother is good, because her child has crossed the sea or the Sahara without dying. So if such a person returns, their mother is bad, that's what the people say. ... So, if you cross, your mother is good; if you return, your mother is bad. (Salif, 11-1-2015)

Whatever kind of behavior the child displays, the mother is indirectly made responsible for it in everyday small talk, and her reputation suffers or improves by turns. If an adventurer is successful, it may even increase people's envy and jealousy. "Our life is difficult," is how Salif evaluated this moral economy relating to the migratory adventure with the mother at its social core, while my co-researcher Birama sat next to me and laughed, bitter and amused at the same time. Salif was describing a hegemonic discourse and everyday practice that I often encountered during my fieldwork: something an outsider might dismiss as mere superstition is the firm local belief of many and may involve severe consequences for the individuals concerned. Not obeying or disrespecting one's husband[30] is considered grounds for severe reproach as it fundamentally undermines the husband's personhood. A refusal to have sexual intercourse would endanger social reproduction and thus the future of the family line, and can be a powerful tool for women, particularly in polygynous constellations. Broulaye remained vague and diplomatic regarding his opinion of mothers' bad faith, which eventually saved his face as well: "Well, I agree that the woman should respect her husband in the correct way; the children they will have will be blessed." Unlike his father, Karim's mother had severe difficulties in accepting her son's "failure": "That's because women love their children so much," he reasoned.[31]

---

29   In French : "*Chacun est dans les mains de sa mère*". Brand, e.g., notes that no one can "go beyond his mother" (2001, pp. 147f).

30   In Bambara: *fourou mousso mi tè à fourou tiè bognan* or *fourou mousso mi tè à fourou tiè kouman kan sabati*.

31   Tellingly, hardly anyone would acknowledge that his own mother had been the subject of gossip. If they admitted anything, it would only be having heard of someone's mother who was.

Women, notably as wives and mothers, are points of reference for various stories in gossip, but also for common beliefs and sayings.[32] Not least, such beliefs should be understood as conveying an implicit fear of women, their existential and creative powers, particularly birth-giving women and their bodies (cf. Ba, 2015). These are part of discourses where women engage with occult powers associated with the bush ("*la brousse*") as the domain of sorcery. In this vein, "misbehaving" women can be perceived as threats to the stability of the community (*badenya*) and the social order (Jansen, 1996, p. 680) that they are supposed to guarantee.[33] In the end, gossip about an adventurer's mother can be seen as a measure to ensure the community's social integrity. Women become suspect at the moment of their son's unwanted and supposedly unsuccessful return. This clearly goes beyond Meiu's discussion of ambiguously successful Samburu men, where mothers are not mentioned any further for their role in everyday gossiping. The fact of mothers' constituting a central theme of everyday gossip under post-deportation conditions, underlines their centrality in the maintenance of social well-being and social order at least; they are highly admired and redoubtable at the same time.

The power of silence

Silence was not only described as a widespread behavior after deportation, in our conversations too people would suddenly stop talking, their voices would become bitter, or they would find an excuse to change the subject or stroll away. As I have said, not everything can be expressed in words. Traumatic experiences play a role in this, but the shame of not having made it and the money lost in the eyes of the others seem to count more, even if we are speaking of a particular and also positive form of shame here. Plambech (2017, p. 150) speaks of the "sealed lips" phenomenon after deportations. Silence seems to have multiple functions. Silence (*fo ye ma fo* [literally "not greeting"] or *ka mougnon*) and silences (Jansen, 2005, p. 334) in Mandé are, among other things, said to have a preserving function in the light of shame and to maintain respect (cf., e.g., Schulz, 2012, 2005; Jansen, 2005; Diawara, 2003b; Brand, 2001). Accordingly, controlling one's emotions and saving

---

32   Heike Drotbohm confirms with others that gossip stories very often include a gender-specific connotation (2010, p. 54).

33   In patriarchal societies, witchcraft is usually associated with dark spiritual female power (cf. Jackson, 2017, pp. 120ff). Jansen (1996) explains women's relation to sorcery in Mandé oral tradition through their mobility: after marriage a woman moves out of her paternal or brother's compound to her husband's. In the process she crosses the bush and arrives as a stranger in her husband's village (cf. Van Hoven & Oosten and Jansen 1996, p. 680). Women's agency may be hidden as much as possible, but everybody is aware of women's secret strategies and power (to manipulate). As long as women do not openly threaten the social order, though, nobody will stop them (Brand, 2001, p. 154).

face, as Salif did, are honorable and desirable actions in circumstances where affect is seldom expressed openly (Brand, 2001, pp. 16ff).

From an analysis of the Bosnian civil war, Eastmond and Mannergren Selimovic (2012) highlight different agentic functions of silence, among other things "to protect social relations and affirm a sense of normal life" and as "a way of protesting and making claims, especially from a marginalized position" (pp. 506ff).[34] This agentic conceptualization of silence fits our context well: through silences people navigate the precarious social field post deportation. Silences may allow a mutually respectful cohabitation to continue in spite of traumatic memories and demoralizations. Lately, silence has received increasing attention in the discussion of kinship relations, of belonging and relatedness. Heike Drotbohm identifies silence as a productive activity, which defines the in- and outside of intimacy.[35] In that sense, Salif preserved and delimited the intimate relationship with his mother through not speaking. This may have also allowed a conspiratorial silence between the two.

The villagers' hegemonic gossip and talk about loss of money generate new hardships and contingencies after deportations. Contrary to the preserving function of silence, speaking about others not only shames them, but can intrinsically harm their well-being (Meiu, 2017, pp. 169f). In this light, mockery of and gossiping about "failed" adventurers and their mothers are particularly powerful acts and signal a warning review of the order of things. Likewise, they can be seen as an outcry against the direful political and social realities brought about by migratory restrictions and deportations. In contrast, within ambivalent family and neighbor contexts, actively keeping silent may be an even more effective "power element" (Drotbohm, 2010, p. 65) to preserve and potentially influence kinship relations as well as the moral and social integrity and order under review. Speaking and not speaking constitute effective social tools, which are mutually interdependent. Mamadou Diawara sees "the Empire of the Word" as the counterpart of silence "on *both* an ontological level and as a hegemonic *social configuration*" (Jansen, 2005, p. 334; cf. Diawara, 2003b, p. 285). His complex analysis of silences in Mandé builds on the Bamana proverb *"la silence est l'aîné de la parole"* ("silence is the elder brother of speech"). This sets silence hierarchically above speech, which links in with Mandé values of not speaking and respect which are inherent in the concept of *maloya*, eventually.

---

34   Eastmond and Mannergren Selimovic (2012) conceptualize silence broadly as "a form of social communication that is as rich and multifaceted as speech and narration. ... There are great cultural variations, ... in the valuation and uses of silence in human interaction, including as a means to approach sensitive or potentially disruptive subjects" (pp. 505f).

35   See conference report online: http://affective-societies.de/2017/aus-der-forschung/the-prize-of-belonging, accessed 31 October 2021.

Gossip and silence after deportations thus seem to reconstitute each other in a kind of productive exchange and complementation. While the reality is highly morally loaded, socially and economically complex, silence and gossiping are ways to get around the loss of money and the difficulties of contributing as expected. Both try to preserve social relations and their order, but at the same time to challenge them, giving space to renegotiate kin, friendship and broader social relations in the village or the neighborhood, along practices of distancing and proximity, intimacy and withdrawal. The mother's position at the center of these practices of gossiping and silence perhaps expresses the intrinsic fear of a deterioration of the social order induced by deportations and migratory "failures" most notably. Simultaneously, knowledge of the hazards of the journey as well as the frequency of deportations has substantially changed over time. Behavior towards and acceptance of *refoulés* have been similarly impacted. The women in Yakouba's family compound, for instance, reported that they had heard from other villagers about the journey's difficulties and possible hardships; dramatic depictions on the radio and television also alerted them. The new "normalcy" of deportations (cf. Galvin, 2015) and migratory constraints has created collectivities of deportees in the villages around, where memories of the journey and sufferings are shared. There seems to be more openness towards such "failures" even if the loss of money, and the consequent difficulty of achieving wealth and becoming someone, constitutes the "real" drama of return. I will further develop these aspects in the chapters that follow.

The ambivalent role of money and debt under post-deportation conditions

I started with the observation that everything seems to be about money, in order to find out more about its social meaning in conditions post deportation. It has become clear that there is not one meaning of money or its loss; rather there are multiple ones which are situationally defined and constantly renegotiated (Parry & Bloch, 1989, p. 23; cf. also Appadurai, 1986), as well as fundamentally questioned and put under constraint by the rupture of deportation. The primordial difference that money makes is to be seen rather in its symbolic value and related reciprocal obligations. More than that, following Parry and Bloch, the symbolism of money may be regarded as only one aspect of a more general symbolic world of transactions (not necessarily monetary or economic), which relate to "some absolutely fundamental human problems" (Parry & Bloch, 1989, p. 28). In conclusion, I want to reflect from a theoretical point of view, on the social repercussions of money loss, which has so far only been discussed in relation to its multiple forms of debt and social obligations.

Revisiting the meaning of money, potential debts and reciprocities

"It's only money that counts here, not the age anymore, nor the wisdom." A former deportee from Libya is depicting a radical world, thoroughly monetized and
commodified, seemingly cold, brutal, and distant, turbo capitalist, neglecting "traditional" values and indicators of respect in West Africa, towards older men in
particular – that is, if we take this quote literally, out of context. Throughout the
chapter, I have developed the dense web of social relations that factually embeds
deportees, observes them, comments on them, and engages in their life after deportation. Despite the danger of being called *fa den sago* – the equivalent of a social
death sentence – people do eventually return and go on. They have taken over moral
and social responsibilities and obligations "fulfilling age- and gender-specific roles
to [their] family and community" (cf. Hernandez-Carretero, 2015) appropriate to
their life course. Money plays an important role here, being necessary to get on in
life and to increase one's life chances and those of one's extended family. Not being
able to contribute means not being recognized according to the established norms
of "gendered authority, status and social mobility" (Guyer, 2004, p. 147).[36]

However, contributions in any direction have become uncertain in light of political inequalities and constraints. Migration is ever more restricted and dangerous,
raising its social, political, human, as well as financial price over recent decades.
Success and contributing through migration are no longer to be taken for granted.
People may have large debts before even leaving for abroad. Deportations throw
the former adventurer, his kin and close social contacts into additional and unexpected debt relations, and thus contribute to economic inequalities, scarcities, and
an overall "moral crisis." The *refoulé* is often no longer able to repay his debt, at least
financially, and thus to participate in (money) exchange and in what is described as
a continuous reconstitution of social relations and the kinship system (cf. Jónsson,
2007, pp. 55ff). He rather increases his dependencies and multiplies debt relations
– potentially in financial, social, emotional, and moral terms; even if he has paid
in large part for the journey himself as Salif and others reported. Deportees often
speak of an individual responsibility for their "failure." Their social relations are
disturbed, tested, and put under constraint. Money cannot take care of shame (cf.
Buggenhagen, 2012). Rather, these relations are actively renegotiated, for instance,
through gossiping and silence. At the same time, *maloya*, the Mandé concept of
shame, implies a positive connotation, as returnees' sensing and applying to it expresses respect for oneself and others, potentially correcting and preserving good
relations and community cohesion.

---

36   Jane Guyer speaks of a "political economy of recognition" – money which "ranks people on a
     scale according to profiles of achievement and good fortune... rather than structural ascrip-
     tion..." (Guyer, 2004, p. 147).

Arjun Appadurai, like others, assigns a particular power to debt: "*Not opposition, but diversion*" as Roitman (2003, p. 214; emphasis in the original) summarizes the appropriate paths and modalities of exchange (cf. Appadurai, 1986, p. 26), debt represents a moment when particular truths about social relations are revealed. Not only in the African context, can debt be seen as very basis of human and social relations (cf. Roitman, 2003, p. 212). According to David Graeber (2005), all human interactions somehow imply some form of reciprocity. Debt "then, is just an exchange that has not been brought to completion," and the relations, which are deeply moral, remain uneven: it is what happens "in between" (pp. 121f). Debt relations can thus be seen as indicators of existential human relations, where potential ambiguity and ambivalence come particularly into play, "the society *is* our debt" (p. 136). On the one hand, economies and networks of trust provide the basis for the possibility of debt for an adventurer's endeavor in the first place. When money is lost or not obtained, reciprocity does not balance out. Hierarchies may remain, or shift depending on whether one has money or not. Likewise, the inherent ambivalence of social relations, particularly with family, entails a large spectrum of fraud, jealousy, and envy, the "negative reciprocity," this demanding, narrow, and tiresome aspect of the family (Geschiere, 2013, p. 71, building on Marshall Sahlins, 1965).[37] The everyday web of social interdependencies and reciprocal relations is particularly challenged. Powerful family networks can, as a matter of course, handle such situations with more facility than looser networks, as can better-off families. Uncertain monetized and commoditized personal relations and networks make those involved in the commodity of the migratory adventure particularly constrained. Former adventurers' brothers may become oppressive and demanding when their money has been lost or has not been obtained as expected; and mothers too may be put under serious constraint.

Janet Roitman (2003) speaks of a "productive power of debt" as a mode of either affirming or denying sociability. She refers to Sarthou-Lajus with "debt breaks with the logic of exchange [...] because it induces deferred exchange, or intervals of time, that reorganize such relations through the multiplication of possibilities" (1997, p. 18; after Roitman, 2003, pp. 213f).[38] Such creative and productive conceptualizations of debt in the context of human relations may eventually give space to the re-creation of social relations, networks and intimacies, and "a multiplication of possibilities" indeed. In the sense of Shipton's "serial entrustments" (2006),

---

37   Peter Geschiere aims to analyze the negative sides of trustful relations created by the social obligation of gift-giving, "observing jealousy and aggression within the intimate circle of the family" (cf. 2013, p. 71).

38   This approach implies that debt is productive of something and that the productivity of debt is not necessarily revealed in those moments where disorder confronts order (Sarthou-Lajus, 1997, p. 18).

an expected favor could "be passed on to someone else and ... keep moving" (p. 17). One's loss of money could be transferred, endlessly passed on, and eventually never repaid.[39] Debt in this sense has the potential to strengthen and reinforce social bonds.

Against this background, nurturing one's contacts and networks is centrally important in every social and migratory respect. Adama was not the only one who relativized this seeming obsession: "In fact, it's not about money only. You have to have good contacts in order to get anywhere." Some parents' wish for their son or daughter to remain after a forced return was linked to their wealth as a person and his/her potential to take care of them on the spot: "If you leave your suffering parents behind without any assistance that's worse than returning with empty hands," Broulaye summarized. He would not leave again even if someone offered him a lot of money. My findings seem to mirror what Molly Roth concluded about Mali: money "represents a far less substantial and durable form in which to store wealth than social relationships" (Roth, 2005, pp. 129ff). Still, both are intrinsically interconnected, with wealth being the ultimate aim. The above quote from a deportee from Libya hints at a change in social values, particularly visible between generations, in which the monetization and commoditization of social relations, against a background of economic corrosion, are of central importance: when the older generation may no longer be able to support the younger as it used to (including helping them depart on an adventure), and when the practices and expectations of contributing are changing. It is like an adjusted reciprocity, in which the debt diminishes, is transferred, or opens up new possibilities. So, building on the notion of a "productive power of debt," on Roitman, Sarthou-Lajus, and Shipiton, such social and familial debts are to be seen as intrinsic parts of relations, of reproducing, renegotiating, and potentially guaranteeing social cohesion.

Concluding remarks

This chapter set out to analyze the social meaning of money after deportation. This has meant empirically developing and contextualizing deportees' departing in search of money with wealth as their ultimate aim but unexpectedly returning with empty hands, within the different forms of (re)creating (exchange) relations and reproduction. After deportation, social relations and positions may be under

---

39   Parker Shipton's concept of entrustment refers to practices of borrowing which permeate social relations between family and community members. Local credits and debts are highly symbolic and potentially cut deep as obligations shaping identities and cultural existences. Such entrustments may include "delayed marriage payments, or school fee payments from elder to younger kin, reciprocated many years later or in indirect ways" (Shipton, 2006, p. 17).

constraint and require substantial readjustment in a society where the relatedness of a person and the social dimension matter particularly. (Missing) economic contributions cannot be thought of outside their relationality and social context. More than that, the entire family may be indebted and suffer from the loss on the adventure in the long run.

The powerful emotion of shame, *maloya* in Mandé terms, plays a central role both by being anticipated and feared, but likewise in preserving as well as potentially recasting social bonds. *Maloya* is thus an ambivalent, but powerful moral, emotional and social signpost. Even if there are many more *refoulés* today than before, stories and gossip about mothers and brothers still play a prominent role, while gaining and losing money remains at the center of observation and accusation. One central thesis has been the difference it makes to obtain money during one's travels and remit it back, even if one is deported in the end. Such "guarantees," as they might be called, build economic and social security and better embed an involuntary returnee economically and socially. He has been able to prepare at least to some degree – a condition that has been widely discussed in academic literature as necessary above all else for a beneficial return and reintegration. Silence and gossip are powerful political tools for reviewing the social and moral order shattered by the political realities of forced returns and may simultaneously constitute potential agentive ways out, not least through retaining some respect and a good name (*tɔ̀gɔ̀ nyuman*).

In the end, it seems *not* to be all about making money in order to obtain wealth. Wealth lies in a person counting up the degree of his or her social embeddedness and value for the common good. These can be recovered and restored even if the person in question is morally condemned at first. Often, the returned son tries to reintegrate into the household as a last refuge, while adapting to the family economy on site. Many respondents describe themselves as being obliged to stay where they are ("*on est obligé*"; "*on n'a pas de choix*"), although the past adventure and a potential new one may continue to form part of their everyday life. The real loss and the memory of the loss may, nevertheless, be constantly present, as Salif's and Karim's cases demonstrate. They centrally impair one's financial capacity and responsibility toward the family. In this sense deportations have to be integrated into the circularity of family livelihood, social adulthood, and reciprocity. Young men post deportation try to recover their dignity by going on to become good people. The next chapter will expound how this is done through recovering and renegotiating one's masculinities.

Chapter 6
"On se débrouille."[1] – (Re)negotiating masculinities after deportation through everyday suffering, hard work, and (im)mobilities[2]

The recovery and renegotiation of masculinities after deportation is a key factor in re-establishing oneself as a member of society and for the purposes of everyday life. In this chapter, therefore, the crisis caused by deportation and restricted mobility will be analyzed as a specific challenge to the masculinities of both younger and older men. Deportation entails a "true danger of emasculation," that is to say that the loss of money involved not only becomes a symbol of "failed" achievement, responsibilities and adulthood, but, more broadly, questions one's personhood, masculinity and membership of society, even though "success" through adventure has become much unlikelier today, especially as a result of EU intervention in sub-Saharan Africa. Chapter 5 focused on showing how gossip and mistrust may presume that one lacks the spirit, ambition, and strength (*fa den sago*) for the hazardous journey, narratively implying one's social death given that "money is at the heart of social exchange and codes of male respectability" (Gaibazzi, 2015a, p. 113; also Osella & Osella, 2000), and that the danger of being economically dependent on someone is the greatest threat to the latter (Gaibazzi, 2015a, p. 78) and a major source of suffering. This chapter complements its predecessor by highlighting masculinity and the strategies employed by former deportees to get by / eke out a living (*"se débrouiller"*) and recover in the post-deportation everyday.

Young men in Mali face multiple constraints today, evoking a sense of crisis that has been discussed in the scholarly literature.[3] Against this background, an

---

1   "One gets by" also in the sense "one ekes out a living."
2   Parts of this chapter have been previously published in Schultz, S. U. (2020b), reprinted by permission of the publisher (Taylor &Francis Ltd, http://www.tandfonline.com).
3   A crisis of youth leads to a crisis of reproduction and a so-called "crisis of masculinity," seen as mostly driven by economic and structural factors (e.g., Cornwall et al., 2016; Weiss, 2004).

increasing number of "young" unmarried men and even full adults have been having, and still have, difficulties in living up to the norm of becoming a breadwinner and the head of a household (Cornwall, 2016; Schulz & Jansen, 2016). At the
same time, their fathers, in their positions as older men and family heads, have
been struggling to support them, which could eventually result in their losing their
sons' respect. Over the last two decades as well, women have increasingly been
contributing financially or even becoming household heads themselves, although
this has not been happening out in the open (Schulz, 2012). Emigration could have
offered those multiply constrained younger men a means of gaining the status and
responsibility of social adulthood, particularly of becoming a "proper fully adult
man," but deportation cut short their journey to social maturity. Possibly immobilized, in Mali as in other countries in sub-Saharan Africa (cf. Honwana & de Boeck,
2005; Comaroff & Comaroff, 2001; Mbembe, 1985), deportees join a generation "in-
the-waiting in the double sense" (Schulz, 2002, p. 806; cf. Schulz & Diallo, 2016, p.
227)[4].

For most men staying and engaging with life where they are after deportation
is often perceived as their only option, and it is often the express wish of their families, shameful and unworthy as it may first appear. The imperative of looking for
money remains, not least to overcome one's suffering. Nevertheless, as described
in deportation studies, former adventurers can convert their suffering into a new
status defined by courage and fearlessness (Schuster & Majidi, 2015, p. 643; cf. Kusow, 2004)[5] and thereby recover and/or reinvent their masculinities. One might
thus assume that only the physically and mentally strongest stay (given the fact
that the journey allowed only some to survive at all), trying to free themselves from
a certain "culpability," recover their dignity[6] and become good people (above all for
the community) (Bredeloup, 2017).

---

4   Not only waiting to gain senior status, but also waiting for their parents, as well as the state, to
    create the conditions to enable them to do so. Deportations only worsen any such conditions.
5   Maher writes that *refoulés* renegotiated their inferior status by creating "a new system of
    counter-honor as a way to manage or "offset" their stigma as "failures" (Kusow, 2004, p. 194,
    after Maher, 2015, p. 351f).
6   Dignity is a meaningful concept, an emotion implying social skills as well as strategies for
    alleviating suffering (Youngsted, 2013, p. 12). It is similar to the Malian concept of *danbé*, lit-
    erally translated as dignity, honor, or reputation. Schulz (1999) describes *danbé* for Mali as
    "the honor and prestige [one] gains from living up to the expectations" of one's people (p.
    282; cf. Whitehouse, 2012, p. 88f).

Studying masculinities and "failed" migration

My analysis here is informed by different aspects of masculinity studies. Raewyn Connell defined hegemonic masculinity as a practice that legitimizes some men's dominant position in society and justifies the subordination of the ordinary male population and women, and other marginalized or complicit ways of being a man (Connell, [1995] 2005, pp. 76ff). Connell's then groundbreaking work remains very useful for considering masculinities in the plural, as made and remade by their specific social, historical, cultural, and geographical contexts and practices, and shaped by power relations, a critical factor in discussing men and migration (e.g., Ingvars & Gíslason, 2018; Hibbins & Pease, 2009).[7] "The dislocations of migration" (Cornwall, 2016, p. 17) present a particularly interesting site for a rooted intersectional analysis. Migrant men's acquired hegemonic ideals may provide support for them in a transnational social space or be enacted in an exaggerated "hypermasculine" fashion to compensate for a marginal position (Hibbins & Pease, 2009, p. 6).

Regarding the Malian and the broader African context, Schulz (2012) suggests asking which aspect of patriarchy is affected, instead of claiming that masculinities are in crisis: difficulties not only derive from relations between men and women, but more substantially from those between men. In a theoretical reformulation of the concept of hegemonic masculinity, Inhorn (2012, p. 30) calls for a concept of "emergent masculinities" understanding "manly selfhood ... as an act that is ever in progress." This concept is particularly helpful for discussing deportees' sometimes volatile and precarious daily life, enabling an understanding of how "men navigate and adapt to their changing social worlds" (p. 60).

After deportation, migrants' constructions of their potential masculinities, which provided support abroad or while in transit, may suddenly be turned upside-down. At the same time, however, the hegemonic foil of becoming a breadwinner and head of a household remains of central importance. This chapter describes how deportees try to navigate their masculinities and form part of their communities, the particular challenges they may face, as well as what they bring in to enable them to go on. It does so by continuing to examine the empirical case of Brahima in Bamako and introducing Seku and his *grin*[8] in the small village close to

---

7   Despite criticisms that it is one-sided, static or simply mistaken (e.g., Broqua & Doquet, 2013; Schulz, 2012; Inhorn, 2012; Beasley, 2008; Lindsay & Miescher, 2003), Connell's conceptualization of hegemonic masculinities in relation to subordinate, complicit, or marginal ones ([1995] 2005, pp. 76ff), has been extensively adopted and cited as useful, including, recently, when discussing men and migration (e.g., Ingvars & Gíslason, 2018; Charsley & Wray, 2015).

8   A local term for a group of people, often men, who gather around a small stove to brew a drink, usually strong green tea, socialize, and pass the time.

Kita. Brahima and Seku offer insights into the concepts and practices that enable them to manage their endangered hegemonic masculinity after deportation. The specific forms of suffering that deportees describe in narrating their deportation experiences (see Chapter 4) may be reinterpreted for the purpose of recovering their dignity and becoming someone (*ka kè waritiguiyé*). Moreover, hard work and courage, as well as getting married, may help them to manage the everyday. Against this background, some kind of recognized "adventure-hood", as I term it, is integrated into a new repertoire of deportee masculinities. In particular, the chapter takes the generational aspect of deportation into account, shedding light on potential differences between younger and older male deportees.

"I am obliged to stay where I am." – Restricted mobilities, suffering, and working in Bamako

The case of Brahima demonstrates the tension between feelings of stuckness, proactive engagement to stay, and a continuing longing to leave after a (forced) return in an urban context. In Chapter 4, I described how Brahima returned to Bamako in 2008, shocked that he could have been deported, facing mistrust and alienation back in the central market among his former colleagues and close friends. He felt obliged to stay, representing himself as "the Spaniard" and being recognized as such, as described in Chapter 3. At the end of 2015, in the second year of our acquaintance, we met for a longer conversation. Birama and I asked Brahima to evaluate his situation in comparison to the previous year:

> Sincerely, it's ok. I'm doing well and I thank God. Leaving for Europe would please me, but there is the problem of means (*moyens*), which I haven't got. I'd still like to leave, but there's the problem of the means. Other than that, I'm doing well. There is nothing bad. It's OK. (Brahima, 12-12-2015)

Seven years after his deportation the central element in Brahima's narrative was his desire to leave for Europe again, as opposed to his inability to do so. Still, he said "it's OK" and he thanked God, summing up his situation and feeling of constrained mobility. Nonetheless, hardship had increased. This placatory framework could also be seen as a narrative strategy to gloss over hardship and discomfort in order to save face – as discussed in the previous chapter. Thus, pretending to be well would have been the specific aim of the narration instead of revealing his actual state of mind and potential suffering. Brahima gave a coherent account, justifying why he needed to stay. The sensation of "stuckedness" (Hage, 2009) that he expresses is somehow legitimized; the theme of leaving again and of having left once already is predominant. It indicates an intrinsic longing to move on in life and become someone as a person. Ghassan Hage called the idea that a viable life presupposes a form of imaginary mobility, "existential mobility" on an "existential quest," a sense that one is "going somewhere" also in "socio-existential" terms (Hage, 2005, p. 471; cf. 2009; cf. Stock, 2019). Stuckness, on the other hand, is "existential immobility." It presumes a clear lack of agency, particularly as a man, as mobility and manhood are intrinsically connected. Most importantly, both can be perceived and imagined, rather than physically existing, and still dominate one's everyday. According to Hage, the "heroism of stuckedness lies in this ability to snatch agency in the very midst of its lack" (2015, p. n.d.). Imaginative talking about leaving, individually or among a group, can create agency. Beyond this, promoting one's decision to stay and justifying one's obligation to do so is a central motif of talk and eventually a lived reality, whether in an adaptive psychological mode or one of proactive acceptance (cf. Carling & Schewel, 2017), which can be likewise agentic. I follow these entanglements throughout the rest of this chapter, not least because they are intrinsic aspects of restoring masculinities.

As I mentioned, however, everyday hardship had increased for Brahima in comparison to the previous year. His expenses had grown and the employment situation had got worse, reminiscent of Salif's descriptions in Chapter 5.

> This year, it's not easy […] It's the work. I eke out a living ("*je me débrouille*") here in the shop (*butiki*). That's not at all my objective, but if you don't have any other possibility, you are obliged to accept. That's obligatory. That's as if I visit you and you prepare *la bouillie* (Bambanakan: *sari*; English: mash) for me. I'll eat it, knowing that there are no other possibilities. (Brahima, 12-12-2015)

Even though he felt expressly constrained, Brahima showed conviction and consistency in the way he kept on going, working and earning his small income. At the same time, his decision to adapt on-site did not rule out the potential of leaving again. To exemplify this obligation to accept everyday hardship and reciprocal responsibility, Brahima referred to the allegory of the traditional mash, "*la bouillie*," the common breakfast among farmers in West Africa.[9] Having *la boullie* for lunch or dinner is considered a sign of lack of means as people generally only eat it in the morning. The traditional lunch and dinner is *tô*, also made of sorghum or from corn. It comes along with a variety of sauces. Having *la bouillie* for all your meals makes it obvious that the family cannot afford to purchase the ingredients for the sauce. In view of the high value placed on hospitality in rural southern Mali, usually

---

9   *La bouillie* is mostly made from one of the many forms of Malian sorghum or from corn. The various forms of sorghum are the most widespread grains in Mali; they grow despite the dry Sahelian soils. They are thus considered to be the grain of the "poor" rural population. (See online, e.g., http://moulindelamousquere.pagesperso-orange.fr/pages/mali/cereales-afrique. htm, accessed 31 Octobe 2021.) For *la bouille*, the corn is pounded, mashed and then boiled, then one adds shea butter and eats it with sugar.

expressed through the abundance of food and drink offered to a guest and often involving the slaughter of poultry or a sheep, serving *la bouillie* as lunch or dinner creates a shameful situation. Whatever the guest might think of being served *la bouillie* for lunch or dinner, however, the imperative of hospitality would prevent him or her from refusing the meal offered by the host. In order to preserve social harmony, there would be no choice but to eat the humble meal offered, or in other words there would be no possibility of Brahima's doing anything other than staying in Bamako for the moment.

After his return from the Canary Islands, Brahima had almost immediately gone back to work, thereby showing masculine courage. His uncle commented approvingly when asked if he was touched by his nephew's unexpected collapse: "Well ... he started to sell mattresses. This is already something." Having accepted that he had to stay in Bamako, Brahima tried to be a breadwinner, even if he described himself as dissatisfied. From that small economic base, he had worked his way up, he was even able to marry back in his village, thus carrying out the role expected of him. In 2015 Brahima was taking care of his sick mother and his wife who stayed with the extended family in Bamako. Still, he preferred to remain in the capital rather than return to his parents' village, and he was very hesitant and evasive when I asked him if we could visit the village together.

Beyond autonomy and anonymity, the city does offer some real economic opportunities such as possibilities for earning a small income through the extensive economic market structure, trade and (inter)national exchange even though it may be on a day-to-day basis; "*le petit business*" as people tend to say. This can be done without much schooling. Further, working on a construction site, as a watchman, or as a gardener may be a possibility. Importantly, the city also offers many different prospects of consumption. Brahima had been a Bamako dweller since he was ten, when his parents sent him there to earn his living with his uncle, and a rural village could hardly keep up with the modern standards of the capital, in Brahima's view. Charles Piot, on the other hand, has aptly illustrated the claim that rural villages (of the Kabre in Togo) are "a site... of the modern, one that is as privileged as any other" (Piot, 1999, p. 178). Others have shown that the rural cannot be so easily separated from the urban in Africa (cf. Ferguson, 2006, p. 167f). This is evident from people's intra-mobility patterns and the high degree of interconnectedness between the rural and the urban nurtured, not least, by the dense social web and embedding of many people, exemplified here by the family's receiving medical care in Bamako.[10] Still, negative perceptions of less desirable, remote rural areas are widespread in the respondents' accounts as well as among the wider population. In Bamako, Brahima seemed to be able to have an active life which corresponded

---

10   The latter relates to the centralized infrastructure in Mali, where some medical treatment is only available in Bamako.

more closely to a "Western" image of "modernity" and urban life: in addition to his many familial and economic caring responsibilities, he practiced taekwondo six days a week. This enabled him to remain physically strong and to somehow partake in, or at least get a taste of, a more popular city life. Without being able to read and write in French, he was very active and connected via Facebook and other social media. He showed off two fancy smartphones, the latest of which had been bought and sent by a friend in France. In this connection, Sasha Newell has analyzed the Ivorian "bluff" (Newell, 2012), a means of gaining prestige not through migration but by producing an image of success based mainly around (Western) clothing that is beyond the men's real economic means.[11] All these seem to be important features of consumption and worldliness, a form of manly maturity or wisdom, which may contribute to Brahima's standing as a (deported) man in the city.

Even if he was obliged to stay, the hegemonic trait of mobility and being an adventurer continued to be omnipresent. His uncle and foster-father joined in the talk about re-emigrating: "If he [Brahima] wants to leave again, I will agree to it," and he repeated the common narrative: "No, I cannot refuse to let him leave. Why? (loud voice) If he leaves, it will be to make money. If he earns a lot of money, it will help everybody in the family. If a child is courageous, he will simply leave!" The courageous man is thus the one who disregards all the hazards and leaves in spite of obstacles and a potential obligation to stay. The cultural trait of emphasizing out-mobility is mirrored by the social situation. Brahima's family is of Soninke ethnicity, which is credited with an extensive migratory heritage. Basic convictions such as "everybody can make it," and even more "a man is made to travel" imbue our conversation and exemplify the expectations of migratory adventure and their intrinsic connection to becoming and being "a man." Brahima is very clear about what he actually aims to do:

> The main objective [laughs] is to leave here from Mali to go to Europe. You see, the first time, I left for Spain; this was for searching for money to continue on to Europe. … Unfortunately, I was deported (refoulé). Since I've arrived here, I don't want to stay in Mali anymore, I feel like returning. Europe and Africa, there is a very big difference between them – at the level of income. In every respect, Europe is different than Africa. Birama [points to my co-researcher] has not been there, but I, nevertheless, know the difference between Europe and Africa well. (Brahima, 12-12-2015)

Despite all the hardships of the journey, his main objective is still presented as being to leave again, not least because the everyday offers few possibilities for a

---

11   Ferguson speaks of postcolonial imitation (2006) and Bhabha of mimicry (1994) which would need to be discussed, of course, against the contradictions and inequalities in the postcolony (cf. Newell, 2012, pp. 14ff, also Mbembe, 2001).

larger and more substantial income (see Chapter 5; also Makhulu et al., 2010). Europe, by contrast, is represented as an economically highly desirable place, even for someone who has been deported from there. That is also based on its symbolic dimension, as shown before. Moreover, these aspirations are built on transnational spaces, knowing, hearing from, exchanging with contacts abroad. In this case, of course, Brahima's own migratory experience counted too, even if it was only 40 days in Tenerife. "In Bamako there is no agriculture, so it can only be little business or leaving on adventure," his uncle added. Brahima had prepared for being an adventurer and for succeeding and earning in Europe. But it did not work out. In Gambia, "hard-working off-farm workers, especially those who travel" are called "hustlers" (Gaibazzi, 2015a, p. 63), while in the literature on youth in Africa, "hustling" has been used as another term for actively getting by through everyday difficulties and uncertainties (cf. Ludwig, 2017a).[12] In this sense, Brahima's "eking out his living" ("*se débrouiller*") through "small businesses," the most widespread expression used to describe everyday getting-by jobs in Mali, is acknowledged as a hard-working attempt to improve the situation, that could, at the same time, be seen as a masculine continuation of the spirit of adventure, complementary to the travel, and even as preparation for potentially heading off again.

Bahima's uncle agreed that there was currently no money to re-emigrate, and Brahima could not leave his wife and three-year-old child behind "just like that." As in the other cases described, it was the economic as well as the social obligation to take care which made him stay. "Still, I think about it, because when you want to achieve an objective, this discourages you." Multiple sufferings, among his memories as well as in daily life, formed part of his milieu. Though physically immobile, at least in international and transcontinental terms, Brahima remained mobile in his imagination at least (Urry, 2007)[13], full of aspirations, and also of a certain conviction that he would get another chance to leave.[14] In Hage's terminology he was

---

12   Since Honwana & de Boeck's "Makers and Breakers" (2005) there has been plenty of literature on youth in Africa and a varied discussion on the phenomenon of everyday getting by in spite of the labor market and other structural constraints, i.e., the "prolonged decline and drastic reduction of social possibilities" (Vigh, 2006, p. 96; cf. Ludwig, 2013). Terminologies such as hustling, eking out a living or navigating, have become synonyms for ways to analytically grasp the everyday reality, the "abject" and often desperate efforts to survive of youth in Africa (cf. Ludwig, 2017a, p. 14; Newell, 2012; Vigh, 2006). This debate has been further extended to study African migrant realities in Europe (cf., e.g., Schapendonk, 2018).

13   Urry differentiates four dimensions of mobility: physical, imaginative, virtual, and communicative. (2007).

14   The "aspiration/ability" model by Carling (2002; revised by Carling & Schewel, 2017) differentiates between aspirations to migrate and the ability to do so. "Feeling obliged to stay" thus implies that the desire to leave and expectation that one will leave are pitted against the ability and capacity to realize this desire, creating a situation of an involuntary immobility (cf. Carling, 2002).

existentially mobile. In his late twenties, Brahima, in fact, had a real chance to leave again; most importantly, because mobility is seen the privilege of the youth. His uncle again explicitly exclaimed: "As he is still young, if he still wants to leave, he can leave! Not so? ... He is like one of my sons (*laughs*)." The uncle expatiates on his expectations driven not least by the hegemonic image of the successful adventurer and man exerting pressure on his nephew to re-emigrate. Brahima's narrative priority of leaving again to achieve something more has in the end to be seen against this hegemonic background too, since it potentially influenced his narrative, making him represent himself as a young ambitious man. His economic endeavors on the spot were almost hidden by it, although his uncle did recognize them too.

After deportation, Brahima joined a generation in waiting in multiple senses. Honwana (2012) used the term "waithood" for the extended phase between youth and adulthood that does not allow young people to follow the established paths to gain social status as preceding generations had. Other than this, however, Brahima seemed to act within the binding structure of sociality and comply with the social roles as much as he could. He tried to comply with hegemonic conceptions of masculinities by taking over social responsibility and engaging where he was. At the same time, representations of masculinity such as being modern, worldly, and oriented to the potentially heroic acts of the adventurer could emerge, as I will explain later. In this vein, his friend confirmed "of course, Brahima is an adventurer!" And he bade farewell in Spanish: "¡Hasta luego!" Brahima's experience of having been abroad in this sense contributed substantially to his reputation. He was not stuck, but enduring and acting: navigating his livelihood between what was and what might come. Even if he stayed in Bamako after his involuntary return he deserved the status of a (former) migrant, also as part of a transnational supporter network formed by emigrants from his village all over the world.

"As a man, you have to be strong where you are!"– Suffering and courage in the rural hinterland

Seku's story more explicitly demonstrates the intersections of everyday suffering post deportation, courage, and masculinities in getting through in a rural context in southern Mali. Seku had not long turned thirty by the time that we met. Like many others in the small village not far away from the larger community of Salif and Karim, he had been deported from Libya in 2010 (see Chapter 2). This, however, was not his first return: in 2002 he had come back triumphant as a successful returnee.

One evening, we were sitting in the small courtyard of Seku's best friend Baba's house. It was the end of a long, hot day. The cement house had roofs made of corrugated sheets, which indicated some wealth in the family (cf. Chapter 5). Seku, Baba and Ousmane were the core of their *grin*, their privileged and trusted space that allowed them to address and reflect on their daily concerns. These specific tea circles have been called spaces to (re)produce and renegotiate masculinities (Bondaz, 2013; Schulz, 2002).[15] Ousmane was in the nearby city, assisting a mechanic and wheel seller as an everyday job; Baba worked in a small shop behind his father's house. Seku spent almost the entire day with us. It was the middle of the dry season and the harvest had been gathered. Mostly small things were left, considered women's work – picking and processing peanuts. A tarred road, built in 2006 and to be reached via a small dusty track through the bushes and along the fields, had changed the situation of the villagers fundamentally, so people said. Now it was easy to reach the city, to do a little business, sell products at the market as well as to leave for Bamako or farther away.

The majority of young males and others used their small Jakartas[16], which had become the standard affordable means of transport for many. Others, mostly the younger ones, took their bicycles. In the district capital, which offered a large range of livelihood opportunities, people pursue small income-generating activities. Since the previous year, a "moto taxi," consisting of a small van body installed on a motor bike, connects the surrounding villages to the nearest bigger town twice a day. It allows those without their own vehicle, mostly women, children and the elderly, to sell their garden vegetables in the marketplace, to buy items not available in the little village kiosk or to visit people. Baba's and Seku's wives were there on that day, too.

In 2008, Baba, Ousmane, Seku, and many others were in Libya. When the conflict in Libya escalated in 2011, almost the entire village youth, and elder males abroad, came back, either repatriated or deported. Others continued on to Europe, even if it was not their original plan. The whole village became involved in the disaster of their imprisoned youth, through the prisoners' distress calls by phone and through the accounts of others returning. Unlike in Salif's village, which is four times as big, here, everyone seemed to have exchanged their experiences. Now, the three are married; Baba already has two wives.

For Seku it was paramount that he left for Libya twice, and that his first return – by plane – was his own decision. He came to visit and show off: "the 11/11/2003 I came," he laughs. "I will never forget this date." He lived "*la belle vie*"; spent all his money, married, and took important steps toward male adulthood. Migratory

---

15   While Schulz (2002, p. 811) described *grins* as something mostly found in urban areas, the practice seems to have spread more widely in the meantime diffusing into local rural forms of socializing. The young men in the village referred to their tea round as a *grin* with its informally appointed president, thus replicating or adapting a previously urban phenomenon. At the same time, the heterogeneity of backgrounds, ages, and style that potentially exists in the city, can hardly be found in a village, even though things vary with the size of the village population.

16   A type of small motorbike imported from China.

success empowered him. During his second migration too, he was able to get to-gether some money and send it home, like Yakouba and Broulaye who were de-scribed in the previous chapter. In this case too his father had died, and the fam-ily needed support. However, this second stay "did not work out." Seku was de-ported to Bamako, "disturbed and confounded"; notably as a result of his treat-ment in the Libyan prison. Still, he immediately started to help with the family farmwork, not stopping to search for other ways to support himself: after harvest, he left for Kéniéba, the largest region for informal gold mining ("*orpaillage*") farther south-west in Mali. To make preparations for winter, he returned, before leaving again to search for gold, this time in neighboring Senegal. Seku followed the estab-lished patterns of seasonal mobility, which for centuries have secured livelihoods, by cultivating peanuts, cola nuts or doing "small business" (Gary-Tounkara, 2008). Seasonal, but also year-long mining in informal gold sites has become the estab-lished alternative and complement to agricultural work, especially when interna-tional mobility is constrained[17], even if it provokes major conflicts about potential dangers and benefits, particularly between generations (Dwell, 2013; Hilson & Gar-forth, 2012).[18] Seku underlined his motivation:

> Well, we get by (*on se débrouille*)... Here are many things. In the case of sickness, we all stay. There, where you are, you must not... you must not lower your arms as a man. One has to understand this. Even here, it's good. If you have got this idea in your head that we are here, but here it's not good. That's not life... As a man you have to be strong where you are! (Seku, 1-28-2016)

Remaining active is characteristic of a proper man and the central category in Seku's depiction. Lowering one's arms (more generally, sitting with your arms folded ["*les bras croisés*"]) relates to laziness, and a potential accusation of *fa den sago* implying a "danger of emasculation," fundamentally questioning one's integrity as a person, a member of society and "a man." Not only in telling their stories, but also in practice, Baba, Ousmane, and Seku tried to carry on in spite of an everyday precarious situation post deportation, remaining active and engaged, and caring

---

17   Gold is a historical, cultural as well as common social good in Mali. Its industrial exploitation through international companies only started around 2000 when the gold price rose on the international market. Simultaneously, informal gold-mining sites emerged, which are usu-ally administered as regards infrastructure by the nearby community. Often a gold-mining site forms part of a village territory itself and the inhabitants form collectivities to distribute the opportunities for obtaining licenses to dig for the metal equally.

18   For the young men, working on the gold mines can, like going on an adventure, serve to create autonomy and enable them to generate income. For the older population, the informal gold mining sites may be a "hotbed of vice," of drug abuse, prostitution, and sexual disease. In the mining regions, Bamako, and civil society fora, debates are heated and international organizations engage in evaluating the potential dangers of the new rush for gold and luck.

for those who were close to them, thus trying to comply with the hegemonic image of the breadwinner and provider.

Active waiting

In light of their arduous and none too profitable efforts, though, Seku revised their situation, constantly thinking about going on an adventure again:

> Last year, I did not go anywhere. I'm in the process of reflecting (*laughs*). There are conflicts in several countries and it's not easy to have the money. That's why I stay here to wait; it's not for anything else. To have a rest is also good for the body (*laughs*).
> Also it's better to have a rest right now as the gold sites used to yield good money, but now that's not the case – so, it's better to have a rest (*Birama and Seku laugh*). (Seku, 1-27-2016)

Just then, he was doing "nothing," he continued: "there are no activities." The winter preparation of the fields had not yet started. Political crises made it difficult to "just go and succeed." He sat and reflected on the alternatives: "That's it. I'm in the process of evaluating, if I should take the road toward Europe again or go somewhere in the subregion or here in Mali. I'm observing the current situation." As if complementing continuous and active searching, staying, waiting, reflecting, and taking a rest are central elements for many young men of their cohort. Seku laughed when he mentioned the benefit of staying for his physical health. Consciousness of a good physical condition has been described as prevalent among other young men, for example in Senegal or the Ivory Coast, aspiring to create masculine values (Prothmann, 2018; Newell, 2012). From this perspective, resting and reflecting are valuable activities for a mature adventurer and responsible man, even one who has been deported. It is not passive waiting, but a meaningful activity. Waiting can be "actively produced, embodied, experienced, politicized and resisted across a range of migrant spaces" (Conlon, 2011, p. 355). All modes of active waiting are "negotiated and incorporated into everyday lives and life projects" (p. 357). This active sense is even more important since immobility might be perceived as a threat to hegemonic masculinity (Gaibazzi, 2015a), or rather as a female characteristic, but from this point of view it becomes part of an emerging and assembling repertoire of (deportee) masculinities.

   In the end, this kind of renegotiation of waiting and taking a rest again links in with discussions about young people's tactical strategizing, navigating, and hustling, or active sitting in African countries today (e.g., Gaibazzi, 2015a; Newell, 2012; Vigh, 2006; Honwana & de Boeck, 2005). Even if, for some deportees, a complete standstill would induce a feeling of stagnation, an "active waiting," defined as a constantly incorporated mode of being, can be seen as a "motion within motion," as Henrik E. Vigh defined social navigating (2006, p. 14), which here consisted in courageously trying to make the best of the possible choices, including by reflecting and physically recovering over time. Active waiting very much resembles, or at least complements, notions such as (social) navigating, hustling or "eking out a living" (*se débrouiller*). Seku tried to work out the most beneficial opportunities to gain a livelihood. He felt obliged to do so as it appeared to be his duty as a man. Effectively, his presence was also needed to take care of his parents, his uncle, his children, and his wife. Still, Seku was torn and in difficulties. A lot of money had been lost through travel. His wife was contributing financially through selling products in the market. Active waiting represents endurance and a constructive use of time in renarrating, renegotiating, or repracticing the established story of the "failed" adventurer. Taking care of others, moreover, goes beyond the (social) value of money, constituting an essential social worth value in itself.

Intersections of courage, suffering, and adventure

Former deportees circumvent the imminent danger of being called *fa den sago* and thus disrespected as a man, by remaining active and engaging locally, as well as caring for close relatives and friends, as the examples of Seku, Baba, Ousmane, and Brahima illustrate. Showing courage is an important masculine value. It functions productively as an intrinsic and also everyday motor for getting along, and has different connotations in the respondents' accounts. In Bamankan, several terms are used to express courage.[19] They relate to very specific conceptions of masculinity in terms of endurance and physical as well as mental strength; and, again, to the central idea of being a full person with body, heart and soul, which signifies "a man" (values, which could also apply to a woman). First of all, courage is a central value in the migratory adventure itself. Only a courageous young man is able to go into the wilderness, learn from being there, and survive. Seku's uncle and social father gave an example:

> If I tell someone to leave, for example. If he leaves and he finds some difficulties, he will return immediately. By contrast, if the person leaves by himself, even if he encounters difficulties, he will try to overcome them to enter the countries of destination. If the person takes the decision to leave on an adventure, he will endure suffering, prison, and other forms of torture.

---

19   *Dusuta*, which means "with heart"; *jageleya*, which would more generally mean "getting over difficulties"; *kiseya*, which signifies energy as well as *timinadja* which more strongly implies a "don't give up" attitude and particularly refers to courage and suffering in agriculture.

The same applies when the person is *refoulé* and looks to re-emigrate:

> This is a person who is looking for ways to leave. For example, if the person cannot stand suffering, he will stay; but if he is courageous and ready to bear the suffering, he will leave. (Seku's uncle, 01-28-2016)

The conception of individual responsibility for the adventure and its implicit "failures" fits into conceptions of becoming somebody, being able to withstand difficulties and suffering, here exemplified as "prison and other forms of torture." The realities of irregular journeys and externalized migratory control are known. For the father, courage is defined through one's potential to bear such suffering, which is what makes an adventurer, and thus "a man." Re-emigration in spite of all the hazards would be a particular sign of courage, while those who stay behind, including those who have failed to leave (again), may appear as cowards. Seku, like Brahima, had not left for anywhere abroad since 2010. When asked if Seku was courageous, the elder man replied: "Seku was deported. When he came back, he built houses. This was a good thing." Although Seku had been deported and was still there, his uncle appreciated his contribution. This underlines the importance of money as social currency, regardless of a deportation, as discussed in the previous chapter: what one has achieved before, during and after the journey may be of major importance. Furthermore, it points to the idea expressed when Seku vehemently exclaimed – "as a man, you have to be strong where you are!" You have to remain active and engage, contribute however you can and take care of those close to you; even if economic currency remains pivotal. This very much recalls what Brahima's uncle said about his nephew.

What is paramount is the courage one has acquired through living through the sufferings of the migratory adventure, which demands endurance of high risks and sometimes death (Dougnon, 2013). It helps to recover one's dignity post deportation. Suffering is culturally, socially, and historically contingent and can take many forms, as discussed in Chapter 4 (Kleinman & Kleinman, 1991, p. 280). In Mali suffering is an everyday and manifold phenomenon, and, like courage, is expressed through a variety of terms and expressions in Bamanakan.[20] We talk about different forms and terminologies of suffering. Interestingly, Seku equates the suffering caused by hazardous everyday economic and living conditions with the sensation

---

20   *Ni ma tooro*, which means "tired heart" ("*cœur fatigué*"), again points to the central organ and essence of life; or *dimi* which usually refers to suffering during physical sickness translating as "pain," "hurt," and explicitly "suffering" (in French: "*douleur*", "*blessure*", "*souffrance*"). Furthermore, suffering is often framed as a productive category as *monnè*, which should rather be translated as "resentment," "bitterness" or "anger" (in French: "*rancœur*", "*rancune*", "*ressentiment*").

of being left behind to suffer from a disease (*dimi*), thus endangering one's health, endangering the human basis of one's existence. While for Seku "*dimi*" and "*monnè*," translated as "resentment," "bitterness" or "anger," meant the same. Ousmane differentiated between the two terms as follows:

> For example, you and me, we can be looking for something, I may have something and you may not. In this case you will be "*monnè*." I consider this as suffering. "*Monnè*" it's like you telling me that I do not know anything to do in life; in this case, I'll be "*monnè*"; this will make me force myself to do what needs to be done. (Small group discussion, 11-7-2015)

Ousmane speaks of the anger of not having achieved anything [acquired money or means] in comparison with others. Jealousy plays an important role here, it being said to be a central tool for autonomy in Mandé (see Chapter 5). Contrary to a more "negative" form of suffering, as described in Chapter 4, here suffering is framed as a particular productive category. Stress and anger at "failure" and accusation may be silenced, but they may incite action instead of submission.[21] The discursive narratives construct suffering and courage as prerequisites for masculinities post deportation, for being a good son, husband, and father.

Even if the courage of the migratory adventure is mainly framed in terms of masculine values, the rare female adventurers can benefit from its glory, as I was able to learn: Baba's cousin had been deported from Spain six years before. "Everybody was very happy" when she went off to Libya all by herself. A friend sent money, but she had saved up herself by working as a tailor in the city. "She is courageous!" everybody nodded. After her return, she was "unhappy," but everyone tried to make her aware that it was bad luck and she should make the best of it. She had married the year before: "man and woman are equal in *warignini*. If somebody decides to leave, we can only encourage that person. This is our wish" (Baba, 01-25-2016). These accounts appear remarkable given that the migratory adventure is mainly defined as a masculine activity, and money is connected to male respectability. Here, the adventure is described equally heroically when the adventurer a woman. It remains to be seen if this hints at a reconceptualization of new adventurer masculinities and femininities.

---

21   Interestingly, this approach invokes the neoliberal idea of the entrepreneurial self, responsible for his or her own performance (Cornwall, 2016) and not least reminds one of Foucault's "technologies of the self" (1988; cf. also Gaibazzi, 2015a, pp. 75f).

On "adventure-hood" and adulthood as a man

The world described here is seen in terms of the migratory adventure being a pivot, a mode of being, and, most importantly, a means to become a "full man." Men are defined in relation to it, as sitters and stayers or as adventurers. Over the last 20 years, deportations have created a new phenomenon, the "failed" adventurer. Despite returning empty-handed, a man in this situation may still be valued for having grown. Overall, the deportees' narrations perfectly reflected the ambivalence of the adventure as "a career which one enters with more or less trumps, that one accomplishes with more or less success and thus one finishes one day or the other, to leave in a more or less honorable way" (Streiff-Fénart & Poutignat, 2006, p. 131). Ousmane's mother found her son much wiser and more courageous afterward. One former deportee pointed out: "the difference consists in the fact that those who have travelled a lot and those who have not travelled cannot be the same, [although they are confronted by the same problems]." In this vein, Brahima, Seku and others represented themselves as experienced and worldly adventurers, and experts in travel, taking migration as the ultimate act of consumption and personal transformation as defined in the last chapter (Newell, 2012, pp. 208ff). Brahima, for instance, displayed his knowledge of the difference between Europe and Africa by explaining it to Birama, my co-researcher, who had never been to Europe, and was not eager to go there. More than that, deportees took to explicitly warning the village youth of the dangers of leaving. Rather than being persuaded, however, the youngsters tended to ask for their advice as experienced travelers: "They want to find out for themselves! And have their own money," one complained. Sometimes, to the sorrow of the older generation, their mothers, and the *refoulés*, the youngsters' restive search for travel abroad and for wealth would persist. The attributes of the experienced adventurer are explicitly masculine, in a society where "adventure-hood," as I call it, a combination of the terms adventure and adulthood, i.e., this specific experience of the migratory adventure, contributes to manhood and "a man has to travel."

Suffering here attains an overarching meaning for masculinities after deportation and for becoming a respectable person. As Seku described it: "A man/person who suffers, explains his experiences to his descendants, like my grandfather; so if you have not experienced anything, what are you going to tell?" Suffering is the equivalent to experiencing. One cannot be a "real man" without suffering, even if this suffering needs to be finally overcome. Significantly, the adventurous experience is depicted in the person of the grandfather, a highly respected man.

Seku even entered a plea for strength and courage to be considered as particular attributes of the Malian adventurer, underlining the function of as an identity anchor in situations post deportation (see Chapter 4):

I did not see anyone from the village or surrounding area who had suffered psychological problems. But the English speakers were psychologically affected a lot in Libya. Because of this, I think Malians can cope with things that the nationals of English-speaking countries cannot bear. Often you see these young English speakers in prison, who get up and bang on the wall; the Malians do not do that. (Seku, 1-27-2016)[22]

Still, such "adventure-hood" does not suffice for becoming an adult, even if one potentially acquires characteristics needed as the head of a household. One may be courageous and willing to take up everyday work, but one faces the same struggles as before. It is still the "autonomy of money" (Quiminal, 1991, p. 142; also, Gabazzi, 2015a, p. 94) that counts most. In places such as Seku's village, where a considerable number of the younger and older men had been deported or repatriated, the collectivity played a central role. Heroically talking about an imagined new adventure, like talking about the previous ones, was acted out in group discussions and informal talk where Brahima's, Seku's and the others' aspirations to travel again were on show. While the ambivalence of money loss and the hazards of the journey and thus some kind of joint recovery were part of it. "The adventure is never easy" was, over and over again, the central conclusion (see Chapter 4).

"Just talking is far from being without aim," as Schulz declares in "The World Is Made by Talk." Malian youth try to perform worldliness, consumption values, and adulthood through listening to the local radio and talking about music culture in Bamako: "talk adds a social dimension to the texture of everyday life that is crucial to a person's being-in-the-world" (Schulz, 2002, p. 812). A "discursive mode of imagining," meaning a combination of debate and imagining, serves as a performative, establishing, and self-ensuring act (ibid., p. 822) In this sense, talking about a previous or future adventure is a deeply agentic act, one that goes far beyond treating the migratory adventure as a form of consumption by collectively reflecting on its hazards and its potentials for personal transformation. It is not that people pretend to be worldly and knowledgeable; they are recognized as such even as deported adventurers.[23] Not least it creates a space for former and future adventurers, and potentially enables the deportees to recover and assemble a new repertoire of supposed deportee masculinities (cf. also Kleist, 2017a, p. 337).

Baba's, Seku's, and Ousmane's *grin* was a small circle of like-minded people and fellow sufferers providing a space of trust for them to share their worries after

---

22   I will not further analyze or contextualize the obvious groupisms inherent here.

23   Similarly, Stefanie Maher described *refoulés* sharing their stories in Senegal as "communal performances that articulated their suffering as a morally and socially valuable experience" (Maher, 2015, p. 59), building on Brad Weiss who aptly demonstrated how the representation of suffering itself is socially meaningful and contributes to building masculinity, where pain becomes "a social mode of consciousness" (Weiss, 2009, p. 120).

deportation – even though Seku's neighbor revealed one day that "there is actually nothing that connects us, the other *refoulés* and me." It was more that, during everyday chats, they were able to exchange bits of information. In a neighboring village, the older generation of deportees would convene. The brother of one of them laughed in a mixture of astonishment, fraternal forbearance, affection, and admiration: the older men exchanged experiences, which nobody else understood, to relieve their mental imprisonment (*"emprisonnement"*). Some of them had travelled collectively, which provided a particular source of connection (see Chapter 4). But otherwise it was an inner circle of like-minded men, a closed system and a performance at the same time, that most of those taking part understood and may also have been strengthened by (cf. Goffman, 1956). Both the younger and the older deportees seemed to create specific alliances, but each within their own age groups, generally speaking. While the older men's time to leave again had passed, the younger ones were still at the age of mobility. For them, immobilization and potential waithood may have been perceived as particular threats as they implied a potential for *not becoming* or "not arriving" (Khosravi, 2018, p. 8), though another chance of a new adventure and "full male adulthood" might come through talking, imagining, working hard, or through caring and contributing, courageously engaging or actively waiting.

Agricultural hardships and "back to the soil" ?

The migratory adventure may appear to be the hegemonic foil and central rite of passage to social adulthood for men, but notions of suffering and courage go far beyond the adventure. In Mandé, suffering is part of everyday life and common in conversations (Diawara, 2003a, p. 70), particularly for illustrating hardships in agriculture. So former deportees describe their experiences within socially recognized codes of suffering. Consequently, deportation and the situation afterwards are a form of (continued) everyday suffering and can be specifically meaningful. According to Paolo Gaibazzi, who worked in a Soninke village in neighboring Gambia, going on an adventure builds on training in agriculture and having proved oneself to be a "real man." Knowing how to suffer is a part of it. A certain amount of hardship in the education of children is widely practiced (Gaibazzi, 2015a, pp. 74ff). Similarly, Michael Jackson defined suffering in Sierra Leone as unavoidable: "though one imagines a better life, a fairer lot, one is taught to stoically accept the inevitability of hardship. What matters most is how one endures it"[24] (Jackson,

---

24   Maher further elaborates the connections between Islam, sacrifice and suffering in the practice of Qur'anic education, which was supposed to be hard for the young, predominantly male, *talibés* (students) in Senegal to obtain higher knowledge (2015, p. 40).

2008, p. 70). Instead of avoiding suffering, one needs to suffer properly (Geertz, 1965, p. 9).

Therefore, immobility does not automatically indicate "failure" in achieving manhood. Even if highly prestigious, the migratory adventure can only be one of several potential life paths. In a region with long-standing cultures of migration, certain people need to stay to keep agriculture and local business going and take care of the family. More generally, it would be false to claim that everybody leaves.[25] In places such as Seku's village, not all the employable men were, or had been, abroad. There, you would also hear: "Everybody wants to succeed at home. But it's difficult here. Over there, you have the possibility; not here." "One of the brothers will always be abroad," Seku's mother asserted: "They cannot all be here; somebody needs to look for money abroad." Even if accounts seem contradictory, staying and leaving condition each other. In that respect, a successful time abroad for one family member enables others to stay through remittances and transnational circuits. The feeling of belonging and references to the village continue to be central as, for example, Brahima's engagement in the transnational support network shows. There are increasingly long-term and structurally oriented projects for family members from abroad or diaspora representatives, even if those left behind complain about being ignored while the travelers follow their own ideas. Many young men, in urban as well as rural areas, however, view agricultural work as ambiguous. They may complain about the hardships of scratching the dry Sahelian soil without proper machines. Seku complains about their small income: "People are unhappy because they work, and they do not make a fortune." The young men explicitly criticized the Malian state for closing down the peanut-processing mills: "We need factories!" "There is no support, no possibilities here" (Group discussion, 11-7-2015). Support and possibilities are linked instead to international experts and NGOs; even if suspicion of them is equally widespread (see Chapter 2). It is a structurally induced "negative" suffering, which creates people's feeling of marginalization; in the Kleimans' words a "routinized form of suffering" (Kleiman & Kleinman, 1991, p. 280), which is what conditions post deportation may become as well (see Chapter 4).

For many young men all this provides a reason to leave, at least for small business activities in the nearest city, to purchase items for consumption or eventually go on an adventure: the latter is often undertaken to obtain materials for progress in agriculture on their return. Eventually this opens the way to urban experience or global connectedness. Despite a reputation for remoteness and backwardness, the value of agriculture remains high. Deeply embedded in the rural, it still aims at more worldly masculinities.

---

25   After a lot of hype about mobility, immobility was newly discovered in migration research (cf., e.g., Van Hear, 2014; Jónsson, 2011).

Deportations, restricted mobility regimes and economic recessions disturb these migratory and livelihood strategies and have to be integrated: nowadays in Seku's village the majority of young men stay. Despite the value of masculine risk-taking, the increasing chance of death and difficulties abroad seem to motivate young men to remain where they are and try to succeed. Particularly schooling can have a significant effect, coexisting with the established adventurous pathways (e.g., Hertrich & Lesclingard, 2017; Daum, 2014). Furthermore, the EU discourse of safe migration, involving (inter)national NGOs, the Malian government, community leaders, family and youth organizations alike, promotes the idea that "one can succeed here" by going "back to the land." It is what the first Malian president, Modibo Keita, preached back in the 1960s. Today, it has become a motto for providing alternatives for the youth (Gary-Tounkara, 2013, 2008). The prospect has even entered the new Malian migratory policy. And it is the EU Trust Fund that finances the "reintegration" of deportees as well as such "alternatives for the youth" (European Commission, 2016), as if leaving for a better life were something unusual and disregarding common sayings and conceptions of circular mobility, such as that "each departure already implies a return" (also Dougnon, 2013). It is questionable whether these prospects are equally attractive for the youth in light of the prestigiousness of established adventurous ways toward social adulthood, worldliness and becoming an autonomous as well as a contributing and caring person. In any case, the (former and/or "failed") migrant perspective seems to express an in-depth desire to be able to decide autonomously about going or staying, not least as an adventurer and as "a man."

Even though they may be difficult, there are "real" economic possibilities for young men in the rural hinterland too. On the one hand, the informal gold mining industry has given rise to a new informal economy and "incomes at the margins" (Roitmann, 2003)[26] providing alternative income beyond the village (even if it is often illegal). Other than that, the nearby city privileges Seku and his friends on account of its economic market structure and possibilities of exchange, even if only on a day-by-day basis, over more remote places offering little in the way of income possibilities. Even so, people still consider themselves as "poor" (see Chapter 5), which, not least, pays tribute to the overarching and omnipresent development discourse and governance of international organizations and NGOs.[27] What could be seen as the result of an objectifying approach easily overlooking people's agency

---

26   According to Roitman (2003), "incomes at the margins" are – in her research often violent – constructions of spaces for the economic empowerment of Cameroonian young men at the periphery of the periphery (cf. Comaroff & Comaroff, 2001).

27   Who direct their aid "to the poor" to reduce "multidimensional" poverty through "pro-poor growth" (cf. Macamo & Neubert, 2012, p. 100). Simmel, in a visionary way, put things into context by acknowledging that a poor person is one who is the object of poverty assistance.

may thus be an agentic act by local people using the established discourses in order to get through. Whether it was the restricted mobility, a growing self-consciousness of where people come from, seniority or desperation, or importantly the need to take care felt and expressed by one's close friends and relatives staying behind, Brahima in Bamako and many in the village felt obliged to stay. They engage locally and thus may have overcome the presumed defeat through deportation, or even use it productively. Still, the adventure seems to be the more desirable – and, in the long term, more promising – path to take at least once in a lifetime.

The question of marriage after deportation

One of the main topics in the everyday conversations with Seku, Baba and Ousmane was women and marriage. Their judgment turns out to be harsh sometimes, as women seem to be assigned the role of being actually responsible for difficulties and evil (also Schulz, 2012). Marriage is a central rite of passage – for both women and men – and one of the foremost exchange relations during one's life course and a step towards adulthood.[28] Deportations intersect with it in a specific way. While many leave to search for money, potentially to finance a marriage, once they have returned, their lack of money hinders their chances of marrying. Previously, the patriarch took care of the son's marriage, selected a wife for him and paid, but fathers and family heads are often no longer capable of doing so. Consequently, the groom's voice in selecting his bride has become more influential, which may eventually question the patriarch's authority.[29]

As a generation "in-the-waiting" men have been marrying later, due to longer education, long phases of unemployment, and (failed) migrations. Setting up a new household is a very costly business; moreover, the bride price and life in general have become more expensive in recent years (as Brahima or Salif explained). Eventually this hinders youths from becoming "full adult men." One respondent in

---

28 Even if, for men, becoming mature and sexually active does not change their status as "young men" (Grosz-Ngaté, 1989, p. 173), as Schulz (2002) pointed out, the numbers of children born out of wedlock has been "skyrocketing over the past fifteen years, to the extent that marriage no longer serves as a marker of female adulthood" (p. 805).

29 While the first marriage would still be one of reason, contributing to the prestige of the entire family and social harmony in or between the families, even the villages, of the married couples, the second or third wife could be chosen out of affection. Although marriage and parenthood are seen principally as vocations for women, much more than for men (also Schulz, 2012, p. 51), women's voices seem to count little in marriage decisions as depicted by the young men. In the urban context, marriage decisions may be taken much more autonomously by the couples.

Bamako refused to be married, when the family offered support after his deportation from France: he wanted to succeed by himself. As his brother commented: "It's shameful not being able to pay yourself." It would call his masculinity into question.

Yet others bitterly regretted that they lost time through the journey: without achieving the objective envisaged, "dispossessed of the time, [they] had before removal" (Martin, 2015; cf. Khosravi, 2018, p. 7), by "temporal disorders" caused by deportation as explained in Chapter 4. They came to a halt behind their age mates, trying to do the impossible and catch up through tedious everyday work. It took Brahima in Bamako several years to gain an economic base that enabled him to marry back in the village, which could be seen as a substantial success after deportation. Seku took the opportunity to get married after his first return from Libya, although he framed his squandering of his money as an "issue of youth." Literature underlines the idea that consumption items, like Brahima's mobile phones, as signs of migratory success have become symbols that constitute masculinity and are potentially even more important than collecting bridewealth (e.g., Rudwick & Posel, 2014; Ungruhe, 2010; cf. Chapter 5).[30] In the village, it is not unusual, if it is financially possible, for unmarried, deported men to be married by their families after their return – "to give [them] an additional reason to stay and an obligation to take care of," one imagines. The aging parents may need their son where they are. Moreover, this underlines the argument developed in Chapter 5 that in the end a person's wealth lies in being a good member of society. Physically caring for people and taking over duties on spot are an essential reason to stay and are often appreciated. Eventually this links in with the sense of obligation that deportees described as underpinning their need to stay, as in Brahima's case. Without further exploring the matter here, marriage seems to gain a particular value after deportation, potentially more important (not least for reconstructing one's masculinities) than reemigration. From the perspective of post-deportation studies, this seems to be a new phenomenon, which may indicate a certain acceptance of normalization and, even more, an integration of deportations into family livelihood strategies and the everyday. At the same time, marital responsibilities and household management, thus taking over one's duties of care are important aspects in the discourse of (hegemonic) masculinities, which places fundamental value on men staying (Gaibazzi, 2015a, pp. 135ff), contributing to recovery, and assembling a new repertoire of masculinities post deportation.

---

30   Successful adventurers, but also gold seekers, usually return with presents, fashionable clothes, and desired consumption items. A young man returning from a gold mining site in Senegal after two years, had even gilded his teeth, something that was visible to everybody: in his home village he wanted to do some building and then leave for Senegal again, he said.

Generational discrepancies and generations of deportees

These potential contradictions and ambivalences of engaging, leaving, and staying torn between aspirations for autonomy and expectations of reciprocity, are embedded within a broader process of intergenerational change in Mali. Notably, the engagement of young men is not recognized in the same way by everybody and in particular by the older generation. The administrative head of the community exclaimed one day: "The older people don't understand the younger anymore! They have adopted the European lifestyle just like that. The people want the money instantly; but you have to work hard!" At least the initiatives built up with a large number of *refoulés* and repatriates and initiated by the International Organization for Migration and the Association des Repatriés between 2006 and 2010 have fizzled out.[31] Seku and Baba protested vehemently: "He is not right at all. We work so much! It's difficult to get anything." A frequent complaint particularly from fathers of the younger generation of deportees, those aged between 25 and 33, is that the younger ones do not contribute as much from their earnings as they did previously. In earlier times one's entire earnings were shared with the *"chef de famille"* (*sòtigi*), today, young men usually keep the larger part for themselves and, potentially, their nuclear family. Still, a substantial fraction is often shared with the extended kin. Seku's uncle shakes his head: "We contributed as much as we could; but times are different today. They have other needs."

All this hints at a major conflict between generations and shifting roles between men in African societies. Fathers may not have their previous power as providers while the young, even if economically constrained, may leave more easily and earn for themselves. Conversely, the elder may designate this as immoral (also Schulz & Diallo, 2016, p. 227). Threats to the status of senior men by juniors have received particular attention in masculinities studies on African settings questioning "traditional" and re-generating new hegemonic or other interrelated masculinities (e.g., Alber et al., 2008; Honwana & de Boeck, 2005; Weiss, 2004; Lindsay & Miescher, 2003). In this vein, widespread autonomous decisions to leave, including earning

31   Today, there are a number of self-organized groups of former deportees in Kita, often made up according to the deporting country, thus continuing potential networks of migration. Occasional informal gatherings may be supported by the AME as well as the transnational network "Afrique-Europe-Interact" and others. Moreover, the reintegration activities of the IOM and other international as well as local NGOs of transit returns from Libya within the framework of the EUTF and the IOM Joint Initiative for Migrant Protection and Reintegration, have clearly shaped the visibility of the return issues (cf. Alpes, 2020). See online: https://ec.europa.eu/trustfundforafrica/region/sahel-lake-chad/mali/renforcement-de-la-gestion-et-de-la-gouvernance-des-migrations-et-le_en and https://www.migrationjointinitiative.org/countries/sahel-and-lake-chad/mali, accessed 31 October 2021.

one's own money for the travel, may, as demonstrated in the previous chapter, be in-dicators of such shifts of authority, even if autonomy of travel is socially sanctioned. In this sense, sharing less money is potentially consequent on having received less support for the travel beforehand within a primordial concept of generalized reci-procity.

In the small villages, deportation itself is an intergenerational issue. Several generations of deportees live there today. Ibrahim, Ousmane's uncle, was also in Libya in 2001 and was deported; caught in the street like his nephew: "It's so long that I've not talked and thought about all this," he reflected: "You cannot be satis-fied when you return with empty hands; but it's God who decides, so you cannot complain." Ibrahim almost died when trying to cross the ocean. He was against his nephew leaving. Ousmane should have continued school. Now, neither their adventures, nor Ousmane's schooling have worked out. Upon his return, Ibrahim restarted agricultural activities, which he is still engaged in. Today, he has been married twice, has eight children, and is established in the village community. While age may have an empowering effect (Christou, 2015), he dates from a gener-ation where deportations were fewer. More than his nephew, he regrets the "failed" adventure: "It helps that there are other deportees, but you cannot forget what you've lost."

Still, between generations men may agree in their evaluation of the political difficulties as against the economic possibilities and chances. Brahima's uncle in Bamako reflected on the difficulties of the migratory adventure today: "There are conflicts kind of everywhere. When we traveled, it did not happen like this. Only God can protect us. At the moment one has stopped traveling to foreign places until peace returns to the country" (Brahima's uncle, 1-10-2016). The difficulties of migration and political restrictions may thus be recognized as hindering and endangering factors. "If it's possible to stay where you are and work, it's good," is the central message. It implies the value of taking care of one's close family through contributing, but also by physically caring for them and taking over little jobs and duties on the spot. The concept of success, through hard work and earning money, remains the central expectation and desire in becoming a man – whether back in the village, in the city or by leaving (again). The hegemonic ideas and expectations, building on previous economic and structural conditions, however, are thwarted by constrained realities and "real" chances, making it often impossible to fulfill generational expectations.

Concluding remarks: assembling deportee masculinities ?

This chapter has shown a set of men's ideas and practices connected with recovering and reproducing, thus assembling a new repertoire of masculinities after deportation, when the hegemonic conception of the breadwinner and head of household as a successful adventurer may be fundamentally endangered. The crisis brought about by large numbers of forced returns may question one's personhood as a man and substantially erode life chances particularly in a Malian context of self-evident values based on circular livelihood mobilities. Masculine values have to be renegotiated. One could assume different types of rural and urban masculinities, but there seem to be universal features that many (young) men struggle to meet, not only after deportation: the adventurer, as a counterpart to the agricultural worker, or the one involved in small-scale business; being courageous, in good physical shape, enduring, achieving, taking care, contributing, and becoming someone. The majority of these characteristics relate to hegemonic notions of masculinities. Deportations challenge this hegemonic image in particular, but simultaneously create a space for recovering and emerging aspects of masculinities, which may at the same time be particularly productive because of a person's deportation.

The deportee brings along a very specific form of "adventure-hood," even if – or maybe even because – it has potentially "failed." It differs in its particular form (i.e., by being caused by the deportation experience) from the sufferings of returnees who decided to return of their own volition, or had somehow prepared for it, even if the latter were potentially "unsuccessful" as well. Against this background, active sitting, waiting and reflecting become valuable, time-appreciating masculine engagements, demonstrating reflective capacity and knowledgeable worldliness, as forms of manly maturity or wisdom, particularly for some of the younger generation, who eagerly reinterpret aspects of supposed (deportee) masculinities as regards physical shape and consumption items.

Even if they are potentially stuck, one would not automatically call the Malian returnees socially dead, as others predicted (e.g., Vigh, 2016; see also Bredeloup, 2017; Kleist, 2017b). Deportees seem to form integral parts of their societies, eking out a living as many of their contemporaries do. It is about their wealth as persons, about trying to be a good member of society, about what deportees actually do (see Chapter 5). Discrepancies between men are based on migratory and deportation experiences, whether one gained money or not, and most notably on one's age and generation. The latter also influences one's capacity for mobility. Some are torn between leaving again and staying, but precarious and volatile situations may reverse their prospects from one day to the next (e.g., through a parent's death, which would require immediate need to take care on the spot) or through leaving and earning more. While deportees need to navigate their specific vulnerability and potential strength, the approach of courageously going on, regardless of difficulties, demonstrates the pressure to comply with the expected role despite the danger of depending economically on somebody.

Even if one must constantly readapt and renegotiate one's potential "failure," hegemonic values of becoming a household head and provider, ideally achieved through a successful adventure, but also through taking care on the spot, persist on a large scale. Rather than testifying to entirely new deportee masculinities in Mali, hegemonic notions provide stability and orientation in contrast to the conflicts between generations, which generate certain changes in Mandé masculinities. Emerging notions such as those of actively waiting and the worldly wisdom as acquired by "failed" adventurers seem to be discursively interwoven into established conceptions. Hence, former deportees assemble and act out a repertoire of masculinities. Whether this suffices for an entirely new category of deportee masculinities, differing from those of others who "failed" in their adventures may need to be researched further. In the end, (re)interpreting masculinities constitutes a narrative strategy to cope with the crisis of deportations itself. In the next chapter, I shall revisit the sense- and future-making of former deportees through "*la chance*" and a broader cosmology that former deportees referred to time and again.

Chapter 7
"Si j'ai la chance."[1] – Final sense- and future-making of "failed" adventures post deportation

Deportees' narratives time and again made reference to a higher spiritual force: to God, more generally to luck, with *"la chance"* (in Bambara: *kunna dija* or *gèrè diège*) featuring very prominently. A whole range of different aspects are in play here, from the role of God and one's supposed destiny to opportunities and "real" chances, all of which interlink, and, not least, to what a person can make out of this by keeping on going – something many deportees showed in their everyday lives, as described in the previous chapter. "Empty hands," for instance, can be explained as God's will. But, faced with the uncertainty caused by the rupture of deportation, *la chance* appears to serve as the ultimate cause in terms of sense- and future-making. So, in this closing analytical chapter, I want to look further into this notion of *la chance*, which links to people's spirituality and cosmology, and, most importantly, to examine how all this relates to their approach to the world and their own future (cf. also Ludwig, 2017a). Here, we come back to, and develop further, the elements of (im)mobility, longing, talking, and sharing about a migratory journey, as well as actually being an adventurer. My aim is to thereby underline the main thesis of this book, namely that, in the end, it is not about (missed) "success" only, or the sheer "failure" of the migratory adventure or returning without what one went out to search for, even if these normative conceptions are fundamentally shattered through deportation experiences, loss of money, and ambivalent social effects in particular, all of which continue to have an impact in specific ways after deportation. These are very complex categories in regard to their social and cultural embedding and, though they may be shattering in the first instance, they can be productive at the same time.

Going on after a deportation is not only a means to recover one's masculinities, in fact, it is central to one's spiritual and moral being and for living one's life as a "good person with body, soul, and heart." In line with Youngsted (2013), these

---

1   "If I am lucky," in Bambara: *ne kunna dijara.*

young men are "surviving in dignity," without fatalism, and, importantly, also in spiritual terms. I will show that trying and searching appears to be a prerequisite for eventually perceiving and obtaining a new chance. All these features again link intrinsically to the characteristics and ascriptions of being an adventurer and "a man." Here, the adventure and memories of it become endowed with spiritual qualities, with the adventure itself potentially becoming a spiritual journey.

In this, the final analytical chapter of the study, I will carefully trace these terms, narratives and practices and contextualize them in the post-deportation setting. First, I will dive into the concept of *la chance* and references to a higher spirituality as used for sense- and future-making empirically as well as theoretically. I will then demonstrate the concept's entanglements with and developments in (post-)adventures, showing specific evolutions and meanings of planning and imagining the future, such as the practice of "*maraboutage.*" Finally, I will revisit the idea of the collective imaginary of migratory success in light of increasing numbers of deportations and deaths, and as collective sense- and future-making. Overall, this is another facet of the ambivalence of the supposed "failed" adventure, how deportees experience, narrate, and deal with the effects of their deportations afterwards and in the longer run, thus making sense – as well as their futures – in rural and urban southern Mali.

Approaches to *la chance* – Adama and the past chance of the adventure

The case of Adama, the "philosopher" in Bamako, as I called him (see Chapter 5), provides an example of the narrative presentation and practice of *la chance* in and after a supposedly "failed" adventure. Almost philosophically, the former deportee, then sewing shoes beside a main street, described his attempt to go to Europe, his deportations and his struggles with borders and authorities. After many hyper-mobile years in the subregion, Adama had got as far as Mauritania, Morocco, and eventually Libya, where he was deported and then deported again, most recently in the year 2000. In his mid-forties in 2014, he remembered and described his tireless and suffering adventurous years in search of money as follows:

> Coming to the border, they leave you in the desert. If you want [to go anywhere], you have to walk. You can do as you want. In any case that's how it works. It was not easy. That's the misery, but at that moment it did not cause too much hardship to us, because we wanted to go to Europe. When you have something in your head, you try to push yourself and to forget the suffering. ... You see, after all, this is suffering. But it's also good to suffer. A man that has not known suffering can never know how the others have succeeded. Somebody who has suffered a lot, that's also an apprenticeship. Suffering is an apprenticeship. We, who have done

such type of journeys, and those, who have not done them, we don't have the same ideas. We have different ideas. That's why there are some who do not understand life. I, I have had *la chance* a little bit. (Adama, 11-15-2014)

His account goes beyond the aspects of hardship and suffering developed before to "having something in your head," endurance and conviction, dedication and going on. Moreover, it goes beyond the meaning of suffering and searching to the adventure as a learning experience and, importantly, as the process of becoming "a man." The political scenario here is a stage for acting on rather than something considered to be structurally responsible for one's individual situation. After all, Adama thinks himself lucky to have lived through these experiences. He had *la chance*, as he calls it, even if only a little bit of it. It was the specific suffering he underwent that was his piece of luck, although he did not succeed in economic terms and never reached Europe.

La chance in actual fact implies much more than luck. His narrative made his journey into something dignified and sublime, even a spiritual experience. He took the opportunity that was offered to him. As he explained: "*La chance* is not only money, you know. *La chance* is also getting to know the life of others, getting to know the culture of others. That's also important. This is important" (Adama, 11-15-2014). He provided a differentiated picture of what *la chance* might be, here creating an opening to the world and a learning experience through others' lives. He is a full-fledged adventurer in his experiences, memories, and narrative representations. His open-mindedness is characteristic of many other former deportees and migrants I met. It can be considered part of their "adventure-hood" as expounded in the previous chapter. As an all-encompassing experience, the adventure gave Adama a satisfaction and a source of dignity that had endured up to the time when we met. His deportations and rejections were just one aspect in the diverse cycles and phases of (im)mobile life. Thanks to his constant activity, he had been able to perceive and obtain *la chance* in his own eyes. More than that, in this way he had grown morally and spiritually through his adventure. Now, however, many years later, the hazards presently accompanying the adventure made it not worthwhile trying again.

No, I decided to stay here. [...] Because I told myself, trying to go on a clandestine migration, I don't want that anymore...This is also not the normal way. If you go clandestinely, you are not in accordance with the rules, and they deport you directly. (Adama, 11-15-2014)

This sounds like a replication of the official discourse of safe migration, as described above, which seemed to have become more established since Adama's day (see Chapter 6). Adama had, he felt, collected sufficient experience and knowledge as an adventurer, and reached a certain age – though age was not an explicit part

of his argument. Most importantly, as he again concluded: "Like this, I have suc-
ceeded a little bit." Adama considered himself to have been the one who took the
decisions – whether to walk on in the desert, and now whether to stay and not
leave again, as this had been an essential prerequisite for a sustainable return and
reintegration, as outlined in Chapter 5. He did not see himself as subjected to external forces and immobilized. He had had *la chance* "a little bit." This can be seen as
a declaration of autonomy and agency against structural constraints and interventions, narratively manifested as *la chance*, which he defines as the luck and the little
bit of success he had had. Within his space of possibilities, Adama was leading a
self-determined life in Bamako. He maintained his ex-wife and his three children
on his small income, and planned to take the children to his mother's village for
further education, as Malian tradition prescribes, he explained. Nevertheless, he
himself did not return to the village, preferring the social distance and anonymity
of the city.

On chances, luck, and destiny

In deportees' narratives, and in everyday life more generally, *la chance* is used to
explain past experiences, present situations as well as the future one may potentially encounter, here in situations after deportation. *La chance*, in Bambara *kunna
dija*, can mean luck, success, and opportunities as described by Adama, as well
as serendipity and the unexpected. In local terms having *kunna* means having the
possibility of success if one commits oneself to it, tries to attain it. More generally, *la chance* is inherent in all essential life stages – education, traveling, farming,
marriage, and aging, all of which are deeply engrained in one's social relations:
"everything that you do in your life is a question of *la chance*." After deportation it
appears to be a specific anchor and signpost as to how to make sense of things and
go about doing them.

   On the one hand, loss and "failure" as a result of deportation can be described
as depending on God and a higher spirituality. Salif illustrated this: "If you win it's
good, but if you lose, it depends on God. ... I did not reach Europe and the economy
that was behind me is lost, thus everything depends on God for me." More explicitly, a common saying is *"On s'en remet à dieu"* (One leaves something up to God) or
as if stating the ultimate reason for something: "everything is an act of God." God's
will may be used interchangeably with *la chance* or the two may be explicitly linked:
"God gave me *la chance* to return in good health." Similarly, people say: "everything
is a question of *la chance*." Also "the adventure is a matter of *la chance*" including
its upsides and downsides. Not only does such argumentation offer a reason for
what happened, and how things are, but *la chance* has a specific orientation towards
the future, providing a repertoire for how to go along. These narrative usages of *la*

chance fit perfectly into the relational ambivalence of the adventure as previously described. It cannot be seen without its broader spiritual and cosmological embedding, closely interlinked with the social order so that *la chance* becomes a very complex phenomenon in narrative presentations of sense-making and practices of how to go about one's life after deportation.

Brahima, "the Spaniard" from the Bamako market, for instance, made sense of his "failed" journey when he summed up: "But if God decides something, one cannot do anything against it." Likewise Ousmane's uncle Ibrahim in the little village framed his own empty hands after being deported from Libya in 2001: "It's God who decides, so you cannot complain." More explicitly than Adama's, these remarks demonstrate a widespread belief in some kind of fate or destiny. They seem to devoutly accept the outcome, but they still stay active in many areas of life, most importantly in fulfilling their socially expected role in light of the danger of being called a coward or lazy (*fa den sago*). More than that, and as also exemplified by Adama and Brahima, they were engaged in a constant search for a higher, spiritual being and personhood through submitting to God.

With respect to elder brothers' accusations against younger brothers on account of the latter's monetary loss and deportation, Broulaye explained as above, "But that's not exactly it. Everybody has his destiny." In this situation, many deportees would feel obliged to leave again in order "to find the money to refund [...] the elder brother," but, he continued, outlining the ambivalence of the situation, "on the contrary, others say to the *refoulés* that it's not that serious, and that the essential thing is to be in good health, so that they can still work to earn." Belief in a predestined outcome enables the young men's inability to enter Europe to be seen as something that they were not fully responsible for and could not influence. It is of the utmost importance that one remains healthy, able to work and to earn money to contribute. The wealth of the person eventually counts most. It is against this background that a "failure" is often characterized by deportees and their family and friends as "the adventure did not work out" (*tounga man ja*), as described in Chapter 5, or "he did not succeed," or more precisely as, "I did not have *la chance*."

La chance and the references to God and luck on the one hand seem to demonstrate a tendency to explain the world by generalizing and more importantly externalizing responsibility onto God, a higher spirituality, and one's destiny, which eventually relates to one's social relationship with one's parents and the role of the mother in particular. At the same time, all this is brought into connection with one's activities and the need and wish to decide and go on, to make something out of it: "That they can still work to earn," as Broulaye put it. In this vein, and as the cases of Brahima, Salif, and others show, a sense of obligation to stay after a deportation can be seen as submission to God and a cosmological belief in *la chance*: this widespread belief makes one "not challenge destiny too much," it is often said. In the following, I will delve further into this tension between human agency, destiny, and fate.

The adventurer's "failures," risks, and chances

Equating *la chance* with luck (like equating it to God) is appropriate, but does not suffice to explain the entire phenomenon. Furthermore, beyond a western or neoliberal discussion about luck in terms of fortune and wealth, the current use of *la chance* needs to be seen in its specifically migratory as well as local context. Recent discussions in studies on African migration (to Europe) and luck are helpful and make further attempts at theorizing. As in the Malian context, luck is described here as intertwining the notions of free individual agency with ideas of fate and a predetermined course (cf., e.g., Gladkova & Mazzucato, 2017; Gaibazzi, 2015b; Nieswand, 2010).[2]

In people's accounts, references to *la chance* have a great deal to do with trying and seeing whether there are opportunities, generally conditioned by uncertainty and crisis. After deportation, a distinct adaptability and flexibility are necessary. Such an attitude furthermore links up with a locally grown flexibility, what Müller (1990) calls "flexibility out of tradition." This is developed from an analysis of economic activity in agriculture, ethnic classification and religiously founded ordering patterns in the central Niger Delta throughout Malian history that are characterized by multiple alternatives and practices, which are realized according to need and possibility and related to adaptations to the extreme climatic conditions of the dry and rainy seasons (Müller, 1990, pp. 139ff). This flexibility is also related to conditions of everyday suffering and hardship and describes a particular cultural repertoire of endurance, adaptability, and a perceptivity for "serendipity" (Gaibazzi, 2015b, p. 228) that enables people to cope with the risk and uncertainty present in the everyday of their precarious life worlds. Not least, this is a supposed essential characteristic of the adventurer as described here in particular.

Susann Ludwig (2017a) conducted a convincing longitudinal study of Malian graduates in which she identified the emic concept of *la chance* as central to people's sense-making as well as their future-making in an environment of uncertainty, which is based on common-sense knowledge. She subdivides the meaning of *la*

---

2   Gladkova and Mazzucato (2017) focus narrowly on "chance encounters," referring to a "migrant's transitory social interactions" with a previously unknown people (p. 4). They identify two different (even if rather simplistic) character types among African migrants whose attitudes translate into how they encounter chances: as opportunities for positive change or as risky endeavors. Chance here empirically relates to God, fate and destiny and appears as something unexpected and hazardously occurring. Even if the authors do not further develop this direction, chance is a moment inspiring change and thus similar to Ludwig's (2017a) conceptualization, a moment separating the present from the past, as will be developed shortly.

chance as follows: "University graduates in Mali create «*la chance*» (opportunities); they take «*la chance*» (chances), but they also simply have «*la chance*» (luck) or happen to find «*la chance*» (serendipity)" (Birzle & Ludwig, 2015; cf. Ludwig, 2017a, p. 33). Her definitions pre-empt and underline deportees' narrative references to *la chance* in a different context, which emphasizes the meaning of the local context. She argues that Malian graduates "open up *la chance*." In terms of its temporal meaning (which I will shortly specify),

> *La chance* separates the present from the future since it enables a different present – something has been imagined as the future in the past. … [L]a chance is ambiguous: it can be accessed and influenced by individual action; but it is also believed to be God's will, which cannot be influenced (Ludwig, 2017b, p. 70).

In Mandé, generally speaking, people believe that every single person has a proper destiny which can be challenged and which has to be invoked through personal activity, but which it is not fundamentally possible to influence (cf. Brand, 2001). This kind of broader embedding and a general belief in destiny, fate, and one's chances, not only serve, as shown, as a last resort for sense-making post deportation, but more generally underlie the way people live their lives and not least make their futures in West Africa. So, as an overall cosmology, it tends to be commonly distributed among young people in Mali.

When we take the cases of deportees presented in the earlier chapters, and the more general narrative and practical relation to *la chance* described so far, this bringing together of the past, the present, and the future appears not to be a question of social standing, education, a particular migratory experience, or having potentially more "real" chances and opportunities than others.[3] The young men in my research used and adapted the concept of *la chance* to their context in a similar way to the young Malian graduates that Ludwig describes.[4] However, *la chance* receives a specific connotation and role under conditions after deportation, not least as it links in perfectly with the approach of the supposed "failed" adventurer.

The accounts of former deportees show that a specific attitude to approaching and opening up *la chance*, "engaging for it" in local terms, is central. Adama understood his suffering and interrupted journeys as his destiny, which he needed to submit to, but which he had shaped as well. He even appreciated the luck he had had and went to work on it actively and constructively. Brahima did not sit and twiddle his thumbs, nor did Seku, Salif and the many others introduced before, even if they were demoralized and in a potentially restless state. "A hustler does

---

3   Even if the issue of "real" chances does self-evidently play a role in everyday life (cf. Schulz & Diallo, 2016; cf. Chapter 6).

4   I would not even call this a specifically Malian or Mandé (cf. Gaibazzi, 2015b) phenomenon; for instance, Cameroonian transit migrants I met in Mali similarly referred to *la chance*.

not sit idly by" (Gaibazzi, 2015a), and "as a man you have to be strong where you are!" are the hegemonic lines to follow as we learned in the last chapter. "Good adventurers" need to be open and adaptable to the unpredictability of *la chance*. As when searching for money, for something else, to become someone, one is looking for luck and the right opportunity to come along.[5] As developed in the last chapter, this goes along with an ethos of hard work and suffering, self-discipline, as well as endurance, which is implanted, above all in rural men, from early on. Not only does this make "a full man" in terms of the ruling idea of masculinity, it prepares one to manage one's own life as well as the lives of those close to one.

It is against this background that former or future adventurers, young and old, may likewise appear vigilant and self-determined when representing themselves as experts in travel (see Chapter 6). Furthermore, people's approach to and perception of *la chance* and their broader cosmology help us to understand adventurers' high level of risk-taking, narratively expressed in such sayings as: "If you go on adventures you have to be aware that you may die or not. But you are going to die in any case." While risk is implied in the concept of the adventure and consciously accepted (Dougnon, 2013), a narrative and practical account of *la chance* is an expression, in part, of the politically and structurally shaped conditions that restrict people's life worlds, as well as an answer to them. This comes over in declarations such as Madou's "at that moment, the idea of a journey had taken over my mind. Either I went on an adventure or I would die, because there is so much poverty in Mali" (see Chapter 4). Madou, who urgently felt the need to re-emigrate after his deportation from Mauritania, demonstrated people's desperation, but at the same time their conviction that possibilities do exist. In situations of deep uncertainty and disillusion, that notion may provide security and a halt.

Risk and uncertainty have been more generally and increasingly discussed in studies on youth in Africa today (e.g., Pratten & Cooper, 2015; Whitehouse, 2012; Weiss, 2004), on modernity (e.g., Beckert, 2016, see below), and in particular on migration (Alpes, 2017; Collyer et al., 2015). Alpes (2012) and others all concluded that death, hardship, and deportations do not frighten people. Beyond the contribution of risk-taking, courage, and endurance to the make-up of a full-fledged adventurer and "man," their belief in their own chances allows us to understand even better the attitudes of so-called "kamikaze" migrants (Hernández-Carretero & Carling, 2012) or "bushfallers" (Alpes, 2017), who readily accept high risks in venturing out. Even if it may appear like fatalism, it is better seen as a feature of the previously described

---

5   People need to be open "to unexpected turns in their careers, to keep moving and to work as a way of remaining alert to the unforeseen occurrences of fortune," Gaibazzi depicts the Gambian hustlers likewise. This "quest for luck" is most intrinsically connected to (im)mobility cultures; it embodies a "kinetic notion as well as existential understanding of destiny" (2015b, p. 227).

spirit of not giving up, becoming a good person and a socially recognized, honorable man through experiencing, searching, earning, and contributing (cf. also Maher for the case of Senegalese *refoulés*, 2015, p. 49). Gaibazzi names this mode of existence "journeying" (2015b), while Monica Belloni (2015) speaks of "gambling" to describe the trial- and-error attitude of Eritrean refugees on their often deadly passages to Italy. Lucht (2017) moreover coined the phrase "eternal existential unrest" to describe the attitude of migrants stuck in Niger, who did not lose faith, but kept on going in the conviction that their efforts would pay off one day – if not before, then in their afterlife (see also Chapter 4). For Adama, his adventure was an existential struggle, which appeared to be sublimated into a sort of spiritual journey toward honor, dignity, and respect that was paying off in his everyday life now.

Religious and ritualistic inscriptions of "failed" adventures

La chance is in the end to be seen within a broader religious, spiritual, and cosmological order. Many deportees grow up with Islam and a widespread spirituality. Taking care of one's family through the adventure is, for instance, part of the commitment of being a good Muslim (cf. Maher, 2015, p. 35) More than that, there is a long-standing practice of coping with contingency and indeterminacy in Africa, including the use of various forms of divination and witchcraft that "probe causal forces inherently thought to lie beyond human control" (Bromber et al., 2015, p. 9). Cosmology and witchcraft have been discussed in particular as integral parts of the neoliberal dispensation in Africa (cf. Gaibazzi, 2015b; Geschiere, 2013; Comaroff & Comaroff, 2011, 2001, 1999; Weiss, 2004). For Henrietta Nyamnjoh (2010) religion fills a gap in the lives of those who do not benefit from the promises of modernity and globalization, and possibly even gives solace in experiences of migrant death, suffering and loss (cf. p. 82).

Luck or chance and success are part of Islamic destiny, as well as part of migratory trajectories, like suffering and "failure." Belief systems that explain humans' "failure" or success as a result of their being torn between human agency and a predetermined destiny are to be found in the cosmological notions in West Africa too.[6] Igor Kopytoff speaks of "pragmatic religion"; for Meyer Fortes these things are "modes of living" and for Evans-Pritchard "part and parcel of social process" (cf. Karp, 1986, pp. 715f). In this vein, analyzing religious or spiritual practices can allow in-depth insights into social relations and their context.

Boris Nieswand further explains that these notions (including a "negative" as well as a "positive destiny"), rather than serving as a thorough explanation of the

---

6   Jackson (2017) says that even in the most fatalist conceptions of destiny in West Africa there
     is a vestige of human agency to be found (cf. Gaibazzi, 2015b, p. 233).

world, form an explanatory foil to specific actions and occurrences (Nieswand, 2010). Against this background, Nieswand develops the concept "enacted destiny" from his work with charismatic Protestant (African) migrant groups/churches in Berlin. It places a positive outcome and success between human agency and pre-determined, divine destiny. Several works on charismatic Protestant movements place the emphasis on free will and the role of human activity and influence as a tribute to modernity (e.g., Van Dijk, 2007; Comaroff & Comaroff, 2001). Similarly, a certain entrepreneurial attitude on the part of Malian adventurers (cf. Chapter 6) and the idea of the adventure as a commodity could be placed within a neoliberal ideology. More than that, however, they are deeply embedded in and part of local narratives and notions. And in this respect the social relation and embedding are of the utmost importance and deeply interlinked with the broader cosmology.

Meyer Fortes, one of the first anthropologists to analyze West African belief systems, concluded that one's social role is intrinsically related to one's destiny. In his famous monograph "Oedipus and Job in West African Religion" ([1956] 2018), he describes how, for the Tallensi: "not fear, ignorance, or superstition, but the moral bonds of the filio-parental relationship are the springs of Tale ancestor-worship" (ibid., p. 409). Similar to the concept of a "debt of life" (Bredeloup, 2017), he explains, "It is because one owes one's life to one's parents, Tallensi say, that one has irrevocable and absolute bonds with them" (Fortes, [1956] 2018, p. 409). According to Fortes' interpretation, this parallels very much Job's recognition of the unquestioned authority of God and his submission to it. "One's destiny should not be challenged too much," as explained above. If this bond between the parents and the child, here the mother in particular, is "abortive," and the child has an "evil Prenatal Destiny," this serves for the Tallensi "to identify the fact of irremediable failure in the development of the individual to full social capacity." In fact, all this links in well with the belief in the importance of the relationship between mothers and children, and the role of mothers in particular (see Chapter 5).

It is no accident that an expression such as "everything is a question of *la chance*" reminds us of the Bambara saying *bè bi ba bolo*, "everything is in the hands of/ depends on your mother" and "everything you have will be owed to your mother," which eventually puts the mother at the center of responsibility for an adventurer's success or breakdown. One's mother is seen as responsible for one's fate and destiny, here related to the migratory adventure and its potential breakdown, which puts her in danger of being blamed and could potentially imply the son's social death (*fa den sago*). Still, there are considerable differences between the two approaches. While *la chance* is a way of explaining one's situation by referring to God and luck, *bè bi ba bolo* is a statement stressing one's moral accountability as described more fully in Chapter 5, not least related to the submissiveness of the mother to her husband. It relates to Fortes' ethnographic conception insofar as he considers destiny to be deeply relational and social. For the Tallensi, this "is neutralized by ritual procedures based on the belief that evil Prenatal Destiny is in the last resort susceptible of control by the ancestors if they so will it" (Fortes, [1956] 2018, p. 411). Thus the Tallensi consider ways to get around even an "evil Prenatal Destiny." In Mandé such a neutralizing effect could also relate, therefore, to the supposed "good" behavior of the mother; however, there is no means of setting the mother in a spiritual, otherwordly position. This would remain something different. More than that, it would set the mother in relation to *la chance* and thus to an overall sense- and future-making.

A supposedly "failed" migratory adventure does not mean "the end of the world" is a saying repeated not only by representatives of the AME (field notes, 10-20-2014). It follows reasonings such as "the travel did not work in the first or second place, but there are other ways to go about it." Although the quest for fortune may have failed at the first attempt, the quest for luck has not, or may deserve another *chance*. Failure and success are thus "two sides of the same coin" (e.g., Voirol & Schendzielorz, 2014, p. 27) or "provisional containers for one another" (Appadurai, 2016, p. xxv). Interestingly, migrants' accounts in Nieswand's study refer relatively little to failure. The latter is either compensated for by a focus on the future, or accounted for as an instance of individual misconduct, as something evil or as a "ritual mistake." In the sense of enacted destiny, success is described as divine and "failure" as human. Maher discussed deportations in Senegal using the image of a "failed ritual" (Maher, 2015, p. 32f), which, if it fails, needs to be fixed.[7] All of this links back to the ancient concept of the adventure as a "rite of passage" and eventually to the generative and transformative power of ritual (cf. Jackson, 2017, 2005). "Failure" in giving space for creating something new, becomes a productive category itself. *La chance* in relation to going on serves as a basis for some recognition, eventually enabling new chances and potential to "fix" such "failure" through other achievements and, maybe, to repair the ritual and neutralize one's destiny as well. It is in this respect that *la chance* is something "ambiguous" between individual agency and divine dependency, something one has to commit oneself to. Not least, from such point of view, one can better understand the ambivalence of the migratory adventure and an assumed "failure" as an intrinsic mode of being of people torn between mobility cultures, social expectations and migratory constraints, and eventually as a productive category.

Maraboutage and calling on higher spirits for *la chance* in adventures
One of these practices of ritualistic repair can be consulting a "*marabout*" or calling on higher spirits. More generally, consulting *marabouts* is an established practice to learn about one's predetermined destiny in tension with individual agency and

---

7   A failed ritual can, accordingly, be the result of a mistake in performing the ritual as well as the failure of the ritual as such, in terms of its efficacy (cf. Bonhomme, 2008).

for activating *la chance*, before, during, and after (failed) adventures, and in many other stages of everyday life. *Marabouts* are local spiritual leaders, usually male[8], in West Africa and previously also in the Maghreb, and mostly in the tradition of Sufism. They were highly renowned and influential representatives of the priesthood in previous centuries, and there is a large diversity of *marabouts* in Mali today.[9] A village usually has at least one *marabout*, who may potentially be in conflict with the local imam. A common *marabout* may combine animistic, shamanic, and esoteric elements with those of the Islamic religion in telling the future. Still a difference is made between a *marabout* and a *"féticheur"* (a fetishist, in English, in the sense of a worshipper of fetishes or priest of an animistic religion) who is often referred to as a mere peddler of superstition and sorcery. While at the same time fetishes and talismans play a central part in everyday life.[10] When someone is going on an adventure the *marabout* or *féticheur* hands over a *giri-giri* for a safe journey (cf. also Nymanjoh, 2010). Otherwise, *marabouts* are renowned and honored for their visionary powers and some have become central public figures in Mali today (Schulz, 2006). For many people, consulting one's *marabout* is a prerequisite at any stage of life. Regarding their central meaning in people's cosmology and being, Brand (2001) describes *marabouts'* activities as taking place in the grey area between fate and destiny, where one's actions are seen to be decisive but unclear in outcome (pp. 148ff). In this way, a *marabout* can be of essential help in providing guidance and orientation within this vague space. More likely, the *marabout's* support will make things more acceptable (p. 29). The latter becomes particularly important retrospectively, after a deportation, but also in relation to the future.

Maraboutage is in its function "inextricably linked to the cultures of migration" (Nymanjoh, 2010, p. 4). In fact, *marabouts* have become part of the commodification of the migratory adventure through broadening their activities towards the lucrative business of foretelling an adventure's potential success or "failure." Ida Marie Vammen calls these *marabouts* "brokers of hope" (2017), as, in light of the uncertainty of adventure, many seek advice to learn about their destiny in order to avoid potential "failures" and capture success, fortune, luck, and *la chance*. For example, an adventurer may consult his *marabout* before leaving, but also before entering the boat in Mauritania or in Libya to ensure a safe journey. Beyond that, spiritual and divination practices are widely established means of receiving advice on the

---

8   AmberGemmeke (2008), however, wrote about female marabouts in Dakar.

9   For some more historic insights and the current *Grand Marabouts* in Mali see Wiedemann (2013). Thiam (2014) defines *marabout* as Muslim religious sage, who can be a Qur'anic master or religious guide.

10   Often children, male as well as female, receive a small leather belly chain which is intended to bring them luck, and many people wear so-called *giri-giris*, necklaces and amulets also believed to bring spiritual blessings and luck.

imponderables of an adventure and ensuring its positive outcome. Often mothers call on the higher spirits and pray for success and blessing for their sons. Salif's mother went to see a *djin*[11] in her home village, to know if his journey would work out successfully. Meanwhile, he consulted a *marabout* and sacrificed an ox. More than that, some *marabouts* have also become part of migration-facilitating networks themselves (Vammen, 2017).

I once participated in a spiritual ritual calling on the wisdom of a caiman, a member of a subspecies of the alligator, which was seen as a spiritual force able to make hopes and desires come true. It was in a little village where we had been staying for several days. Very early in the morning Birama and I accompanied a small group of villagers to express our wishes to the sacred caiman. In an excited and solemn atmosphere, wearing white clothes[12], we followed the eldest son of a family of hunters[13] who had inherited the legacy of calling the caiman, to a small lake about two kilometers into the woods. One after the other people went to the ritual master, telling him their wishes, handing over their sacrifices, mostly cola nuts and living poultry, which the master slaughtered in calling the caiman. A woman in a festive white dress and veil with little colorful flowers around the edges stood out. She shouted out loud and vehemently. Birama translated in a whisper: "I wish my son luck in passing the ocean! He is in Algeria. I want him to succeed in crossing to bring happiness and fortune to the entire family. I wish he may be strong and courageous!" It appeared to be of the utmost importance and seriousness how she framed and openly displayed her wish for her son's success.

Not only did this underline how successes and "failures" in adventures are incorporated in spiritual practices, but the woman's performance also emphasized the necessity of publicly demonstrating her support and dedication to the realization of that success. It appeared as if this would enable her to deeply hope for and rely on the survival of her son, not to mention his support – maybe also well aware of all the constraints he might face in order to achieve these aims. More than that, it might be a necessary demonstration to underline her backing and benediction as a mother, which are believed to be decisive for a son's success, and finally also to prevent defamatory speech by the villagers – even if the latter can only be a presumption. In this respect, it could be interpreted as a demonstration of how the linkage of destiny and fate depends on the child–parent relationship and its ritualistic invocation as described by Meyer Fortes. The caiman appeared after some

---

11 Here a woman, who is said to have great visionary capacities.

12 White is considered the color of initiation and in Africa usually worn for initiation rituals htt p://dictionnairedessymboles.com/2016/03/le-symbolisme-du-blanc.html, accessed 31 October 2021.

13 Mandé hunters are considered to be great sorcerers and part of the bush ("*la brousse*"), the domain of sorcery, where they perform their hunting activities (Jansen, 1996, p. 680).

time. It was barely visible though. Some waves indicated its appearance. Still excited, but satisfied, we left the place and returned to the village.

There were other occasions, in cases of deportation, where the *marabout* had obviously made a wrong prediction before the adventurer left, or a spiritual medium,
such as the caiman or a *djin*, failed to make the wish expressed – and not least paid
for – come true. "That's how I lost 200,000 F CFA just as a matter of course[14] – just
for a forecast, without even any transport!" – Salif was angry about his mother's
intervention with the *djin* and the *marabout* at the same time. Blaming the spiritual
mediator could also serve as a way of externalizing his anger. Others would consult a *marabout* again, although the previous journey had not worked out: "it's not
good to do things haphazardly," which means, proper guidance is needed. Yakouba
killed and sacrificed four sheep, before leaving, at the *marabout's* request. The intervention of a *marabout* or other spiritual mediator is seen as a kind of insurance
for the risky journey and for its continuation afterwards, providing certainty at the
moment of doing something, which matters even more than the retrospective evaluation of the prediction. Consulting the *marabout* after a forced return helps make
sense of the unexpected thing that happened, moreover one receives guidance for
one's next steps. Such an approach also indicates some acceptance of the "failed"
attempt and the wrong prediction as well; most importantly, it is about a new certainty at this moment disclosing another way to go about things. In contrast to
that, Karim refused, being clearly resigned: "When I was deported, I was very sad
(literally: "my heart was suffering"; see Chapter 5). I did not go to a *marabout* again"
(Karim, 11-1-2015). Others would openly deny ever consulting a *marabout*, even less
a *féticheur* or other spiritual guide.

Although *maraboutage* plays such a central role in people's lifeworlds on the basis of the prominence and long standing of practices of divination and witchcraft, I
encountered a certain social secretiveness and embarrassment when people openly
acknowledged that a wrong prediction had been made by a *marabout*. In a discussion with a group of deportees in Seku's village one afternoon, nobody answered
my question about who went to the *marabout* before leaving. Then, there was some
ashamed laughter. One of them confessed that he went, and everybody laughed,
first a hidden chuckling, then a resounding roar. Overall, there was an abashed atmosphere. The majority of young men sitting there in the animated circle seemed
to agree with the general practice of *maraboutage* with respect to the adventure.
"If you fail, you go to the *marabout* for a second try and turn of adventure, and if
you fail again, you may choose to go to another *marabout* to ensure you get good
advice in case you want to leave again and have a third try," one said and everybody
nodded, though some started laughing again.

---

14   About 300 €.

The practice of consulting the *marabout* to learn about the future outcome of the adventure was not questioned – in the event of a failed prediction you tried another *marabout*. While this links in with the general attitude of trying and seeing and not giving up, they seemed to be afraid of losing face in front of one another, as well as vis-à-vis me and Birama. At the same time, testing another *marabout* subverts the belief in one's destiny, or to put it a better way, the role and capacity of *maraboutage* is challenged. Almost all the young men sitting there had "not made it" so far. Apparently, the misleading consultation and a certain secrecy surrounding the fortune-teller, connected to the "failed" attempt, created embarrassment when socially shared in the group. It could be that it might reveal that somebody had a negative destiny, and consequently that his mother had been guilty of wrongdoing that had so far not been able to be compensated for or "neutralized" in any way. The mystical ability of the *marabout* becomes an integral part of what is believed to be destiny or a mother's "failure." While *maraboutage* is an everyday practice, particularly in relation to the migratory adventure, these vague arguments underline a specific uncertainty and disorientation of the everyday at the same time. Deportations contribute to that as well. Still, continuing these spiritual practices provides a source of certainty against the uncertain present and, above all, the uncertain future ahead.

Approaching the future – (un)certainties and contingency under post-deportation conditions

Deportations have been prominently introduced in this study as ruptures affecting the past, the present, and the future – ruptures with long-lasting effects, challenging material, social and emotional relations deeply, and potentially ruinous to family harmony (cf. Jackson, 2017, p. 151). In the event of a temporal discontinuum, through deportation a significant future is put at risk, and becomes potentially impossible to achieve. The *marabout* or *djin* may have predicted wrongly, and the desires linked to the adventure have not been fulfilled.

A deportation may also represent a turning point. As research has shown, uncertainty can become a precondition for hope, aspirations, and not least for productivity, as long as there is an "awareness of it and willingness to act in it" (Kleist & Jansen, 2016, p. 379; cf. Cooper & Pratten, 2015; Johnson-Hanks, 2005).[15] In a similar vein, increasingly literature on African youth links to imaginations, aspirations, desires, future-making, and the role of the future itself (cf., e.g., Carling

---

15   In this sense, Kleist and Jansen define "hope as a phenomenon [that] is characterized by simultaneous potentiality (in its broadest sense) and uncertainty of the future" (Kleist & Jansen, 2016, p. 379).

& Schwewel, 2017; Vigh, 2009b)[16], in connection with migration in particular (e.g., Stock, 2019; Kleist & Thorsen, 2017). More than that, imagining and aspiring are seen as the first steps to, and prerequisites for, any action and potential change: the concept of "vital conjunctures"[17] put forward by Johnson-Hanks (2002) proves to be particularly relevant for the context discussed here. "Vital conjunctures" point towards the uncertainties of the future, which makes the term particularly useful, when the crisis of deportations adds to everyday uncertainties. Johnson-Hanks defines them as follows: "These are the moments when seemingly established futures are called into question and when actors are called on to manage durations of radical uncertainty. Conjunctures are navigated in reference to their horizons – the imaginable futures that are hoped for or feared" (p. 878). Former deportees are thrown into an unexpected situation and need to find a new way and narrative to make sense of their everyday experience as well as their future. So far, I have shown how this is done through references to and reinterpretations of suffering, hard work, courage, caring, contributing, and leaving again, furthermore through a narrative relation to *la chance*. Eventually, such ruptures and turning points can give space to "another potential future"[18], too.

In southern Mali these imaginable futures have for many been postulated as those of successful departure and return as reference points for people's actions. The "horizons of the conjuncture," as Johnson-Hanks (2002) terms them, remind us of the "horizons of expectations" after Koselleck (2004). Both concepts refer to the horizons of what is imaginable, can be expected and thus can eventually be done at a specific point in time and space, given one's experiences, knowledge, and situation.[19] Here, the imaginable futures, which are the collective imaginary

---

16   Although obviously running the risk of inaccurately lumping the unlike together with the same, I want to consider the similarities of these concepts as they all constitute ways to deal with uncertainties and contingency in light of constrained mobilities, deportations, and migrants' deaths.

17   The term derives from Johnson-Hanks' work with young, educated Cameroonian women about their future plans, specifically as regards having children. Many of them said they could not make any plans due to their uncertain environment (cf. Engeler & Steuer, 2017). Johnson-Hanks calls "judicious opportunism" (2005, p. 370) the quality that allowed women to respond to an extremely volatile situation.

18   According to Johnson-Hanks, these are "experiential knots during which potential futures are under debate and up for grabs" (p. 872).

19   "Koselleck applied two formal abstract categories – experience and expectation – that interrelate past, present and future, and frame human action with respect to time." (Bromber et al., 2015, p. 4) According to Koselleck, "experience is present past, whose events can be incorporated and remembered through a process of permanent reworking of individual and 'alien' experience." The past as a whole, as diverse interpenetrating and overlapping layers of time, is a "space of experience" (*Erfahrungsraum*). "Expectation" as Koselleck puts it, both individual as well as interpersonal, is "future made present." Expectation is directed at the non-ex-

of migratory success, constitute the hegemonic foil now set in contention through deportation and thus potentially in need of being reinvented.

Susann Ludwig, who worked on Malian university graduates, calls an unexpected, yet desired, rupture of the everyday the "sprout"[20] of *la chance* – in a context where *la chance* divides past, present, and the future. Deportations do indeed usually come unexpectedly and rupture a migrant's life in a country of destination or transit. However, even if rather exceptional, there is a relative probability of the administrative implementation of a deportation: it is more likely in specific political situations such as where there are restrictive migratory policies against "illegal aliens" or a rigorous implementation of EU externalized border controls, in other words elements of the established practice of the global deportation regime. Even so, they are experienced often as happening unexpectedly, when people are caught in the street and returned carrying the symbolic plastic bag, for instance.

Likewise, deportations are in the vast majority of cases said to be undesired, even if deportees and their close friends and relatives may interpret them as not having had *la chance* or having suffered ill luck (*"mauvaise chance"*).[21] At the same time, the rupture through deportations may open up a space for "another potential future" and eventually a new chance. Ludwig's findings reveal how *la chance* provides a tool and guidance for Malian graduates to deal with the past, the present, and the future. Instead of predicating a specific kind of life course, the future implies *la chance* of whatever kind. Similarly, former deportees refer to *la chance* and new chances and their (imagined) futures, and thereby potentially create new certainties within an omnipresent contingency, as I will show.

Future plans and aspirations – between planning and vague disorientation

The future is the object of multiple forms of social and religious practice and imaginations, as we already have seen with respect to the practice of *maraboutage*. Even if people have no possibility of knowing the future for certain,[22] "the future matters!" as Beckert outlines in his essayistic analysis explaining capitalist dynamics (2016, p. 270). Generally speaking, there are two different ways of approaching the future: to relate it to the past and past experiences, like a memory transferred into time ahead (Koselleck, 2004; Schütz, 1967, p. 61); or to relate to it from the present,

---

perienced, but confronts a limit, which Koselleck (2004) called the "horizon of expectation" (*Erwartungshorizont*). This incorporates hopes, fears, rational predictions, and speculations.

20   This is based on a respondent's expression (cf. Ludwig, 2017a, p. 12, n. 9).

21   More than that, not having had this chance needs to be accepted as a part of one's destiny, which "everybody has, as people say."

22   Knowing what will eventually happen is impossible, even though it has long been humankind's desire and is intrinsically connected to conceptions of progress in modernity (e.g., Bromber et al., 2015).

as something newly imagined and "yet to come" (Bloch 1986 [1954]). More generally, the future is contingent (Beckert, 2016), undetermined, and contains endless possibilities (Bromber et al., 2015; cf. Ludwig, 2017a, p. 147). This contingency is approached differently in different contexts.[23]

In the Malian context in question, contingency may create uncertainty and fear, but likewise joy or confidence after a forced return (as Salif outlined, for instance). Calling on higher spiritual forces through a *djin*, a *féticheur* or a *marabout* is a way to deal with this contingency and uncertainty. Supposed unawareness of the future[24] can thus be a productive component in general cosmological explanations in West Africa, within the tension between destiny and human agency, where one's future may be outlined, but open for human activation at the same time. Related to this, Charles Piot (2010) speaks of a "nostalgia for the future," developed in West Africa since the fall of the Berlin wall. It describes a positive longing for the future, based on the wish to change the present and the conviction that anything else would be better than present suffering. Belief in a certain destiny, even if that destiny needs to be activated, can provide certainty; a narrative use of *la chance* after deportations links in here, as I will show.

Respondents appeared to approach the contingencies and unexpectednesses of the future through planning and aspiring, imagining, or longing. The future projections of former deportees were not central to my research, but often formed part of our conversations. References to the future, in fact, often came up without my explicitly asking about their visions and ideas for their later lives, most obviously with regard to their aspiration of leaving again, but also in connection with other projects and future plans that they wanted to share. Not least, many people's everyday activities may eventually relate to preparing for the future, such as Seku's reflecting on and actively waiting for upcoming possibilities. Some respondents talked about their future endeavors in a quite open-ended and vague way, while others had very concrete plans and visions. In this context, *la chance* was related to a specific orientation toward the future. The unexpected "sprout" of *la chance* would, in fact, in this case become something desired. Simultaneously, this narrative relation provided a repertoire of how to get along. Thus, a conversation might go "if he has *la chance*, he will be able to leave again" referring to a new potential

---

23 Central works on future-making in modernity, dealing with this contingency, are related to money, risk, and capitalism (cf., e.g., Beckert, 2016; Appadurai, 2013; Taleb, 2007). Risk and luck, success and failure are the most central terminology here.

24 Predicting "the future, based on what we already know, is the major source of uncertainty, because it leaves us vulnerable to surprise" (Ludwig, 2017a, p. 103). Ludwig draws on Taleb's analogy with the black swan and circumstance that we "continuously refuse to expect the unexpected" (2007).

success in adventure, or "he will be able to set up a business," or "he will be successful with his agricultural work," referring to concrete economic opportunities arising on the spot. Often, these narrations were very similar to expressions of the supposed adventurer's way of trying and seeing not least what makes "a man."

Broulaye, for instance, was committed to setting up a business. At the time he was making preparations, so he regularly commuted between the nearby larger city and the tiny village in order to establish contacts and plan what his little business could be about. Realistic opportunities were to step into the mobile phone sector by selling credit and sim cards, to trade agricultural products, or to do some kind of support work in the market – for instance, selling mattresses, as Brahima did in Bamako, or assisting a wheel seller, like his friend Ousmane. He reasoned, "If I have *la chance*, it will work out. If not, I will need to see whether I have to go and search for money elsewhere." In his view, there was a possibility that a chance might come along that would allow him to realize his plan and set up a business. He could not be sure that this would occur, but it might happen, as he had observed from other cases where things had worked out similarly. The least he could do was to prepare, actively engage, and look out for his chance if it came. For the time being, his future was bound up with staying and engaging where he was.[25] If things didn't work out, he would need to adjust and look for an alternative. *La chance* in this respect provided narrative guidance and certainty. There might be a new chance in the future.

The commonest way of framing a new adventure was to introduce *la chance* between vague imagining and concrete planning, as one oscillated between staying and leaving. Former deportees' and other young men's planning and aspirations were being centrally impacted by today's constrained mobilities. Particularly those who had already made several attempts at leaving and risked potential deportation, often expressly refused to go on a clandestine migration again, reminding us of the state discourse of safe migration. The argument would be: "If I have *la chance*, I will be able to get a visa. I do not want to take the land route" (cf. Chapter 6). Adama's comment was: "This is not the normal way." Some would reflect on "normal" or rather "safer" ways in a manner that was sometimes scarcely realistic. One respondent said that, if he were to leave again, he would rather go by plane and continued: "If I can't get hold of enough money, I may go by land instead. But if I do find the money, I would rather stay and use it to establish something here" (Group discussion, 11-1-2015). The "if," which implies a new chance, repeatedly points to the critical relevance of money in relation to leaving in a "safe" and legal way rather than "unsafely" and clandestinely over land. If his financial situation allowed, he

---

25   Many conversations with young deported men during field work were on their possible future projects, similarly prefaced with "if I have *la* chance".

would either take off again by plane or build up something on the spot – the latter option resembling Broulaye's reference to *la chance*. These comments hint at the contingency of the future and a person's potential chance of leaving or staying, but also at indecisiveness about what would be the right way. This kind of vague argumentation and uncertainty might well be interpreted as a sign of disorientation.

Contingency and indeterminacy are integral parts of the everyday for this age group in particular (e.g., Schulz, 2002). According to Beckert (2016), "fictionality points to the openness of the future, which makes expectations contingent." What will happen eventually is unknown. However, "contingency negates the idea that expectations are correct in the aggregate" (p. 10). "Fictional expectations" on the one hand mean actors' images of "future states of the world, the way they visualize causal relations, and the ways they perceive their actions influencing outcomes," which could be related to common-sense knowledge of *la chance*; while "rational expectations" propose "that actors' expectations, at least in the aggregate, equal the statistically expected value for a variable" (ibid.).[26] Both seem to be intrinsically impossible. Nothing can be sure, even if expectations build on experiences one has previously had. In other words, there can be no "reliable" expectations, rather humans act against a background of unawareness, risk, and contingency, and need to be flexible and continuously revise and adjust their expectations and actions according to contingent outcomes and experiences over and over again. Imagined futures are thus a crucial component of the social, economic, and political order itself (ibid., p. 11). Even if former deportees in southern Mali act against a background of supposed destiny, which implies that part of a person's future is predetermined, the role of contingency is central, as stated above. Expectations may be raised but remain permanently fictitious. More than that, for adventurers to stay active and open to the unexpected appears very (post)modern in the end, taking (post)modern ascriptions of flexibility, adaptability, and openness into account.

Some deportees seemed to be very specific – one might even say "rational" – in their planning of future activities. They concretely prepared for *la chance* to come. Brahima, for instance, had very concrete plans for re-emigrating. One day, after all his talk about longing to leave, all his insistence on the impossibility of doing so and on his obligation to stay (cf. Chapter 6, *la bouillie*), he declared to my surprise:

> I'm in the process of preparing. I've done all my papers. I have prepared all the papers that allow going on an adventure through the legal channels. Everything

---

26   Beckert explains further: "According to rational expectations theory, actors make use of all available information, which suggests that outcomes do not differ systematically from the forecasts made by the dominant economic model" (2016, p. 10). His argumentation very much refers to a materialist, capitalist world, but he says it is also applicable to societies shaped by other cosmologies and religions less related to the economy (2016, p. 3).

is ready. I don't have the visa yet, but all the papers you have to file to get the visa. I looked for all these papers. (Brahima, 12-12-2015)

His aim was to obtain a visa to Europe, which he considered a (symbolically) much "better" place than Africa (see also Chapters 4 and 6). When I asked more questions, he detailed the steps he had already taken to get a tourist visa: getting a certificate to show he had a secure income in Mali, an invitation from a host in a European country, and a guarantee of insurance while abroad. Everything sounded structured and planned. In the end, however, his plan never came to anything. Possibly his plans were merely the product of some kind of wishful thinking recreated only in our conversation. Up to the present time of writing, Brahima remains in Bamako. Even if he actually was in the process of organizing his administrative papers, he would never have been able to obtain a visa. It would be highly unlikely for somebody like him, lacking substantial financial resources, education, and the necessary close networks, to be able to acquire such a document. Doing so depends on external forces – in this case the decision of the embassy. But his planning and organizing kept him busy in the meantime. And it was the only thing he could do. He put himself in a position of readiness: he prepared. As a narrative strategy, moreover, it created the impression – for himself as well as his interlocutors – that he would be taking off again soon, thus continuing physically mobile and active. Narrating, sharing, and imagining again appear not only as deeply agentic acts in light of given constraints, but also as preparatory ones. Through stories we make meaning out of the past, the present, and the future.[27] Brahima's state of immobility included a very concrete, albeit still imagined, state of mobility in the future. In this forward-looking spirit, his being was constitutively and existentially upgraded.

For others, this kind of *chance* of leaving again or setting up a business would eventually be realized someday. Yakouba, for instance, managed to establish a small fish-culturing project through a family friend who had a contact in an NGO. Little by little, he was able to contribute to the family income. The youth in the village now talk about his project, and say that they want to do the same. Success becomes a source of envy and role model for others – no matter whether achieved through migration or not. Idrissa, another deportee in Bamako, on the other hand, emigrated again to France eight years after his deportation (after he had been unfortunately and unexpectedly caught in a Paris street without papers during daylight hours). For years afterwards, it seemed he had primarily been living and longing to return to Europe. "Everything is much better than here in Africa," he said, following the

---

27   Nancy Scheper-Hughes (2008) speaks of the "narrativity" of "living to tell the tale" in reference to Clifford Geertz: "the only thing that humans could not seem to live with is the idea that life might be utterly random, meaningless and absurd. Resilient narratives reframe adverse events in order to make them meaningful, purposeful, and, ... 'for the best'" (p. 44).

same narrative as Brahima before. "If I have the money, I will go back to France," he repeated frequently.[28] It seemed like an immovable fixation. Idrissa lived partly on "*petits jobs*," but mostly on money sent by a cousin in France in whose house he was living in Bamako. "He has to go abroad," the cousin's wife declared firmly. Half a year later, Idrissa actually arrived at Paris airport. A relative with French citizenship had written a letter of invitation and the powerful family networks provided the obligatory resources – a full bank account and insurances – that fortunately enabled him to obtain a visa. Today, he is even married to a French woman, originally from the Ivory Coast, and has finally received a residence permit. At last, he has had *la chance*.

When former deportees "make" the future, *la chance* is intrinsically connected to imaginations, aspirations, and hope, but importantly also to the certainties and securities of real-life chances and social becoming after deportations, even if they do not necessarily withstand statistical evidence. This is most obvious in respect to the hegemonic foil of leaving (again) and one's real migratory chances. A short comparison with the Gallup World Poll (GWP)[29], for instance, is useful: This well-established survey found that "32% of respondents in sub-Saharan Africa had a desire to emigrate, 4% planned to do so within the next year and 1% were making relevant preparations" (Carling & Schewel, 2017, p. 5), like Brahima and Idrissa. Obviously, making preparations still differs considerably from actually leaving in the end, but this percentage seems minimal. Considering the overarching administrative mobility restrictions, it is almost negligible. Such expectations can thus barely be called "rational." And yet, after deportation, many people continue to aspire to leave again or try to do so, and some actually make it in the end. Mohammed, another former deportee, in Seku's village, illustrated the point convincingly:

> My elder brother left on an adventure in 2000, and was deported in 2001. I got ready to leave as well. He recommended me to stay as he would not want me to confront the same difficulties. I said no, I would leave because everybody's chances differ: It's possible that I would not see the same difficulties as him. Later, when I was also deported, I handed the same advice to my little brothers: They did not accept it either. The one that comes right after me is in a gold mining site. It's now two years that he has been there in Senegal. (Small Group discussion, 11-7-2015)

---

28   This was most obvious, when Modibo, Idrissa's childhood friend, visited for holidays. We met on the patio of the house where I was staying in Bamako. Idrissa wanted me to get to know his friend. Both kept talking about Modibo's life in France as a (today regularized) night guard and the time they spent together in Paris back then. Idrissa needs to return was their continuously repeated joint conclusion.

29   Since 2005, the GWP has tracked "over 100 crucial world issues affecting people's lives" in 160 countries worldwide in the form of representative surveys. Migratory aspirations are one part of it: https://www.gallup.de/182702/gallup-world-poll.aspx, accessed 31 October 2021.

Repeated deportations do not act as a deterrent, even if underlined by an elder brother, as this quote clearly illustrates. The success of a neighbor, or some acquaintance, can suffice to convince someone that they have a similar possibility of success.[30] To put it another way, even if there is a low probability of making it, the fact that "somebody has made it" is enough reason for somebody else to try it too (cf. also Belloni, 2015, p. 110).[31] In Koselleck's sense, building on past as well as "alien" experiences (cf. Koselleck, 2004, p. 259) – the same may appear in vital conjunctures experienced by others[32] – manifests a knowledge of the possibility and thus creates the expectation (even if "fictional") of a "real" and new intervention of *la chance* to enable not only a successful migratory adventure, but also the building-up of a small project on the ground. Ludwig has convincingly shown how such knowledge of the existence of *la chance* can eventually build into an everyday certainty for Malian graduates (cf. Ludwig, 2017a). It is knowledge transferred from the past to the future (p. 169), and Malian deportees do very much the same thing insofar as all the contingencies lived out through imagining and aspiring at first are then applied to what Beckert termed "fictional expectations," pointing to the openness of the future.

In this way, *la chance* is a means and motor to keep people hoping and imagining, planning and potentially realizing new futures.[33] Brahima concretely prepared and Idrissa eventually took off. Yakouba had a small project and Broulaye prepared for a little business. In sum, future-making by former deportees and adventurers was narrated and practiced through remaining open to the unexpected, yet required *la chance* if it was to be taken further, if people were to leave again and eventually have success. Noemi Steuer, Michelle Engeler, and Elisio Macamo (2017) speak of "elusive futures" for many African youth, who assume that any kind of action implies the possibility of acting in the same way again in the future (p. 13).[34] Through experiencing, narrating, collectively sharing and most importantly

---

30   Ludwig describes how there can be 1000 Malian graduates applying for one position in the *concours* (competition) for the public service, making success a statistical impossibility, but still people try and believe in *la chance* (2017a, p. 136).

31   "Perceived luck can play a major role in people's key decisions" as authors from gambling studies have suggested (Smith et al., 1996; cf. Belloni, 2015, p. 111).

32   Alber (2016) widens the concept of vital conjunctures that form individual experience to include those that also affect a person's social context.

33   Jackson even discusses luck as the only chance for youth in Africa against a backdrop of violence which appears "as the logic of imagination loses touch with the logic of social practice, desperate fantasies and actions are born" (2005a, p. xxiii).

34   With the aim of going beyond concepts such as "extended presence" (Nowotny, 1989) or "waithood" (Howana, 2012), the young adults Steuer, Engeler, and Macamo describe also lack a large range of opportunities in comparison to times before, but are not waiting for adulthood. They go on in different spheres of their social lives and thus are socially becoming everyday (2017, p. 22).

actively going on and taking care, not least in terms of their spiritual and moral development, former deportees effectively contribute to preparing the ground for a new future. "Collective immobility" (Kahn, 2013, p. 529) has become a shared experience and reality; (collectively) imagining new futures may do the same. In ending this chapter, I want to question what the reality of massive deportations and immobilizations could eventually imply for the social imagery of migratory success and its supposed "failure" likewise.

Revisiting the imaginary of migratory success

Under conditions post deportation, the primary and also newly imagined future in which one leaves again appears to be part and parcel of people's being, remembering, and aspiring. Against the background of taken-for-granted mobility cultures and horizons of expectation that imply that one will leave, the intense talking and longing connected with leaving again constitute old and new (imagined) realities and futures, which are essential for people's (social) being and self-image, particularly when narrated and collectively shared – thus "discursively imagined" as described in the last chapter (cf. Schulz, 2002, p. 822). In the end, does this imply a change in the imaginary of migratory success?

In Mali and other countries, migration has become a phenomenon "fetish," like "a god-thing" (Bazin, 2008), as described above, due to the importance of the income generated and the political construction accompanying it (Lima, 2005; Quiminal, 2002). Thus denunciations of the adverse effects of this (migratory) culture, made through safe migration campaigns and by demonizing "irregular" migration and reinforced by the externalization of European borders, are hard to accept, even if these effects are traumatic and deadly in their contemporary form. Simultaneously, a longing for abroad is increasingly part of the conflict between the need for youth to move – and its being taken for granted that they will move – on account of a lack of prospects on the spot and the constraints placed on their doing so. Deportations and border restrictions contest and even reverse these practices and imaginations, spoiling previously entertained hopes and aspirations that relate desires for consumption to family expectations. Jackson speaks of a "failure of hope" (2005, p. xx) and Kleist refers to the "mobility paradox" (2017b) in a similar way. And yet, after deportation, many people continue to aspire and go on where they are or try to leave again. The imaginary of traveling is overwhelmingly convincing and established (e.g., Kleist & Jansen, 2016; Gaibazzi, 2015b; Mbembe, 2007); more than that, it is based on the conviction that one still has chances oneself, built on the security of others' migratory success.

One can argue that the uncertainty that many encounter after deportation, particularly when stuck in situations of immobility, has led to narratives of progress and success being increasingly linked to the "global horizons" (Graw & Schielke,

2012) of migrant destinations: "People repeatedly equate migration with their hopes for a secure future, for themselves, but especially for their families and children" (Boehm, 2009, p. 354). Based on a respondent using the metaphor of the trampoline to talk about Portugal as a destination, Henrik Vigh figured that "migration in itself comes to function as a technology of the imagination in which envisioned migratory trajectories open up imagined worlds and possibilities" (Vigh, 2009b, p. 105). Thus migration, itself an imagined aim, opens the way to new imaginaries and futures perceived through the experiences of migrants and potentially deportees as well (pp. 92f; cf. Gardner, 1995).

Political interventions by the European Union have substantially externalized, constrained and reversed migrations within sub-Saharan Africa today (Gaibazzi et al., 2017) and have rendered "success" through adventure much less likely, but even after several "failed" migratory attempts the hegemonic notion of success through migrating largely persists in the collective imaginary, connected to courage, masculinity, and worldliness as well as potential social mobility for one's entire kin. There are still few alternative discourses that discourage people from undertaking these perilous adventures. Rather, the collective imaginary stigmatizes the immobility of young people considering it a breakdown in the adolescent life cycle (Gonin & Kotlok, 2012), especially for men. Simultaneously, ever more restrictive migratory policies increasingly challenge these hegemonic conceptions. A change of attitude seems to be developing not least in light of the large number of deportations, and more recently humanitarian and transit returns, from Libya and other African countries and thousands of deaths in the Sahara and the Mediterranean – even though, as I suggested, intra-African deportations are considered less grave than deportations from Europe. "Individual failure" still needs to be halted, though, in view of the collective conception. Consequently, a "failed" adventure may be internalized and silenced or become an issue between mother and son in order to retain respect, as I have shown before, and not least to keep up the societal hope (Hage, 2003).

Even so, as I have said, in recent years there have been more young people and their families declaring that they will stay and engage on the spot, and more community initiatives supporting them. Interestingly, their discourses resemble those of the state and the EU. Moreover, the state is promoting a double discourse, on the one hand "fighting" irregular migration, and on the other valorizing migrants' roles and promoting legal ways simultaneously. One can hear stories about successful returnees in many places. For instance, "Samakirikora" a development project of former migrants who left around 1960 from the region of Kayes has contributed to developing the villages around the area and become well known (field notes, 10-

28-2015).[35] This contributes to the "horizon" of expecting a successful and dignified return for the benefit both of oneself and one's close family and friends. For many, the adventure remains "the last way out," but it could also be "the next possible option," while others stay.

I have framed deportations as turning points and vital conjunctures, thus providing space, or rather enforcing space, to develop new imaginations and aspirations. Literature has also discussed imaginations and aspirations as fundamental motors for action and (potentially radical) change, which may provide a new repertoire of "more fundamental ways of grappling with the future" (Bromber et al, 2015, p. 3).[36] Hannah Arendt, who was never able to fully develop her theory of imagination, emphasized the power of imagination for both cognition and action and the capacity to change facts.[37] Likewise, as often cited, Arjun Appadurai (1996) coined the idea of the "capacity to aspire," as a navigational capacity, which essentially means that there is agency as long as people can aspire. Consequently, imaginations and aspirations are not only central to any kind of agency, but at the core of our activity including the possibility for creating new or alternative ways to go about things. Bottici complements Arendt's individual approach with the psychoanalyst Cornelius Castoriadis defining the imaginary as something fundamentally social and related to the very being of humankind. It is based on the idea that each social entity needs an imaginary to exist and vice versa. Thus, "imagination is before the distinction between 'real' and 'fictitious.' In other words, it is because radical imagination exists that 'reality' exists for us – and, therefore, one can act, it exists *tout court*" (Castoriadis, 1994, pp. 321f; as quoted by Bottici, 2011, p. 62).[38] While Arendt sees in (individual) imaginations something that is absent, for Castoriadis the social imaginary makes our "reality" in the form of a complex entanglement of individuals which can only exist within this social context and imaginary.[39] With-

---

35   Together with people of other nationalities, Senegalese, Algerians, Burkinabe, Guineans, they returned voluntarily from France, installed themselves in a village and built up a sound agriculture.

36   As Bromber et al. (2015) argue "Witnessing accelerated change and thereby the inherent openness of the future seems to give rise to more fundamental ways of grappling with the future in the form of ideologies, revised forms of social semantics and socialization" (p. 3).

37   Imagination is the faculty that mediates between the universal and the particular by providing both schemata for cognition and exemplars for action (Arendt & Beiner, 1982, pp. 72ff).

38   The term 'radical' needs to be understood as follows: "its political meaning points to the need of rethinking imagination in relation to the project of autonomy, which, as we will see, is a crucial concern for Castoriadis. On the more general philosophical level, the term radical ... is also what can be called a primary imagination. This consists in the faculty of producing images in the largest possible sense (that of 'forms', 'Bilder'), that is, images without which there would not be any thought at all, and which, therefore, precede any thought" (Bottici, 2011, p. 62).

39   For further explanation see Bottici, 2011, pp. 63ff.

out further scrutinizing this concept, I want to highlight Castoriadis's contribution – to posit that the social imaginary makes reality underlines its encompassing character and existential meaning, in this case in relation both to the migratory adventure and success ruptured by deportations and potential new chances.

In Arendt's sense, imagination is, furthermore, the basis for critical thinking on the political, because it enables us to reflect on others and to think from within others' shoes. This allows scrutinizing and reflecting upon the community and, eventually, potentially creating change. For deportees and their social circles, change, in the form of an unexpected situation created through the rupture caused by deportation, is first of all radically enforced from the outside. It incites a reversal of the migratory project and has long-lasting effects. This turning point may lead to a standstill, stuckness and (bare) immobility or, as this study has shown, multiple, agentic and navigational ways of going about things and continuing under conditions post deportation. In this, the capacity to aspire, imagine, and long for the future – possibly a new adventure, but also a business on-site and eventually taking care for one's close relations in whatever sense – plays a central role in everyday lives and is a potential motor for productivity, evolution, and potential change from within on the actor's part.

According to Arendt, however, imaginations may be ambivalent: a source of both autonomy and heteronomy (Bottici, 2011, pp. 60f), which means they can be a means of emancipation and thus a critique of what is given, but also a means of subjection to it.[40] Castoriadis sets the creation of images in a primary imagination before any imaginary and reality. Fundamentally concerned with autonomy, it is here that he sees the source of any critique: in the radical capacity to question one's own images lies the possibility of critique (p. 66). Accepting this, Bottici develops the "imaginal" as "what is made from images" to build a bridge between Arendt's individual concept of imagination and the social imaginary, which eventually allows one to navigate between the two, making absent imaginations present in the double sense of creating something new, but also of denying facts. It is a theoretical tool, as she says, to grasp how to come up with new imaginations in a world full of established images.

In terms of the imaginary of migratory success constituting people's "reality," which is made from images, this would mean that people needed to fundamentally question the images produced in this way and come up with alternatives. In addition to the contingent and uncertain everyday, deportations link in here unexpectedly and may question the images established. This is where Johnson-Hanks sees space for another potential future. On the one hand, people may resist European borderscapes by denying the danger of death and the impossibility of making it.

---

40   Imaginations may lead to denying factual truth (cf. Arendt, 1972, p. 5), which in politics, for instance, may foster citizens' subjectivations.

However, increased migration might lead to ever more restrictive migratory policies, unprecedented levels of migratory brokerage, more detentions, deaths, and
deportations, with the political system continuing to brutally subject individuals.
Simultaneously, others would continue to "succeed" or to return autonomously and
contribute to "development," which would help to keep up the established imaginary. Alternative ways out could rather be imagined by creating sustainable possibilities for self-determined development, thus enabling people to stay or building
realistic safe and legal migratory opportunities, albeit circular ones for many – even
if such images would almost fall under Beckert's label of "rational expectations" as
they are close to realistic and also pragmatic scenarios. Radical reimaginations,
in Castoriadis's sense might rather direct toward global freedom of movement,
mobility, and staying as well, a world of equals and of justice, or toward suprater-
ritorial communities of refugees and migrants (such as the proposal for *Refugia* by
Cohen & Van Hear, 2019); all these could be labelled utopian as well. Still, successful
leaving and returning and autonomous decisions to stay after deportation are what
regenerate people and provide new experiences that may persist, while potentially
also widening the "horizon of expectations" and reference for their imaginations
and further actions, by criticizing current conditions and engendering new images
and eventually new realities.

According to Appadurai, the "capacity to aspire" allows those with more expe-
riental knowledge a wider spectrum of possible goals to envision and reach for,
which are usually unequally distributed among richer and poorer populations and
thus economically, socially, and politically shaped. In modernity, however, this connection between experiences and expectations is said to be increasingly falling
apart. Globalization and new media have opened unprecedented ways of consum-
ing "alien" experience.[41] Things can be aspired to that were not imaginable before.
Moreover, our world seems to have become even more contingent or at least is
perceived as such. It was international migration itself that created the imaginary of success, built on established migratory cultures in Mali and thus enabling
"global horizons" in the last decades. Migrations that are forcefully reversed or
prove fatal produce more and more experiential knowledge, collectively shared,
of the complexities of today's world. Adventurers and, in a particular way, the deported demonstrate a specific kind of worldliness and wisdom, gained through
their suffering, even if it may be silenced. But the realities they have experienced
question the "seemingly established future." Still, it remains an oscillation between
leaving and staying, disoriented, vague, subverting, and deeply agentic at the same
time.

---

41   From a case study of the urban poor in Mumbai, Appadurai figures that their activist engagement and multiple connections lead to a widening of horizons.

In order to enhance the capacity to aspire and, in Arendt's terms, the capacity for change through imaginations, Appadurai appeals to a "compulsory cosmopolitanism" that consists in drawing on "the habit of imagining possibilities, rather than giving in to the probabilities of externally imposed change."[42] It is similar to Beckert's fictional and rational expectations. As I have said, deportations are externally imposed and probable, therefore, changes of the latter kind. Former deportees do, in fact, go on and imagine possibilities, narratively framed by *la chance*. A society put under constraint by migratory restrictions, immobilizations, involuntary and forced returns, has no other choice than to go on. On the one hand, the migratory success story is kept up – sometimes by only supposedly successful migrants, in France but merely visiting until they have sufficient earnings to distribute gifts, often showing up in a neat suit or even driving a new car up to a remote village (field notes, 12-28-2015). Others never return or break their ties with the family for shame at not having made it. These illusions suggest one's ability to participate in the globalized world of consumption, but more importantly, to move oneself and one's (extended) family up the socio-generational scale and become someone. It is like grasping at straws to retain dignity, where external forces render an autonomous life impossible and deeply endanger one's dignity as a good person and one's prospects of becoming someone.

At the same time, the large numbers of deportees in Mali, their organizations and the air of everydayness and normalcy associated with them have created conspicuous social realities. The deaths in the Mediterranean are commemorated and ritualized, and bereaved parents, communities, and the diaspora step in, trying to create alternatives for their youth. Still, the economic and educational alternatives really existing on the ground have not been able to compete with the adventurous ways so far, and there are literally no safe or legal ways. Rather migrants may be exalted as "martyrs" and, together with the commemoration of the shipwrecked, incorporated into the cultural heritage of migration (see Sylla & Schultz, 2020) that this study began with. At the same time these moves and actions constitute a vivid resistance against the externalization of the European border regime. Obviously, the established images have been questioned, but there is quite some way to go. So far, the so-called horizons of expectations may have been adjusted, diversified,

---

42   "By the ethics of possibility, I mean those ways of thinking, feeling, and acting that increase the horizons of hope, that expand the field of the imagination, that produce greater equity in what I have called the capacity to aspire, and that widen the field of informed, creative, and critical citizenship. ... By the ethics of probability, I mean those ways of thinking, feeling, and acting that ... are generally tied to the growth of a casino capitalism which profits from catastrophe and tends to bet on disaster. ... I offer these two contrasting ethical styles to suggest that beneath the more conventional debates and contradictions that surround what we call globalization there is a tectonic struggle between these two ethics." (Appadurai, 2013, p. 295).

and widened, but they have hardly completely changed. Meanwhile, people go on imagining and believing in *la chance*.

Concluding remarks

The aim of this chapter was to build a bridge between the conditions of uncertainty and potential stuckness that former deportees are subjected to after deportation, and their finding and expressing intrinsic subjectivities in the narrative as well as a practical relation to *la chance*, *kunna* in Bamanakan, future making, and a broader cosmology, eventually providing another level of meaning. To this end, I have reflected on deportations as rupture-like events, examining their processual character and vital conjunctures, building ground for productivity and potential change over time.

In deportees' narratives and practices, spirituality and religion, sense- and future-making, luck, success, failure and *la chance* coalesce in a very specific form. People imagine and go on, between the tensions of destiny and agency. *La chance* links in here. Practices, such as consulting the *marabout*, and speaking of a new *la chance*, show ways to deal with the contingency and uncertainty of the everyday and the future, under conditions post deportation. They create certainty and not least new potential imaginations and possible futures. The supposed unawareness of the future can thus be a productive component in general cosmological explanations in West Africa, within the tension between destiny and human agency, where one's future may be outlined, but that is open for human activation at the same time.

Susann Ludwig coined the phrase "the happy Sisyphus" or rather "the conscientious Sisyphus" (2017b, p. 173) to describe the Malian graduate. Similarly, former deportees go on – sometimes, however, in a state of severe restless stress. In reference to Clifford Geertz, she concludes *la chance* does not make the world less uncertain, but it renders randomness intelligible. *La chance* supports graduates' feeling that they are "on top of things" and thereby "makes action possible for [them] at all" (Geertz, 1975, p. 12). Former deportees may be deeply constrained in their everyday, but *la chance* may provide them with a sensation of additional autonomy and agency, as if having *kunna* implies a secure belief in success if one engages for it.

Not least, through collective sharing and narrating meaning is recreated, even after deportation. In this sense, the supposed "failure" of the migratory adventure, can productively allow space for creating alternatives and new certainties, not least for surviving with dignity and a more spiritual quality in one's social relations. The immobility–mobility continuum, from bare immobility via imagined mobility to a new and real mobility is often the pivot and mode of being. While massive "failures" have led to the collectivization and normalization of deportation experiences, the imagery of migratory success appears largely a hegemonic, even if debated, foil.

Chapter 8
Conclusion

This book set out to tell an alternative story, based on the narratives and practices of former deportees in southern Mali, of supposedly "failed" migratory adventures and their ambivalences, caused by and endured after deportation. To this end, it examined the social, material, cultural, emotional, political, temporal, and spatial dimensions of life after deportation. Now, in this concluding chapter, after a short summary of the main lines of argument, I will revisit the leading theme, the notion of the "failed" migratory adventure with respect to its sociological ambivalence, before taking my leave with some final reflections on the political dimension of the post-deportation situation in southern Mali and beyond, touching on the role of the researcher in particular and on what remains to be done.

Facing conditions post deportation in southern Mali – a short summary

The dominant discourse on migration that relates to the adventurer's supposed success – leaving to search for money (as "there is nothing here"), earning, then returning to contribute to the social uplifting of the family – is contradicted by the effects of the global deportation regime and the EU's externalization of its borders and migratory controls onto the African continent. The opening scene of the book, which described families commemorating the loss at sea of community members, their sons, fathers, and brothers, in a city to the west of Bamako, offered a powerful image of the response to this disruptive condition. Moreover, the overwhelming number of deportees, repatriates, and other returnees and former migrants participating in the event was a strong testimony to the ruptures and frictions affecting established migratory and social patterns and multiple transnational entanglements in the region. In terms of this dominant narrative, a supposed "failure," is condensed into the drama of returning with empty hands as a result of a deportation. Against this background, the book focused on how former deportees cope with a central dilemma arising from their deportation experience: that of going on over the long term with shattered socio-economic prospects and, most importantly, while still enmeshed in the dense web of social relations and obligations that many had at first tried to flee.

Mali is a special case as regards the number and variety of deportations to which its people have been subject. They started in the 1960s, when many African states gained their independence, and continued with forced returns from Europe after increasing migratory restrictions in the 1970s, first of all from the former colonial power, France, and then from Spain, and finally Italy. The number of forced returns increased with the strengthening and outsourcing of a European external border to the African continent in the 2000s, a process that gained momentum in the aftermath of the European "refugee crisis" and the human rights violations committed in North African detention centers. The Malian state, meanwhile, never implemented large-scale deportations itself, though it has lately taken up the practice of so-called "assisted voluntary returns." Multiple political crises – in Libya around the fall of President Gaddafi in 2011; in northern Mali from 2012, spun off as one consequence of the Libyan case; latterly the European "refugee crisis" – have, furthermore, formed the political context in which the post-deportation situation is discussed. All this adds to a widespread sense of economic, social, intergenerational, and allegedly gender-related crises among people. Oriented along the general lines of grounded theory, the book provides a multi-sited, in-depth ethnographic view of the global deportation regime in operation over an extended field site stretching from the deportee organizations in Bamako to the administrative district of Kita Cercle in the region of Kayes, and towards the region of Sikasso in the direction of the Ivory Coast. All these places are characterized by particular regional, historical and (reversed) migratory settings and, above all, a high level and frequency of migration and (forced) returns, as well as a certain amount of organization on the part of the deportees in question.

The majority of the men in this book (young and old) were deported during and after the peaks in the 2000s, particularly during the Libyan crisis, but more generally during the first wave of externalization from Mahgreb countries and in the aftermath of the attacks on the border fences of Ceuta and Melilla in 2005. Some were sent back by air, but a substantial number were also put on trucks and set down in the desert. Many eventually returned to their villages of origin: some after many deportations and violent push-backs, after phases of protracted waiting, and "forced immobility" (Stock, 2019). Others came from European countries, often after long experiences of being undocumented, spending periods in detention and facing sometimes arbitrary deportation practices. Most of them called themselves *refoulés*. These people, mostly men from a rural or urban background even if they lived in urban areas, retained substantial connections with their villages of origin. Many had left on an adventure after something had not worked out: leaving became an "exit option," which was subsequently torpedoed by another breakdown and supposed "failure" as the objective of social becoming and uplifting the entire family did not "work out" either. Many had been back "home" for several years.

Deportees retrospectively narrated their deportation experiences in accounts of (social) suffering summed up in the phrase "the adventure is not easy" – feelings of restlessness, violence, fear, stress, and anger were repeated patterns; they also depicted the deportation regimes running from European countries through North Africa that had caused these forms of social suffering. The central narrative of suffering revolved around the loss of money and the emblematic "empty hands" that they returned with having left on a quest for money, a quest that has to be seen in light of the social norms of contributing, reproduction, and the management of social relations in which money and wealth occupy a specific symbolic position fundamentally related to the social order. Post deportation, this leads to conflicting social dynamics conditioned by deportees' feelings of shame, which, in the form of the Mandé concept of *maloya*, is ambivalent, being seen also as status-enhancing, inasmuch as it maintains respect and one's inner sense of self. Gossip can serve as a regulator and also a revisor of the social order; silences may be strategies to counteract gossip; both equally are attempts to preserve or re-establish social harmony. They can condition each other. Mothers, who in Mandé are given a central, moral role in beliefs linked to the performance and success of their children and vice-versa, are especially impacted by gossip.

Fa den sago – without spirit, lazy, cowardly – is the narrative denotation of social death, something one might be said to undergo after deportation, when one runs the risk of narrative emasculation because obtaining money and providing for the family through the migratory adventure are central masculine features. Deportees in urban and rural areas have to navigate their immobilities and masculinities after deportation – and eventually over the longer term – getting by through hard work, showing courage, marrying, and, most importantly, through (re-)interpreting the suffering both of the journey and of the everyday, eventually reconverting it into what I term "adventure-hood," which may provide them with some new (masculine) self-confidence, dignity, and autonomy. It remains to be seen to what extent these realities and renegotiations contribute to emerging deportee masculinities that complement the existing repertoire of hegemonic and other masculine features.

The deep ambivalence that the deportees are thrown into is countered in the end by the emic notion of *la chance*, which appears to dominate in everyday conversations generally and receives a particular meaning in situations post deportation. As a final effort at sense- and future-making, deportees narrate and practically relate to *la chance* as a way of coping with the contingencies and uncertainties of their past, their present, and their future. Within a broader context of cosmology, religion, and spirituality in Mali and West Africa, chance is deeply socially embedded in everyday practices. Set between conceptions of fate, destiny, and human agency, such an approach enables people to provide guidance – most importantly on how to go about creating the certainty that there will be another chance, often either through leaving again or building up something on the ground.

The book has shown how deportations impact individuals differently depending on a number of factors. In addition to time spent abroad and the time since one's return, age, gender, and generation play a central role since mobility, and the migratory adventure in particular, are related to different aspects of masculinity as one grows up and becomes someone. This links in with one's economic positioning and embedding before, during, and after migration, as well as one's capacity to contribute and other people's expectations that one will contribute. Moreover, the type of migratory journey one undertook, and the specific experiences, hardships, and suffering one underwent determine one's condition after deportation substantially. It fundamentally matters, as I have shown earlier, what people lived through while abroad and on the way. The months or years between leaving and returning are of critical importance. Insofar as they form one's experience of adventure or migration, they may enable embeddedness and preparedness, even in cases of unplanned, unexpected, and involuntary, forced returns, in which, according to Cassarino, preparation is quasi "non-existent" (2004, p. 19). The same applies to experiences of deportation, the way that people are returned, and the violence that accompanies it, which is also of central importance. There is even a certain hierarchy as regards the means of transport used for one's deportation, by air or over land. Moreover, the starting point of a deportation carries symbolic value in terms of its gravity, related above all to particular characteristics ascribed to the deporting state. As far as social embeddedness is concerned, it is one's social networks and relations before, during, and after return, that have been shown to be most relevant for re-embedding after deportation and, at the same time, most challenging in relation to the central loss of money and one's ability or inability to contribute. Whether one was able to earn some money while abroad and remit it back home, or managed to return with something anyway can substantially influence the economic and social conditions of one's life post deportation. Not least one's place of settlement after deportation – in a rural or an urban area – influences one's position in relation to economic and mobility opportunities and autonomy, and also to one's development and social being. In the end, what matters, it is said, is the wealth of being a full person, caring and contributing with body, heart, and soul for that signifies being "a man" as well.

Supposed "failed" migratory adventures and sociological ambivalence

Deportees are forced into an unwanted situation in which they must confront un-
met expectations of reciprocity and contributing and are forced to navigate in a
charged social environment where a person normatively counts only in terms of his
or her relatedness. This situation is deeply ambivalent and contradictory in many
dimensions as it is impossible for the involuntarily returned migrant to take on the
expected role of breadwinner and provider, given that he may become dependent
on his family instead, at least for the interim; this is a severe blow to someone's personhood and may impair it substantially, even over the longer term. On the other
hand, the deportee has survived and has come back healthy and alive – ideally,
given that many return psychologically and physically impaired – and is thus able
to go on.

Ambivalence has relatively recently been rediscovered as a subject for sociology
(e.g., Boccagni & Kivisto, 2019; Arribas-Ayllon & Bartlett, 2014; Wegar, 1992; Bau-
mann, 1991; Billig et al., 1988). Most significantly, Robert K. Merton borrowed the
concept from psychology (originally psychoanalysis) making "sociological ambivalence" insofar as it is "built into the structure of social statuses and roles" (1976,
p. 5) fruitful for sociological theory. Different from ambiguity, inconsistency, uncertainty, or disorientation, ambivalence "is the coexistence of opposing emotional
and cognitive orientations toward 'the same person, object or symbol'" (Boccagni
& Kivisto, 2019, p. 6; cf. Smelser, 1998, p. 13).[1]

Within sociology, ambivalence has been mostly discussed with respect to family and kin relations, as well as immigration (Boccagni & Kivisto, 2019, p. 4). For the
latter, a shifting and contrasting of roles and identities in different lifeworlds and
cultural value systems, in the sending, potentially the transit, and the receiving society, is a practically unavoidable matter of fact. As shown extensively in this book,
migration itself may be deeply ambivalent, full of hope, hardships, and happiness,
"sometimes resulting in a protracted emotional experience" (ibid., p. 6), requiring
constant navigating, repositioning, and negotiating. Analytically, ambivalence allows individual emotional depth, which at the same time needs to be seen in light of
"the competing role-based normative expectations [and] the broader societal contradictions that engender it" (ibid.). Ambivalence may be a time-specific or place-
specific experience or a protracted condition (p. 11). In this vein, ambivalence makes
it possible to grasp and discuss social complexity, linking the individual experience
to the social dimension as well as the historical and structural context.

---

1   Merton's definition of sociological ambivalence is notwithstanding a psychological one, as
    ambivalence cannot be thought of without "an emotional, conative, or cognitive response"
    (Boccagni & Kivisto, 2019, p. 5).

In the current book ambivalence has been developed as a helpful analytical lens to study deportees' experiences and lifeworlds starting from what I have called the ambivalence of the "failed" migratory adventure. Deportations are the result of a political administrative measure that is potentially economically driven. Still, deportees are thrown into what many consider to be "failure," a morally and emotionally charged judgment (cf. Appadurai, 2018). Deportees cannot resolve this dilemma, at least not at first. It is the morality of "failure" and judgmental behavior, based on normative and hegemonic conceptions, which can cause emotional extremes of stigmatization, shame, and, even if only rarely, social (self-)exclusion for deportees. The term "relational ambivalence" best describes the complex social dynamics that occur within family and village or neighborhood spaces through the drama of return. Monika Palmberger (2019) emphasizes the relational approach to ambivalence in a study of Turkish labor migrants in Austria, according to which, ambivalence "can neither be seen solely as an individual experience, as residing within the individual, nor as a result of differing social status and roles alone. Rather it is a product of relationships individuals engage in" (p. 14). This defining addition of the social relationality of ambivalence is of major importance in the context under discussion, where people consider themselves not as having relationships but as being relationships (cf. Piot, 1999). Moreover, relational ambivalence has shown itself to be the most significant analytical lens for examining the (re)negotiations described as taking place through gossiping and silence post deportations.

Sociological ambivalence is, furthermore, considered to be a transitional stage to be overcome (Belloni, 2019). Migrants' ambivalence is often thought to resolve itself once they are back in their country of origin, but returning migrants may, in fact, carry with them cultural values from abroad that cause new ambivalent sensations. In the case of deportations, expectations and realities collapse altogether, once deportees are back, potentially leaving them torn. More than that, deportations cause ever more extreme emotional experiences of ambivalence. In this sense, I appreciate Monica Belloni's appeal for sociological ambivalence to be considered as an "ongoing condition" (Belloni, 2019, p. 5) and emotional experience, illustrated here by the protracted normative inconsistencies deportees confront during and after their migrations and deportations, caused "from above" by the deportation regimes.[2] Protracted ambivalence may be experienced in deportees' immobilization and sense of stuckness. The social dynamics in kin and family relations are particularly challenging since they condense the contradictory expectations and

---

2   This is different to the case of the Eritreans that Milena Belloni discusses, where contradictions are produced in the country of origin itself with opposing expectations – becoming a breadwinner through migration, as against a lifelong obligation to do military service in the home country (Belloni, 2019, pp. 14f).

ambivalent reactions of joy, sadness, and hope. This may be added to by intergenerational ambivalences, as I have shown.

At the same time, a supposed "failure" has generally been summed up by deportees and their circles in the phrase "the adventure did not work out." In this sense, wealth and value lie in the person, who is healthy and alive and able to go on in most cases. "It's not the end of the world," as the staff of deportee organizations say too. What is important is the space left for going on. Deportations may bring about a turning point and vital conjuncture. In this sense, I developed "failure" as a productive category as well. Deportees have a range of strategies for dealing with things, as shown. Considered a *rite de passage* towards adulthood and becoming somebody, in West Africa the migratory adventure still also functions partly as a ritual intended to transform the adventurer as well as his social circle. Even if deportees "have not made it" in the expected way, they have the air of having been "there," or at least somewhere else, and of having acquired some "adventure-hood." In this respect, the adventure has worked out as some form of transition. Like the memories of hardships and shame, this "acquisition" may endure over time as well to be potentially integrated into the ambivalent experience of a supposed "failure," collectively shared and thus also becoming somehow normalized.

"Failure" and ambivalence can also be seen in Appadurai's view as "nothing bad": if you fail, "fail early, fail often" (2016, p. xxiii), he suggests, trying to grasp the contemporary conception in capitalist modernity. One might also be reminded of Samuel Beckett, the "maestro of failure" (Power, 2016), and his literary work, once dubbed "the art of failure" (Coe, 1964, p. 4; cf. Burton, 2005). For Beckett, failure was the only artistic goal, the single act of expression worth trying to articulate,[3] most prominently in *Worstward Ho* (1983): "Ever tried. Ever failed. No matter. Try again. Fail again. Fail better": it is about the value of trying, even if one fails and suffers.[4] Malian adventurers are not artists in the literal sense, but they are definitely artists of life. A supposed "failure" may become part of their being and eventually a productive category. In the artistic sense, "failure" and suffering are not only inevitable, but even to be glorified.[5] All this links in with the existential quest of leaving and returning in the concept of the migratory adventure with suffering at the core of sense-making post deportation: memories of suffering, suffering in everyday life, but also suffering that can be reinterpreted as a new chance.

---

3   "To be an artist is to fail, as no other dare fail, that failure is his world and the shrink from it desertion" (Beckett, 1983, p. 145).

4   Eventually, failure is seen as suffering in Beckett's literature as well: "I suffer, thus I am" (cf. Burton, 2005, p. 60).

5   Silence is also given a prominent place in the discussion of failure in Beckett's work: "silence as an authentic response to failure", and actually the only legitimate response. Burton refers further to Wittgenstein and his similar appreciation of silence (cf. Burton, 2005, p. 57).

So, who is the one judging a supposed "failure" or success and who is the one that is forced to accept the judgment (cf. Appadurai, 2016, p. xxxi)? Hegemonic social conceptions are challenged by increasing numbers of deportations. A "failure" is not denied, but potentially externalized, to God as ultimately responsible, to one's mother, to higher spirits, and increasingly to politics and structural causes. Notwithstanding, though, the migratory adventure also remains an individual endeavor to attain responsibility and manhood. The radical change Malian deportees experience through deportation has long-lasting effects for themselves and their communities. This turning point may lead to standstill and immobility as well. The form of ambivalence experienced seems to change over time and according to each situation and case; but it is hardly ever resolved completely. It is more a matter of reducing its strength by continuing. In some cases, ambivalence may be resolved – when one earns money or potentially becomes someone through setting up a small project on the ground or with the support of a relative. It can be the ambivalence of the situation itself that generates multiple agentic and navigational ways of going about things, and continuing. In this way, deportees redefine, adapt, and negotiate their roles continuously. In the end, perhaps, it is questionable whether ambivalence can or needs to be dissolved after all.

La chance can be a narrative and practical means of going on with this dilemma. In this sense, ambivalence can be hopeful as well; hope can emerge out of uncertainty (cf. Kleist & Thorsen, 2017).[6] Hannah Arendt even considers imaginations to be ambivalent in their political potential to change facts (1972, p. 5, cf. Bottici, 2011, p. 61). Within the cosmological, spiritual, and social order in West Africa and Mali, people are used to mastering contingency (cf. also Bromber et al., 2015) – in the light of ambivalences too, one might say. And inside this cultural repertoire of openness and flexibility, there may also be space to adapt the dominant narrative of migration and the humanly judged concept of "failure" too, not least because its ambivalence and productivity may be a motor for social change as well. As Beckert suggests, imagined futures can be crucial components of the social, economic, and political order itself (2016, p. 11).

Back to the political and what remains to be done

For most people in Mali, migrations, mobility, and deportations have been shaping their lifeworlds and society in recent decades. With changing political realities,

---

6   For Palmberger (2019), migrants' undecidedness constitutes a strategy to cope with difficult situations, weighing different opinions, moral and social stances, thus not adopting one single position or judgment.

people have been responding differently, by adapting migratory strategies and, if necessary, redefining what they are and may become as well.

Migrants' restless going on against migratory constraints and after deportations seems deeply agentic. Lucht even makes a political act out of migrants' restlessness and desperation, defining "the death-defying journeys in the desert and the Mediterranean" as "ways of transgressing the borders imposed on them in more than one way." Migrant suffering and sometimes death would therefore not constitute "political acts *per se*," but "forms of iconoclasm that question the moral legitimacy of the system" (2017, pp. 157f).[7]

Even if deportees' situations may sometimes be an ongoing experience of ambivalence and suffering, one may frame deportees' restless continuing in Lucht's terms instead as morally questioning the established deportation regimes through "forms of iconoclasm" to political acts. The works of Dünnwald and Lecadet highlight the associations of former deportees in Mali, which have built a remarkable activist legacy in their country and the region. These continue to frame and take part in the political debate and reality with respect to EU externalizations and deportations in Mali today. Cécile Canut and Alioune Snow show with the *"théâtre des expulses,"* who performed in 2008 in Bamako under the direction of ARACEM and AME (back then their founding members had recently been deported themselves), how the play *Essingan* demonstrates the ambivalence of the dominant narrative of migratory success. It differentiates the difficulties of the journey and the possibilities of a common "failure," which places the weaknesses of the individual traveler and his "lapsed moral attitudes." This should be "understood as an integral part of the group's attempt to negotiate new theatrical representations and new discourses on migration" (Canut & Snow, 2008, p. 10). Since then, the numbers of deportees in the country have been rising. Experiences of deportation have become ever more collective, even if individual and social ambivalences persist. Protests against state practices of externalizing borders and their corollary effects, the deaths of migrants and their forcible return, have received unprecedented urgency and visibility. This is also a collective endeavor to cope, as in the commemoration of the shipwrecked, public opposition to restrictive migratory policies, and former deportees organizing themselves, accusing the state of "forcing people to leave" and pleading for "real" alternatives on the ground. In this sense, the political and public discourses surrounding migrants' "failure" seem at least to have turned against a Malian state and the EU which "kill," even if the narrative of migratory success persists.

---

7   In a similar vein Alvarez (2016) observes "Despite their small size and relatively small numbers, the small boats that ply the Strait's [i.e., the Strait of Gibraltar's] clandestine routes were often figured as physical and metaphorical vehicles for (imagined) assaults on the integrity of the European body politic. Furthermore, the immigrants they carried were regarded as potential assaulters of the physical and social security of individual Europeans" (p. 121).

In the aftermath of the "refugee crisis" and in the course of the current Valetta process, the new funds for return and reintegration available under the EUTF have given place to new activities and associations of migrants and others. "Assisted voluntary return and reintegration" has become the dominant paradigm also in light of the so far stagnating negotiations on forced returns in the asymmetric architecture of the EU Migration Partnership Framework of 2016 (Schultz, 2020a). Framed as more humane and flexible – and being so in real terms – it is also an option preferred by African states over the highly criticized and contested procedure of forced return in West African societies as developed here (cf. Adam et al., 2019; Zanker et al., 2019). It is only recently that conditions post return and deportations have been discussed as becoming sustainable; notwithstanding, the focus on security remains (Cassarino, 2016, pp. 219f). These (re)integration projects are as much intended to Europeanize the question of deportations and expulsions in Mali and the subregion (cf. Sylla & Schultz, 2019) as to address the fundamental discrepancies between adequate activities on the ground, potential funding, and uneven communication, known as development collaboration.[8] In this respect, former deportees and potential migrants are made development actors themselves through EUTF-programs, marking a clear nexus of deportation and development. More than that, these "assisted voluntary returns" are not necessarily appreciated by assisted returnees themselves, civil-society actors, or the returnees known as *refoulés* either. It is to be assumed that, with the latest increase in assisted returns, above all in the form of transit and emergency returns from North African countries (Alpes, 2020; Zanker & Altrogge, 2019), collective experiences have become an ever more integral part of the societal everyday, with memories and narrations being widely shared. This hints at there being a new quality of return and reintegration realities and society in Mali.

Several of my findings mirror what the existing work on post deportation and return research suggest. These include upholding the migration cycle to permit an eventual sustainable return and reintegration (e.g., Cassarino, 2016), given that deportation may incite renewed migration and worsen matters at the point of departure, and enabling returns to be prepared for, decided on, and multiply embedded (cf. Ruben et al., 2009; Davids & van Houte, 2008.). In terms of development through return for the countries of origin, Collyer (2018) summarizes three central aspects (p. 123): the possibility for migrants to gain work experience and knowledge that will need to be valued and integrated once they come back; the social capital of the returnees before leaving, while abroad and after their return; and migrants' ability to plan their return. This underlines the necessity of enabling a dignified and autonomous, prepared and embedded return, as well as the possibility of mobility,

---

8   Even if the aims may be similar, the approaches vary widely and do not necessarily communicate, but are characterized by misunderstanding and a clear North–South inequality.

in order to contribute to development and social well-being too. Currently these aspects are not to be found in deportations and only partially in so-called "assisted voluntary returns" (AVRs) (e.g., Kalir, 2017; Kuschminder, 2017; Koser & Kuschminder, 2015) most of which are perceived as *refoulements* by migrants themselves.

Few of these findings, however, have been transferred into political practice. In Germany, for instance, for researchers' analyses and suggestions to be integrated into policy discussions and the evaluation of return and reintegration programs has become acknowledged as a critical tool (cf. Biehler et al., 2021; SVR, 2020; Schmitt et al., 2019). Hasselberg in this sense questions the role of the researcher. She asks how we can make our findings more public and enter policy circles and public debates (2018, pp. 31f). Essentially, a large gap remains between academic and public policy discourses, which, not least, derive from different role perceptions and ascriptions. Thus, the social sciences' conception of their public function is usually a more indirect one, that of producing "orientation and meaning in the local, national, and global public spheres" (Faist, 2018, p. 28), in other words providing explanatory and analytical knowledge. On the policy side, the researcher is considered more valuable for policy consultancy, which is to be provided on the basis of "evidence-based" research, often referring to concrete numbers that will generate clear-cut results to inform policy makers.

From this point of view, the complexity and ambivalence of sociological and ethnographic research, as it has been promoted here, is hard to translate into such clear-cut advice directly. More than that, there is a major lack of more systematic research and data on forced returns, their impacts and adverse effects on the societies and people concerned: longitudinal analysis, statistical and mixed-method data generation are necessary to enable broader comparisons to be made and also for the work to be potentially taken more seriously by public-policy discourse; even if one runs the risk of being policy-driven thereby (cf. Castles, 2010). So, much more social science and ethnographic research is needed on fine-grained social dynamics post deportations, and the impact of deportations over time. This research, moreover, should be conducted not only from a socio-economic point of view but in relation to the social and emotional costs and implications particularly of the debt relations involved with the emblematic loss of money caused by forced return, and take into account how all this translates into relations with family and kin and other types of social relations (cf. Buggenhagen, 2012, p. 169), which are highly ambivalent in how they relate to the shame of being unable to provide in the expected sense. Not least, the useful analytical lens that sociological ambivalence offers for grasping the complexity of deportees' social lifeworlds, which I could only touch on here, should be explored on a broader scale and with greater seriousness. Overall, more space and in-depth detail are indispensable to a better contribution to understanding returnees' survival and dignified and autonomous reintegration and way to go on – as well as how, in the end, this links in with actors' entanglements and the broader discourse and practices of migration and potential social change.

More than discourse, debate, and narration, this book has encouraged action to this end on the practical level. Even if individual deportees and their families do not necessarily recognize structural causes as responsible for their suffering, the highly active civil society in Mali, in the subregion, and transnationally is calling for an all-encompassing transformation of relevant institutions and recognition of migrants' rights, including their right to self-determined development, stay, and mobility. Eventually, this would imply fundamental changes in the world trade system, plus stricter regulation of financial flows (cf. Faist, 2018, p. 29), and, not least, the formal integration of mobility. From this point of view, it is essential to discuss and approach migratory and deportation policies within a broader framework of political, legal, social, and economic transformation. What does the deportation and assisted return of individuals, citizens and groups do to societies at large? More than that, it would require an open dialogue between all actors involved – policymakers, activists, and migrants, ordinary citizens and other civil society and economic actors – which is aware of power asymmetries and aimed at reciprocity and equal sharing. Even though there appears to be a long way to go, it is worthwhile thinking about this, discussing it, and writing it down. In that sense, this book has provided a view from the south Malian actors' side on the effects of the global deportation regime in this particular historical moment and context, characterized by EU externalizations into the African continent and a great many deportations and returns, as well as on how people cope with the realities of deportation on the ground. It is meant to be a contribution to an understanding of how people's social lifeworlds are carved up, disrupted, and shaped by current global structural inequalities and how they react to it. As such, it builds a basis for further engagement by deportation studies in how this can have a profoundly transformative effect on the society at large and what shape that transformation will take – without ever letting deportation be the last word.

Glossary

These are the main terms and expressions in Bambara, the main local language in Mali, which are used most often in the book, with their English and in some cases their French equivalents.

ba	mother
bè bi ba bolo	everyone is in the hands of their mother
bololankoloun	empty hands (French: "les mains vides")
ka segin bololankoloun	returning with empty hands
bonya	respect
danbé	dignity, honor, reputation
dimi	pain, hurt, suffering (French: "la souffrance")
ka gwa dèmè	to contribute
fa	father
fa den	child of the same father
fa den sago	the will of the father's children or, better, of his family, is not fulfilled
fadenya	jealousy
fatagna	powerlessness
geleya	difficulty
grin	group of people, often men, who gather around a small stove to brew a drink, usually strong green tea, socialize, and pass the time.
hòrònw	nobility
kunna dija/gèrè diège	luck (French: « la chance »)
maloya	shame (shyness, embarrassement)
monnè	resentment, bitterness, anger
wari ko gèlèyara	money affairs have become difficult
ka taaga wari gnini/warignini	to try to get money (French: "chercher de l'argent")
ka kè waritiguiyé	to become someone
sago	will, desire
senankuya	joking relationships
sòtigi	head of the family (French: "chef de la famille")

ni ma tooro	"tired heart" (French : "cœur fatigué")
tògò nyuman	good name
tounga	the migratory journey, travel, "the adventure" (French: "l'aventure")
tounga man ja	the trip/the adventure did not work out

Bibliography

Adam, I., Trauner, F., Jegen, L., & Roos, C. (2019). *West African interests in (EU) migration policy* (Policy Brief No. 4). United Nations University.

Adepoju, A. (1984). Illegals and Expulsion in Africa: The Nigerian Experience. International Migration Review, 18(3), 426–436.

Adepoju, A. (2003). Continuity and Changing Configurations of Migration to and from the Republic of South Africa. *International Migration*, 41(1), 3–28.

Adepoju, A. (2016). *Migration within and from Africa: Shared policy challenges for Africa and Europe* (Delmi Research overview No. 5). Swedish Government Inquiries.

Adida, C. L. (2010). *Immigrant Exclusion and Insecurity in Africa*. Doctoral Thesis. Stanford University.

Agamben, G. (1998). *Homo Sacer: Sovereign Power and Bare Life*. Stanford University Press.

Aghazarm, C., Queada, P., & Tishler, S. (2012). *Migrants caught in Crisis: The IOM Experience in Libya*. Geneva. International Organization for Migration.

Agier, M. (2011). *Managing the undesirables: Refugee camps and humanitarian government*. Polity Press.

Alber, E., & Drotbohm, H. (Eds.). (2015). *Anthropological Perspectives on Care: Work, Kinship, and the Life-Course*. Palgrave Macmillan.

Alber, E., van der Geest, S., & Reynolds Whyte, S. (Eds.). (2008). *Generations in Africa: Connections and Conflicts*. LIT Verlag.

Alpes, M. J. (2012). Bushfalling at All Cost: The Economy of Migratory Knowledge in Anglophone Cameroon. *African Diaspora*, 5(1), 90–115.

Alpes, M. J. (2014). Imagining a future in 'bush': Migration aspirations at times of crisis in Anglophone Cameroon. *Identities*, 21(3), 259–274.

Alpes, M. J. (2017). *Brokering high-risk migration and illegality in West Africa: Abroad at any cost*. Routledge.

Alpes, M. J. (2018). "Non-admitted": Migration-Related Detention of Forcibly Returned Citizens in Cameroon. In S. Khosravi (Ed.), *After Deportation: Ethnographic Perspectives* (pp. 231–252). Palgrave Macmillan.

Álvarez, D. (2016). Unstable Vessels: Small Boats as Emblems of Deaths Foretold and as Harbingers of Better Futures in Figurations of Irregular Migration across the

234 "Failed" Migratory Adventures?

Strait of Gibraltar. In L. Mannik (Ed.), *Migration by Boat: Discourses of Trauma, Exclusion, and Survival* (pp. 117–134). Berghahn Books.

Amselle, J.-L. (1978). Migration et société néo-traditionnelle: Le cas des Bambara du Jitumu (Mali). *Cahiers D'Études Africaines, 18*(72), 487–502.

Amselle, J.-L. (1987). L'ethnicité comme volonté et comme représentation: À propos des Peul du Wasolon. *Annales. Histoire, Sciences Sociales, 42*(2), 465–489.

Anderson, B., Gibney, M. J., & Paoletti, E. (2011). Citizenship, deportation and the boundaries of belonging. *Citizenship Studies, 15*(5), 547–563.

Andersson, R. (2014). *Illegality Inc.: Clandestine Migration and the Business of Bordering Europe*. University of California Press.

Andrijasevic, R. (2010). From Exception to Excess: Detention and Deportations across the Mediterranean Space. In N. De Genova & N. Peutz (Eds.), *The Deportation Regime: Sovereignty, Space, and the Freedom of Movement* (147-165). Duke University Press.

Appadurai, & Arjun (Eds.). (1986). *The Social Life of Things: Commodities in Cultural Perspective*. Cambridge University Press.

Appadurai, A. (1996). *Modernity at Large*. Routledge.

Appadurai, A. (2013). *The Future as cultural fact: Essays on the global condition*. New York. Verso Books.

Appadurai, A. (2016). Failure: An Introduction. *Social Research, 83*(3), xxi–xxvii.

Arendt, H. ([1943] 2018). *Wir Flüchtlinge*. Reclam.

Arendt, H. ([1963] 2000). *Eichmann in Jerusalem: A report on the banality of evil*. Penguin Books.

Arendt, H. (1972). *Crises of the republic: Lying in politics; civil disobedience; on violence; thoughts on politics and revolution*. Harvest Book Harcourt Brace & Company.

Arendt, H., & Beiner, R. (Eds.). (1982). *Lectures on Kant's political philosophy*. University of Chicago Press.

Arhin, K. (1995). Monetization and the Asante State. In J. I. Guyer (Ed.), *Money Matters: Instability, values and social payments in the modern history of West African communities* (pp. 97–110). Heinemann.

Arribas-Ayllon, M., & Bartlett, A. (2014). Sociological Ambivalence and the Order of Scientific Knowledge. *Sociology, 48*(2), 335–351.

Atkinson, R., & Flint, J. (2001). Accessing Hidden and Hard-to-Reach Populations: Snowball Research Strategies. *Social Research Update* (33).

Ba, A. H. (1973). La Notion de Personne en Afrique Noire. In G. Dieterlen (Ed.), *La notion de personne en Afrique noire, Paris 11-17 octobre 1971* (pp. 181–192). Éditions du Centre national de la recherche scientifique.

Badiane, O. & Kinteh, S. (1994). *Trade pessimism and regionalism in African countries: The case of groundnuts* (IFPRI, Research Report No. 97). International Food Policy Research Institute.

Bakewell, O. (2008). 'Keeping Them in Their Place': the ambivalent relationship between development and migration in Africa. *Third World Quarterly*, 29(7), 1341–1358.

Bakewell, O., & Haas, H. de. (2007). African Migration: Continuities, discontinuities and recent transformation. In P. Chabal, U. Engel, & L. de Haan (Eds.), *African alternatives* (pp. 95–118). Brill.

Ballo, M. (2009). *Migration au Mali : PROFIL NATIONAL 2009*. International Organization for Migration.

Banton, M. (Ed.). (1965). *Anthropological Approaches to the Study of Religion*. Tavistock Publications.

Bartels, I. (2020). Abschiebung global. *PERIPHERIE – Politik • Ökonomie • Kultur*, 39(3), 343–368.

Barten, J. (2009). *Families in movement. Transformation of the family in urban Mali, with a focus on intercontinental mobility*. Master's thesis. African Studies Centre.

Bauman, Z. (1991). *Modernity and ambivalence*. Cornell University Press.

Bazin, J. Retour aux choses-dieux. In A. Bensa & V. Descombes (Eds.), *Des clous dans la Joconde* (pp. 493–520). Éditions Anarchardis.

Beasley, C. (2008). Rethinking Hegemonic Masculinity in a Globalizing World. *Men and Masculinities*, 11(1), 86–103.

Beckert, J. (2016). *Imagined Futures*. Harvard University Press.

Beckett, S. (1984). *Der Ausgestossene: L'expulsé. The expelled*. Suhrkamp.

Belloni, M. (2015). Refugees as Gamblers: Eritreans Seeking to Migrate Through Italy. *Journal of Immigrant & Refugee Studies*, 14(1), 104–119.

Belloni, M. (2019). Refugees and citizens: Understanding Eritrean refugees' ambivalence towards homeland politics. *International Journal of Comparative Sociology*, 60(1-2), 55–73.

Benjamin, C. E. (2008). Legal Pluralism and Decentralization: Natural Resource Management in Mali. *World Development*, 36(11), 2255–2276.

Benjaminsen, T. A., & Ba, B. (2019). Why do pastoralists in Mali join jihadist groups? A political ecological explanation. *The Journal of Peasant Studies*, 46(1), 1–20.

Bensaâd, A. (2012). *La Libye révolutionnaire: Décentralisation et incertitude en RDC, état et rébellion en Centrafrique*. Karthala.

Bergamaschi, I. (2013). French Military Intervention in Mali: Inevitable, Consensual yet Insufficient. *Stability: International Journal of Security & Development*, 2(2), 20, 1-11.

Bergamaschi, I. (2016). *The politics of aid and poverty reduction in Africa: A conceptual proposal and the case of Mali* (Global Cooperation Research Papers No. 16). University of Duisburg-Essen.

Berry, S. S. (1995). Stable Prices, Unstable Values: Some Thoughts on Monetization and the Meaning of Transactions in West African Economies. In J. I. Guyer

(Ed.), *Money Matters: Instability, values and social payments in the modern history of West African communities* (pp. 299–313). Heinemann.

Besnier, N. (2009). *Gossip and the Everyday Production of Politics.* University of Hawai'i Press.

Bhabha, H. (1994). *The Location of Culture.* Routledge.

Biehler, N., Koch. A., & Meier, A. (2021). *Risiken und Nebenwirkungen deutscher und europäischer Rückehrpolitik. Ein außen-, sicherheits- und entwicklungspolitischer Beipackzettel* (SWP-Studie S 12). Stiftung Wissenschaft und Politik.

Billig, M., Condor, S., Edwards, D., Gane, M., Middleton, D., & Radley, A (1988). *Ideological dilemmas: A social psychology of everyday thinking.* SAGE Publications.

Bloch, A., & Schuster, L. (2005). At the extremes of exclusion: Deportation, detention and dispersal. *Ethnic and Racial Studies, 28*(3), 491–512.

Boccagni, P., & Kivisto, P. (2019). Introduction: Ambivalence and the social processes of immigrant inclusion. *International Journal of Comparative Sociology, 60*(1-2), 3–13.

Boeck, F. de, & Honwana, A. (2005). Introduction. In A. Honwana & F. de Boeck (Eds.), *Makers & Breakers: Children & Youth in Postcolonial Africa* (pp. 1–18). Africa World Press.

Boehm, D. A. (2009). "¿Quien Sabe?": Deportation And Temporality Among Transnational Mexicans. *Urban Anthropology and Studies of Cultural Systems and World Economic Development, 38*(2/3/4), 345-374.

Boehm, D. (2016). *Returned: Going and Coming in an Age of Deportation.* University of California Press.

Boesen, E., & Marfaing, L. (2006). Entre ville et désert: Mobilité, activités et urbanité dans l'espace Sahara-Sahel. *Revue Européenne Des Migrations Internationales, 22*(3), 253–258.

Bohannan, P., & Dalton, G. (1968). *Markets in Africa.* Northwestern University Press.

Bondaz, J. (2013). *Le thé des hommes: Sociabilités masculines et culture de la rue au Mali. Cahiers D'Études Africaines, LIII*(209-210), 61-85.

Bosworth, M., Hasselberg, I., & Turnbull, S. (2016). Punishment, citizenship and identity: An Introduction. *Criminology & Criminal Justice, 16*(3), 257–266.

Bottici, C. (2011). Imaginal Politics. *Thesis Eleven, 106*(1), 56–72.

Boyer, F. (2017). Les migrants nigériens expulsés d'Arabie Saoudite. *Espace Populations Sociétés* (1).

Brachet, J. (2018). Manufacturing Smugglers: From Irregular to Clandestine Mobility in the Sahara. *The ANNALS of the American Academy of Political and Social Science, 676*(1), 16–35.

Brand, S. (2001). *Mediating Means and Fate: A Socio-Political Analysis of Fertility and Demographic Change in Bamako, Mali.* Doctoral Thesis. University of Leiden.

Bredeloup, S. (1995). Tableau synoptique : expulsions des ressortissants ouest-afri-
cains au sein du continent africain (1954-1995). *Mondes En Développement*, 30(91),
117–121.

Bredeloup, S. (2008). L'aventurier, une figure de la migration africaine. *Cahiers In-
ternationaux De Sociologie*, 125(2), 281.

Bredeloup, S. (2017). The Migratory Adventure as a Moral Experience. In N. Kleist
& D. Thorsen (Eds.), *Hope and Uncertainty in Contemporary African Migration*
(pp. 134–153). Routledge.

Breidenstein, G., Hirschauer, S., Kalthoff, H., & Nieswand, B. (2013). *Ethnographie:
Die Praxis der Feldforschung*. UVK.

Bromber, K., Gaibazzi, P., Roy, F., Sounaye, A., & Tadesse, J. (2015). *»The possibilities are endless«: progress and the taming of contingency* (ZMO Programmatic Texts
No. 9). Zentrum Moderner Orient.

Broqua, C., & Doquet, A. (2013). Examining Masculinities in Africa and Beyond.
Cahiers D'Études Africaines, LIII(209-210), I–XXXII.

Brotherton, D. C., & Barrios, L. (2009). Displacement and stigma: The socialpsy-
chological crisis of the deportee. *Crime, Media, Culture*, 5(1), 29–55.

Bruijn, M. de. (2007). Agency in and from the margins: Street children and youth in
N'djaména, Chad. In M. de Bruijn, R. van Dijk, & J.-B. Gewald (Eds.), *Strength
beyond Structure: Social and Historical Trajectories of Agency in Africa* (pp. 263–284).
Brill.

Bruijn, M. de, van Dijk, R., & Foeken, D. (Eds.). (2001). *Mobile Africa: Changing patterns of movement in Africa and beyond*. Brill.

Bruijn, M. de, van Dijk, R., & Gewald, J.-B. (Eds.). (2007). *Strength beyond Structure:
Social and Historical Trajectories of Agency in Africa*. Brill.

Bruner, E. M. (1986). Experience and Its Expressions. In V. W. Turner & E. M.
Bruner (Eds.), *The Anthropology of experience* (pp. 3–32). University of Illinois
Press.

Bryman, A. (2012). *Social research methods*. Oxford University Press.

Buggenhagen, B. (2012). *Muslim Families in Global Senegal: Money Takes Care of Shame*.
Indiana University Press.

Burton, B. (2005). The Art of Failure. *Irish Studies Review*, 13(1), 55–64.

Cagnol, M. (2012). Le travail social dans un contexte de "double espace". *Hommes &
Migrations* (1286-1287), 134–137.

Calandre, N., & Ribert, E. (2012). Les pratiques alimentaires d'hommes ouest-afri-
cains vivant en Île-de-France. *Hommes & Migrations* (1286-1287), 162–173.

Calenda, D. (2012). Return Migration to Mali: Examining Definitions and Statistical
Sources. *CRIS Analytical Note* (2). European University Institute.

Calenda, D. (2014a). Return Migrants in Mali. In J.-P. Cassarino (Ed.), *Reintegration
and Development* (pp. 49–70). European University Institute.

Calenda, D. (2014b). Return Migrants' Remittance Behaviour. In J.-P. Cassarino (Ed.), *Reintegration and Development* (pp. 141–165). European University Institute.

Camara, B., Traoré, B. F., Dicko E., B., & Sidibé, M. (2011). *Migration et tensions sociales dans le sud du Mali* (Rapports de recherche du CODESRIA No. 9).

Canut, C., & Sow, A. (2014). Testimonial Theater and Migration Performance. *Africa Today*, 61(2), 3–18.

Carling, J. (2002). Migration in the age of involuntary immobility: theoretical reflections on Cape Verdean experiences. *Journal of Ethnic and Migration Studies*, 28(1), 5–42.

Carling, J. (2016). West and Central Africa. In M. McAuliffe & F. Laczko (Eds.), *Migrant Smuggling Data and Research: A Global Review of the Emerging Evidence Base* (pp. 25–53). Geneva, International Organization for Migration.

Carling, J., & Erdal, M. B. (2014). Return Migration and Transnationalism: How Are the Two Connected? *International Migration*, 52(6), 2–12.

Carling, J., & Hernández-Carretero, M. (2012). Protecting Europe and Protecting Migrants? Strategies for Managing Unauthorised Migration from Africa. *The British Journal of Politics & International Relations*, 13(1), 42–58.

Carling, J., & Schewel, K. (2017). Revisiting aspiration and ability in international migration. *Journal of Ethnic and Migration Studies*, 44(6), 945–963.

Carsten, J. (2004). *After Kinship*. Cambridge University Press.

Cassarino, J. P. (2004). Theorising return migration: a revisited conceptual approach to return migrants: European University Institute. *EUI Working Papers*, (02).

Cassarino, J. P. (Ed.). (2014). *Reintegration and Development*. CRIS Analytical Study. European University Institute.

Cassarino, J.-P. (2016). Return migration and development: The significance of migration cycles. In A. Triandafyllidou (Ed.), *Routledge Handbook of Immigration and Refugee Studies* (pp. 216–222). Routledge.

Castillejo, C. (2017). *The European Union Trust Fund for Africa: A glimpse of the future for EU development cooperation*. 2016/22. Deutsches Institut für Entwicklungspolitik.

Castles, S. (2010). Understanding Global Migration: A Social Transformation Perspective. *Journal of Ethnic and Migration Studies*, 36(10), 1565–1586.

Castoriadis, C., ([1964] 1974). *Redefining revolution*. Solidarity pamphlet (44).

Castoriadis, C. (1994). Radical imagination and the social instituting imaginary. In D.A. Curtis (Ed.), *The Castoriadis Reader* (pp. 319–338). Blakewell.

Ceesay, O. (1998). State and Civil Society in Africa. *Quest*, 12(1), 123–130.

Chabal, P. (2009). *Africa: The Politics of Suffering and Smiling*. Zed Books.

Charles-Dominique, L. (2014). La patrimonialisation des formes musicales et artistiques. *Ethnologies*, 35(1), 75–101.

Charsley, K., & Wray, H. (2015). Introduction: The Invisible (Migrant) Man. *Men and Masculinities*, 18(4), 403–423.

Chastanet, M. (1992). Survival strategies of a Sahelian society: The case of the Soninke in Senegal from the middle of the nineteenth century to the present. *Food and Foodways, 5*(2), 127–149.

Choplin, A., & Lombard, J. (2014). On West African roads: everyday mobility and exchanges between Mauritania, Senegal and Mali. *Canadian Journal of African Studies, 48*(1), 59–75.

Christou, A. (2015). Ageing masculinities and the nation: Disrupting boundaries of sexualities, mobilities and identities. *Gender, Place & Culture, 23*(6), 801–816.

Cissé, M. (1999). *Parole de sans-papiers.* La Dispute.

Cisse, P., & Daum, C. (2009). *Migrations internationales maliennes, recomposition des territoires migratoires et impacts sur les sociétés d'origine.* Institut Supérieur de Formation et de Recherche Appliquée (ISFRA).

Cisse, P. (2009). Migration malienne au Cameroun. *Hommes & Migrations* (1279), 38–51.

Clarke, A. E. (2005). *Situational analysis: Grounded theory after the postmodern turn.* Sage Publications.

Cliggett, L. (2003). Gift Remitting and Alliance Building in Zambian Modernity: Old Answers to Modern Problems. *American Anthropologist, 105*(3), 543–552.

Cohen, R., & van Hear, N. (2019). *Refugia. Radical Solutions to Mass Displacement.* Routledge.

Collinge-Germain, L. (2009). Cultural In-Betweenness in "L'expulsé" / "The Expelled" by Samuel Beckett. *Journal of the Short Story in English, 52.*

Collyer, M. (2007). In-Between Places: Trans-Saharan Transit Migrants in Morocco and the Fragmented Journey to Europe. *Antipode, 39*(4), 668–690.

Collyer, M. (2015). *Conditions and risks of mixed migration in North-East Africa* (Study 2). Mixed Migration Hub.

Collyer, M. (2018). Paying to Go: Deportability as Development. In S. Khosravi (Ed.), *After Deportation: Ethnographic Perspectives* (pp. 105–126). Palgrave Macmillan.

Comaroff, J., & Comaroff, J. L. (1999). Occult Economies and the Violence of Abstraction: Notes from the South African Postcolony. *American Ethnologist, 26*(2), 279–303.

Comaroff, J., & Comaroff, J. L. (2001). *Millennial Capitalism and the Culture of Neoliberalism. A Public Culture Book.* Duke University Press.

Comaroff, J., & Comaroff, J. L. (2011). *Theory from the south, or, how Euro-America is evolving toward Africa.* Routledge.

Conlon, D. (2011). Waiting: Feminist perspectives on the spacings/timings of migrant (im)mobility. *Gender, Place & Culture, 18*(3), 353–360.

Connell, R. W. ([1995] 2005). *Masculinities.* University of California Press.

Connell, R. W., & Messerschmidt, J. W. (2005). Hegemonic Masculinity: Rethinking the Concept. *Gender & Society, 19*(6), 829–859.

Cooley, C. H. (1922). *Human Nature and the Social Order.* Scribner's.

Cooper, E., & Pratten, D. (Eds.). (2015). *Anthropology, change and development. Ethnographies of uncertainty in Africa*. Palgrave Macmillan.

Corbin, J., & Strauss, A. (1990). Grounded Theory Research: Procedures, Canons, and Evaluative Criteria. *Qualitative Sociology*, 13(1), 3–21.

Cornwall, A., Karioris, F. G., & Lindisfarne, N. (Eds.). (2016). *Masculinities under neoliberalism*. Zed Books.

Coulibaly, F. (2014, August 6). Le ministre des Maliens de l'extérieur, Abdrahamane Sylla à propos du récent naufrage en Libye d'une embarcation clandestine. *ABamako.Com*.

Coutin, S. B. (2013). Place and presence within Salvadoran deportees' narratives of removal. *Childhood*, 20(3), 323–336.

Coutin, S. B. (2015). Deportation Studies: Origins, Themes and Directions. *Journal of Ethnic and Migration Studies*, 41(4), 671–681.

Dannecker, P., & Englert, B. (Eds.). *Qualitative Methoden in der Entwicklungsforschung*. Mandelbaum.

Daou, O. (2016, January 9). Gabon: 185 Maliens expulsés. *L'indicateur Du Renouveau*.

Daphi, P., Deitelhoff, N., Rucht, D., & Teune, S. (2017). *Protest in Bewegung? Zum Wandel von Bedingungen, Formen und Effekten politischen Protests*. Nomos.

Darwin, C. (1872). *The Expression of Emotion in Men and Animals*. John Murray.

Daum, C. (1998). *Les associations des Maliens en France: Migrations, développement et citoyenneté*. Karthala.

Daum, C. (2005). *Les immigrés et le co-développement* (CERAS revue projet, 288).

Daum, C. (2014). Entre individualisation et responsabilités familiales : les mobilités des jeunes de la région de Kayes au Mali. *Revue Européenne Des Migrations Internationales*, 30(3-4), 163–180.

Davids, T., & van Houte, M. (2008). Remigration, Development and Mixed Embeddedness: An Agenda for Qualitative Research? In P. d. Guchteneire, M. Koenig, & J. P. Cassarino (Eds.), "The Conditions of modern return migrants". *International journal on multicultural societies*, 10(2) (pp. 169–193).

Davies, C. A. (1999). *Reflexive ethnography: A guide to researching selves and others*. Routledge.

Dedieu, J. P. (2018). The Rise of the Migration-Development Nexus in Francophone Sub-Saharan Africa, 1960–2010. *African Studies Review*, 61(1), 83–108.

De Genova, N., & Peutz, N. (Eds.). (2010). *The Deportation Regime: Sovereignty, Space, and the Freedom of Movement*. Duke University Press.

De Genova, N. P. (2002). Migrant "Illegality" and Deportability in Everyday Life. *Annual Review of Anthropology*, 31(1), 419–447.

De Genova, N. (2018). Afterword. Deportation: The last word? In S. Khosravi (Ed.), *After Deportation: Ethnographic Perspectives* (pp. 253–266). Palgrave Macmillan.

Délégation Générale des Maliens de l'Extérieur (DGME). (2015). *Unpublished Statistics and Data Bank*. Bamako.

Dembele, D. (2010). *Le Mali et la migration irrégulière.* CARIM – Consortium pour la recherche appliquée sur les migrations internationales.

Diawara, M. (1985). Les recherches en histoire orale menées par un autochtone, ou L'inconvénient d'être du cru. *Cahiers D'Études Africaines,* 25(97), 5–19.

Diawara, M. (2003a). Ce que travailler veut dire dans le monde Mandé. In H. D'Almeida-Topor, M. Lakroum, & G. Spittler (Eds.), *Le Travail en Afrique noire: Représentations et pratiques à l'époque contemporaine* (pp. 67–80). Karthala.

Diawara, M. (2003b). *L'Empire du Verbe et l'Eloquénce du Silence: Vers une Anthropologie du Discours dans les Groupes dits Dominés au Sahél.* Rüdiger Köppe Verlag

Diombana, L. (2009). *Migration au Mali: Document thématique 2009. La gestion de l'émigration au Mali.* Organisation Internationale pour les Migrations.

Donaldson, M., Hibbins, R., Howson, R., & Pease, B. (Eds.). (2009). *Migrant men: Critical studies of masculinities and the migration experience.* Routledge.

Douglas, M. (1966). *Purity and danger: An analysis of the concepts of pollution and taboo.* Routledge and Kegan Paul.

Dougnon, I. (2012). Migration of Children and Youth in Mali: Global versus local discourses. In G. Spittler & M. Bourdillon (Eds.), *African Children at Work: Working and Learning in Growing Up for Life* (pp. 143–168). LIT Verlag.

Dougnon, I. (2013). Migration as Coping with Risk and State Barriers: Malian Migrants' Conception of Being Far from Home. In A. Kane & T. H. Leedy (Eds.), *African migrations: Patterns and perspectives* (pp. 35–58). Indiana University Press.

Drotbohm, H. (2009). Horizons of long-distance intimacies. *The History of the Family,* 14(2), 132–149.

Drotbohm, H. (2010). Gossip and social control across the seas: Targeting gender, resource inequalities and support in Cape Verdean transnational families. *African and Black Diaspora: An International Journal,* 3(1), 51–68.

Drotbohm, H. (2011). On the durability and the decomposition of citizenship: The social logics of forced return migration in Cape Verde. *Citizenship Studies,* 15(3-4), 381–396.

Drotbohm, H. (2012). It's like Belonging to a Place That Has Never Been Yours: Deportees Negotiating Involuntary Immobility and Conditions of Return in Cape Verde. In M. Messer, R. Schroeder, & R. Wodak (Eds.), *Migrations: Interdisciplinary Perspectives* (pp. 129–140). Springer.

Drotbohm, H. (2015). The Reversal of Migratory Family Lives: A Cape Verdean Perspective on Gender and Sociality pre- and post-deportation. *Journal of Ethnic and Migration Studies,* 41(4), 653–670.

Drotbohm, H. (2016). Frozen Cosmopolitanism: Coping with Radical Deceleration in Cape Verdean Contexts of Forced Migration. In T. Hylland Eriksen & E. Schober (Eds.), *Identity Destabilised. Living in an Overheated World* (pp. 42–58). Pluto Press.

Drotbohm, H., & Hasselberg, I. (2015). Introduction. Deportation, Anxiety, Justice: New Ethnographic Perspectives. *Journal of Ethnic and Migration Studies*, 41(4), 551–562.

Dubuis, E. (2017, December 13). Le cimetière marin. 15 000 hommes, femmes et enfants sont morts en Méditerranée depuis 2014. *Le Temps*.

Dünnwald, S. (2011). Failed Migrants in Bamako. *Centro De Estudos Africanos*.

Dünnwald, S. (2012). *The deportee in a country where migration is always successful*. W086 „Deportation, Justice, and Anxiety". European Anthropological Society Association (EASA), Nanterre.

Dünnwald, S. (2017). Bamako, Outpost of the European Border Regime? In P. Gaibazzi, A. Bellagamba, & S. Dünnwald (Eds.), *EurAfrican Borders and Migration Management: Political Cultures, Contested Spaces, and Ordinary Lives* (pp. 83–107). Palgrave Macmillan.

Dwell, M. (2013). Undermining the 'Local': Migration, Development and Gold in Southern Kayes. *Journal of Intercultural Studies*, 34(5), 584–603.

Eastmond, M., & Mannergren Selimovic, J. (2012). Silence as Possibility in Postwar Everyday Life. *The International Journal of Transitional Justice*, 6, 502–524.

Ellermann, A. (2009). *States against migrants: Deportation in Germany and the United States*. Cambridge University Press.

Ellermann, A. (2013). When Can Liberal States Avoid Unwanted Immigration? Self-Limited Sovereignty and Guest Worker Recruitment in Switzerland and Germany. *World Politics*, 65(03), 491–538.

Engeler, M., & Steuer, N. (2017). Elusive Futures: An Introduction. In N. Steuer, M. Engeler, & E. Macamo (Eds.), *Culture and social practice. Dealing with elusive futures: University graduates in urban Africa* (pp. 9–25). transcript.

Englert, B., & Dannecker, P. (2014). Praktische und ethische Aspekte der Feldforschung. In P. Dannecker & B. Englert (Eds.), *Qualitative Methoden in der Entwicklungsforschung* (pp. 233–265). Mandelbaum.

European Commission. (2011). *Communication from the Commission to the European Parliament, the Council, the European Economic and Social Committee and the Committee of the Regions: The Global Approach to Migration and Mobility*. COM(2011) 743 final.

European Commission. (2016). *Joint Communication to the European Council and the Parliament: A renewed partnership with the countries of Africa, the Caribbean and the Pacific*. JOIN(2016) 52 final.

European Commission, Malian Ministry of Foreign Affairs. (2014). *Union Européene – Mali. Programme Indicatif National 2014-2020*.

European Council (2003). Council Directive 2003/86/EC of 22 September 2003 on the right to family reunification. *Official Journal of the European Union* (12).

Faist, T. (2018). Forced Migration in a Moral Polity and the Public Role of Migration Research. *COMCAD Working Papers* (163).

Faist, T., Gehring, T., & Schultz, S. U. (2021). *Mobilität statt Exodus: Migration und Flucht in und aus Afrika*. Springer VS.

Falconnier, G. N. (2016). *Trajectories of agricultural change in southern Mali*. Doctoral Thesis, Wageningen University.

Fassin, D., & Rechtman, R. (2009). *The empire of trauma: An inquiry into the condition of victimhood*. Princeton University Press.

Fekete, L. (2005). The deportation machine: Europe, asylum and human rights. *Race & Class*, 47(1), 64–78.

Feldman, A. (1991). *Formations of Violence: The Narrative of the Body and Political Terror in Northern Ireland*. The University of Chicago Press.

Feldman, G. (2012). *The Migration Apparatus: Security, Labour, and Policymaking in the European Union*. Stanford University Press.

Féliz, M., & Rosenberg, A.L. (Ed.). (2017). *The Political Economy of Poverty and Social Transformations of the Global South*. ibidem.

Ferguson, J. (1999). *Expectations of Modernity. Myths and Meaning of Urban Life on the Zambian Copperbelt*. University of California Press.

Ferguson, J. (2006). *Global Shadows*. Duke University Press.

Ferguson, J., & Gupta, A. (1992). Beyond "Culture": Space, Identity, and the Politics of Difference. *Cultural Anthropology*, 7(1), 6–23.

Feyerabend, P. (1981). *Wider den Methodenzwang: Skizze einer anarchistischen Erkennt-nistheorie*. Suhrkamp.

Flahaux, M. L. (2015). Return Migration to Senegal and the Democratic Republic of Congo: Intention and Realization. *Population-E*, 70(1), 97–126.

Flahaux, M. L., Eggerickx, T., & Schoumaker, B. (2017). Les migrations de retour en Afrique. *Espace Populations Sociétés*. 2017/1.

Fortes, M. (1936). Culture Contact as a Dynamic Process an Investigation in the Northern Territories of the Gold Coast. *Africa*, 9(1), 24–55.

Fortes, M. (1949). *The web of kinship among the Tallensi: The 2. part of an analysis of the social structure of a Trans-Volta tribe*. Oxford University Press.

Fortes, M. ([1956] 2018). Oedipus and Job in West African religion: The 1956 Frazer Lecture. *HAU: Journal of Ethnographic Theory*, 8(1-2), 394–413.

Foucault, M., Gros, F., Ewald, F., & Fontana, A. (2005). *The hermeneutics of the subject: Lectures at the Collège de France, 1981-1982*. Palgrave Macmillan.

Friedrich-Ebert-Stiftung (FES) Mali. (2020). *Mali-Mètre XI: Enquête d'opinion politique "Que pensent les Malien(ne)s?"*. 11 au 26 novembre 2019.

Gaibazzi, P. (2015a). *Bush, Bound: Young Men and Rural Permanence in Migrant West Africa*. Berghahn Books.

Gaibazzi, P. (2015b). The quest for luck: Fate, fortune, work and the unexpected among Gambian Soninke hustlers. *Critical African Studies*, 7(3), 227–242.

Gaibazzi, P., Bellagamba, A., & Dünnwald, S. (2017). Introduction: An Afro-Europeanist Perspective on EurAfrican Borders. In P. Gaibazzi, A. Bellagamba,

& S. Dünnwald (Eds.), *EurAfrican Borders and Migration Management: Political Cultures, Contested Spaces, and Ordinary Lives* (pp. 3–28). Palgrave Macmillan.

Gaibazzi, P., Dünnwald, S., & Bellagamba, A. (2017). *EurAfrican borders and migration management: Political cultures, contested spaces, and ordinary lives*. Palgrave Macmillan.

Galatowitsch, D. (2009). Co-Development in Mali: A Case Study of a Development Phenomenon Exploited by Immigration Policy. *Independent Study Project (ISP) Collection* (737).

Galvin, T. M. (2015). 'We Deport Them but They Keep Coming Back': The Normalcy of Deportation in the Daily Life of 'Undocumented' Zimbabwean Migrant Workers in Botswana. *Journal of Ethnic and Migration Studies*, 41(4), 617–634.

Gardner, K. (1995). *Global migrants, local lives: Travel and transformation in rural Bangladesh*. Clarendon Press.

Gary-Tounkara, D. (2008). *Migrants soudanais/maliens et conscience ivoirienne: Les étrangers en Côte d'Ivoire (1903-1980)*. L'Harmattan.

Gary-Tounkara, D. (2009). La dispersion des Soudanais/Maliens à la fin de l'ère coloniale. *Hommes & Migrations* (1279), 12–23.

Gary-Tounkara, D. (2013). La gestion des migrations de retour, un paramètre négligé de la grille d'analyse de la crise malienne. *Politique Africaine*, 130(2), 47.

Gary-Tounkara, D. (2015). A reappraisal of the expulsion of illegal immigrants from Nigeria in 1983. *International Journal of Conflict and Violence*, 9(1).

Gaudio, A. (1988). *Le Mali. Collection Méridiens*. Karthala.

Geertz, C. (1965). Religion as a Cultural System. In M. Banton (Ed.), *Anthropological Approaches to the Study of Religion*. Tavistock Publications.

Geertz, C. (1975). Common Sense as a Cultural System. *The Antioch Review*, 33(1), 5.

Gemmeke, A. B. (2008). *Marabout women in Dakar: Creating trust in a rural urban space*. LIT Verlag.

Geschiere, P. (2009). *The Perils of Belonging: Autochthony, Citizenship, and Exclusion in Africa and Europe*. The University of Chicago Press.

Geschiere, P. (2013). *Witchcraft, Intimacy and Trust: Africa in Comparison*. The University of Chicago Press.

Geschiere, P., & Nyamnjoh, F. B. (2000). Capitalism and Autochthony: The Seesaw of Mobility and Belonging. *Public Culture*, 12(2), 423–452.

Gibney, M. J. (2004). *The Ethics and Politics of Asylum: Liberal Democracy and the Response to Refugees*. Cambridge University Press.

Gibney, M. J. (2008). Asylum and the Expansion of Deportation in the United Kingdom. *Government and Opposition*, 43(2), 146–167.

Giebeler, C., & Meneses, M. (2012). Geben und Nehmen im Forschungsprozess. Reflexionen über trans-, inter- und intrakulturelle Räume im Forschungsprojekt. Juchitán – die Stadt der Frauen: Vom Leben im Matriarchat. Eine Retrospektive nach 20 Jahren. In O. Kaltmeier & S. C. Berkin (Eds.), *Methoden dekolonialisieren*.

Ansätze zur Demokratisierung der Sozial- und Kulturwissenschaften. Westfälisches Dampfboot.

Gladkova, N., & Mazzucato, V. (2017). Theorising Chance: Capturing the Role of Ad Hoc Social Interactions in Migrants' Trajectories. *Population, Space and Place*, 23(2), e1988.

Glick-Schiller, N., & Salazar, N. B. (2013). Regimes of Mobility Across the Globe. *Journal of Ethnic and Migration Studies*, 39(2), 183–200.

Gluckman, M. (1963). *Order and rebellion in tribal Africa*. Cohen & West.

Goffman, E. (1956). *The Presentation of Self in Everyday Life*. University of Edinburgh.

Golash-Boza, T., & Navarro, Y. C. (2020). Reintegration nach Abschiebung.: Erfahrungen von aus den USA abgeschobenen Dominikanern und Brasilianern. *PERIPHERIE – Politik • Ökonomie • Kultur*, 39(3), 369–388.

Golash-Boza, T. M. (2015). *Deported: Immigrant policing, disposable labor, and global capitalism*. New York University Press.

Gonin, P., & Kotlok, N. (2012). Migrations et pauvreté : essai sur la situation malienne. *CERISCOPE Pauvreté*.

Graeber, D. (2011). *Debt: The First 5,000 Years*. Melville House Printing.

Graw, K., & Schielke, S. (Eds.). (2012). *The Global Horizon: Expectations of Migration in Africa and the Middle East*. Leuven University Press.

Grosz-Ngaté, M. (1989). Hidden Meanings: Explorations into a Bamanan Construction of Gender. *Ethnology*, 28(2), 167–183.

Guignon, C. B., & Pereboom, D. (2001). *Existentialism: Basic writings* (2nd ed.). Hackett.

Gupta, A., & Ferguson, J. (1997). Discipline and Practice: "The Field" as Site, Method, and Location in Anthropology. In Akhil Gupta & James Ferguson (Eds.), *Anthropological Locations: Boundaries and Grounds of a Field Science* (pp. 1–46). University of California Press.

Guyer, J. I. (Ed.). (1995). *Social History of Africa. Money Matters: Instability, values and social payments in the modern history of West African communities*. Heinemann.

Guyer, J. I. (2004). *Marginal Gains: Monetary Transactions in Atlantic Africa*. The University of Chicago Press.

Haan, A. de, & Rogaly, B. (Eds.). (2002). *Labour mobility and rural society*. Routledge.

Haas, H. de. (2007). *The myth of invasion: Irregular migration from West Africa to the Maghreb and the European Union*.

Hagberg, S., & Körling, G. (2012). Socio-political Turmoil in Mali: The Public Debate Following the Coup d'État on 22 March 2012. *Africa Spectrum*, 47(2-3), 111–125.

Hage, G. (2005). A not so multi-sited ethnography of a not so imagined community. *Anthropological Theory*, 5(4), 463–475.

Hage, G. (Ed.). (2009). *Waiting*. Melbourne University Press.

Hage, G. (2015). *Alter-Politics: Critical Anthropology and the Radical Imagination*. Melbourne University Press.

Hahn, H. P. (2004). Zirkuläre Arbeitsmigration in Westafrika und die „Kultur der Migration". *Afrika Spectrum, 39*(3), 381–404.

Hahn, H. P., & Klute, G. (Eds.). (2007). *Cultures of Migration: African Perspectives.* LIT Verlag.

Hamès, C. (1997). Le premier exil de Shaikh Hammalah et la mémoire hammaliste (Nioro-Mederdra 1925). In D. Robinson & J.-L. Triaud (Eds.), *Le temps des marabouts. Itinéraires et stratégies islamiques en Afrique Occidentale Française 1880-1960* (pp. 337-360). Karthala.

Hammar, T., Brochmann, G., & Tamas, K. & Faist, T. (Eds.). (1997). *International migration, immobility and development: Multidisciplinary perspectives.* Berg.

Hart, K. (1982). On Commoditization. In Esther N. Goody (Ed.), *From Craft to Industry: The Ethnography of Proto-Industrial Cloth Production.* Cambridge University Press.

Hart, K. (1988). Kinship, Contract and Trust: The Economic Organization of Migrants in an African Slum City. In D. Gambetta (Ed.), *Trust and Cooperative Relations* (pp. 176–194). Basil Blackwell.

Hasselberg, I. (2016). *Enduring Uncertainty: Deportation, Punishment and Everyday Life.* Berghahn Books.

Hasselberg, I. (2018). Fieldnotes from Cape Verde: On Deported Youth, Research Methods, and Social Change. In S. Khosravi (Ed.), *After Deportation: Ethnographic Perspectives* (pp. 15–36). Palgrave Macmillan.

Hernández-Carretero, M. (2015). Renegotiating Obligations through Migration: Senegalese Transnationalism and the Quest for the Right Distance. *Journal of Ethnic and Migration Studies, 41*(12), 2021-2040.

Hernández-Carretero, M., & Carling, J. (2012). Beyond "Kamikaze Migrants": Risk Taking in West African Boat Migration to Europe. *Human Organization, 71*(4), 407–416.

Hertrich, V., & Lesclingand, M. (2013). Adolescent Migration in Rural Africa as a Challenge to Gender and Intergenerational Relationships: Evidence from Mali. *The ANNALS of the American Academy of Political and Social Science, 648*(1), 175–188.

Hibbins, R., & Pease, B. (2009). Men and Masculinities on the Move. In M. Donaldson, R. Hibbins, R. Howson, & B. Pease (Eds.), *Migrant men: Critical studies of masculinities and the migration experience* (pp. 1–19). Routledge.

Hilson, G., & Garforth, C. (2012). 'Agricultural Poverty' and the Expansion of Artisanal Mining in Sub-Saharan Africa: Experiences from Southwest Mali and Southeast Ghana. *Population Research and Policy Review, 31*(3), 435–464.

Holas, B. (1956). Fondements spirituels de la vie sociale Sénoufo. *Journal De La Société Des Africanistes, 26*(1), 9–31.

Honwana, A. M. (2012). *The Time of Youth: Work, Social Change, and Politics in Africa.* Kumarian Press Pub.

Honwana, A., & Boeck, F. de (Eds.). (2005). *Makers & Breakers: Children & Youth in Postcolonial Africa*. Africa World Press.

Hummel, D., Doevenspeck, M., & Samimi, C. (2012). *Climate Change, Environment and Migration in the Sahel: Selected Issues with a Focus on Senegal and Mali* (Micle Working Paper No. 1).

Hüsken, U. (ed.) (2007). *When Rituals go Wrong. Mistakes, Failure, and the Dynamics of Ritual*. Brill.

Huschke, S. (2015). Giving back: Activist research with undocumented migrants in Berlin. *Medical Anthropology*, 34(1), 54–69.

Idelman, E. (2009). *Decentralisation and boundary setting in Mali* (IIED Issue Paper No. 151).

Ingvars, Á. K., & Gíslason, I. V. (2018). Moral Mobility: Emergent Refugee Masculinities among Young Syrians in Athens. *Men and Masculinities*, 21(3), 383–402.

Inhorn, M. C. (2012). *The new Arab man: emergent masculinities, technologies, and Islam in the Middle East*. Princeton University Press.

International Organization for Migration. (2014). *IOM Regional Strategy West and Central Africa 2014 - 2016*.

International Organization for Migration. (2018). *Migration governance profile: Republic of Mali*.

Jackson, M. (2005a). *Existential Anthropology: Events, Exigencies and Effects*. Berghahn Books.

Jackson, M. (2005b). Storytelling Events, Violence, and the Appearance of the Past: West African Warscapes. *Anthropological Quarterly*, 78(2), 355–375.

Jackson, M. (2008). The Shock of the New: On Migrant Imaginaries and Critical Transitions. *Ethnos*, 73(1), 57–72.

Jackson, M. (2017). *How lifeworlds work: Emotionality sociality and the ambiguity of being*. The University of Chicago Press.

Jamana (1987). Les émigrés maliens. « Quel destin? ». *Jamana, Revue Culturelle Malienne* (3), 1–69.

Jansen, J. (1996). The Younger Brother and the Stranger: In Search of a Status Discourse for Mande. *Cahiers D'Études Africaines*, 36(144), 659–688.

John, R., & Langhof, A. (Eds.). (2014). *Innovation und Gesellschaft. Scheitern – Ein Desiderat der Moderne*. Springer VS.

Johnson, J. W. (1986). *The Epic of Son-Jara: A West African Tradition*. Indiana University Press.

Johnson-Hanks, J. (2002). On the Limits of Life Stages in Ethnography: Toward a Theory of Vital Conjunctures. *American Anthropologist*, 104(3).

Johnson-Hanks, J. (2005). When the Future Decides: Uncertainty and Intentional Action in Contemporary Cameroon. *Current Anthropology*, 46(3), 363–385.

Jónsson, G. (2007). *The Mirage of Migration: Migration Aspirations and Immobility In a Malian Soninke Village*. Master's Thesis. University of Copenhagen.

Jónsson, G. (2011). Non-migrant, sedentary, immobile, or 'left behind'? Reflections on the absence of migration. *IMI Working Papers Series* (39).

Kafka, F. (1971). *The Complete Stories*. Schocken Books.

Kahn, N. (2013). A Moving Heart: Querying a Singular Problem of '"Immobility' in Afghan Migration to the UK. *Medical Anthropology: Cross-Cultural Studies in Health and Illness*, 32(6), 518–534.

Kalir, B. (2017). Between 'voluntary' return programs and soft deportation. Sending vulnerable migrants in Spain 'back home'. In Z. Vathi, & R. King (Eds.), *Return Migration and Psychosocial Wellbeing: Discourses, Policy-Making and Outcomes for Migrants and Their Families* (pp. 56-71). Routledge.

Kane, A., & Leedy, T. H. (Eds.). (2013). *African migrations: Patterns and perspectives*. Indiana University Press.

Kanstroom, D. (2010). *Deportation nation: Outsiders in American history*. Harvard University Press.

Karakayali, S., & Rigo, E. (2010). Mapping the European Space of Circulation. In N. De Genova & N. Peutz (Eds.), *The Deportation Regime: Sovereignty, Space, and the Freedom of Movement* (pp. 123–144). Duke University Press.

Karp, I. (1986). *Oedipus and Job in West African Religions. By Meyer Fortes, with an essay by Robin Horton*. Cambridge University Press.

Kasfir, N. (1998). Civil society, the state and democracy in Africa. *Commonwealth & Comparative Politics*, 36(2), 123–149.

Keita, S. (2013). Migrations internationales et mobilisation des ressources: Les Maliens de l'extérieur et la problématique du développement. In V. Baby-Collin, G. Cortes, L. Faret, & H. Guétat-Bernard. (Eds.), *Migrants des Suds* (pp. 217–235). IRD Éditions.

Khosravi, S. (2016). Deportation as a Way of Life for Young Afghan Men. In R. Furman, D. Epps, & G. Lamphear (Eds.), *Detaining the Immigrant Other: Global and Transnational Issues* (pp. 169–181). Oxford University Press.

Khosravi, S. (Ed.). (2018). *After Deportation: Ethnographic Perspectives*. Palgrave Macmillan.

Khosravi, S. (2018). Introduction. In S. Khosravi (Ed.), *After Deportation: Ethnographic Perspectives* (pp. 1–14). Palgrave Macmillan.

Kipp, D., & Koch, A. (2018). Auf der Suche nach externen Lösungen Instrumente, Akteure und Strategien der migrationspolitischen Kooperation Europas mit afrikanischen Staaten. In Stiftung Wissenschaft und Politik (Ed.), *Migrationsprofiteure? Autoritäre Staaten in Afrika und das europäische Migrationsmanagement* (pp. 9–22). SWP-Studie 3.

Kleinman, A. (1995). *Writing at the Margin: Discourse between Anthropology and Medicine*. University of California Press.

Kleinman, A., Das, V., & Lock, M. (Eds.). (1997). *Social Suffering*. University California Press.

Kleinman, A., & Kleinman, J. (1991). Suffering and its professional transformation: toward an ethnography of interpersonal experience. *Culture, Medicine and Psychiatry*, *15*, 275–302.

Kleist, N. (2017a). Disrupted migration projects: The moral economy of involuntary return to Ghana from Libya. *Africa*, *87*(02), 322–342.

Kleist, N. (2017b). Introduction: Studying Hope and Uncertainty in African Migration. In N. Kleist & D. Thorsen (Eds.), *Hope and Uncertainty in Contemporary African Migration* (pp. 1–20). Routledge.

Kleist, N. (2017c). Returning with Nothing but an Empty bag: Topographies of Social Hope after Deportation in Ghana. In N. Kleist & D. Thorsen (Eds.), *Hope and Uncertainty in Contemporary African Migration* (pp. 173–192). Routledge.

Kleist, N., & Jansen, S. (2016). Introduction: Hope over Time—Crisis, Immobility and Future-Making, *27*(4), 373–392.

Kleist, N., & Thorsen, D. (Eds.). (2017). *Routledge Studies in Anthropology. Hope and Uncertainty in Contemporary African Migration*. Routledge.

Knoblauch, H. (2001). Fokussierte Ethnographie. *Sozialer Sinn: Zeitschrift für hermeneutische Sozialforschung*, (2).

Koch, A. (2013). The Politics and Discourse of Migrant Return: The Role of UNHCR and IOM in the Governance of Return. *Journal of Ethnic and Migration Studies*, *40*(6), 905–923.

Koch, A., Weber, A., & Werenfels, I. (2018). *Migrationsprofiteure? Autoritäre Staaten in Afrika und das europäische Migrationsmanagement* (SWP-Studie 3). Stiftung Wissenschaft und Politik.

Koenig, D. (1986). Social Stratification and Labor Allocation in Peanut Farming in the Rural Malian Household. *African Studies Review*, *29*(3), 107–127.

Koenig, D. (2005a). Multilocality and Social Stratification in Kita, Mali. In L. Trager (Ed.), *Migration and Economy: Global and Local Dynamics* (pp. 77–102). Alta Mira Press.

Koenig, D. (2005b). Social Stratification and Access to Wealth in the Rural Hinterland of Kita, Mali. In S. Wooten (Ed.), *Wari Matters: Ethnographic Explorations of Money in the Mande World* (pp. 31–56). LIT Verlag.

Konaté, F. O. (2012). La migration féminine dans la ville de Kayes au Mali. *Hommes & Migrations* (1286-1287), 62–73.

Konaté, F. O., & Gonin, P. (Eds.). (2016). *Le Role des Migrations au Mali: Cercles de Kita, Banamba et district de Bamako*. L'Harmattan.

Konzett-Smoliner, S. (2016). Return migration as a 'family project': Exploring the relationship between family life and the readjustment experiences of highly skilled Austrians. *Journal of Ethnic and Migration Studies*, *42*(7), 1094–1114.

Korvensyrjä, A. (2017). The Valletta Process and the Westphalian Imaginary of Migration Research. *Movements*, *3*(1), 192–204.

Koselleck, R. (2004). *Futures past: On the semantics of historical time*. Columbia University Press.

Koser, K. (2015). *Promoting the Assisted Voluntary Return and Reintegration of Migrants* (Occasional Paper Series No. 16). Australian Government. Department of Immigration and Border Protection.

Koser, K., & Kuschminder, K. (2015). *Comparative Research on the Assisted Voluntary Return and Reintegration of Migrants*. International Organization for Migration.

Kotlok, N. (2012). Le "développement solidaire". *Hommes & Migrations* (1286-1287), 268–278.

Kuschminder, K. (2017). Taking Stock of Assisted Voluntary Return from Europe: Decision Making, Reintegration and Sustainable Return – Time for a Paradigm Shift. *EUI Working Paper* RSCAS (31). European University Institute

Kusenbach, M. (2003). Street Phenomenology. *Ethnography*, 4(3), 455–485.

Kusow, A. M. (2004). Contesting Stigma: On Goffman's Assumptions of Normative Order. *Symbolic Interaction*, 27(2), 179–197.

Lachenmann, G. (1986). Rural development in Mali: Destabilisation and social organisation. *Quarterly Journal of International Agriculture*, 25(3), 217–233.

Lachenmann, G. (2010). Methodische / methodologische Herausforderungen im Globalisierungskontext: komplexe Methoden zur Untersuchung von Interfaces von Wissenssystemen. *Working Papers in Development Sociology and Social Anthropology* (364).

Lacher, W. (2013). The Malian crisis and the challenge of regional security cooperation. *Stability: International Journal of Security & Development*, 2(2), 18.

Lassiter, L. E. (2005). *The Chicago Guide to Collaborative Ethnography*. The University of Chicago Press.

Latour, É. de (2003). Héros du retour. *Critique Internationale*, 19(2), 171.

Le Courant, S. (2014). « Être le dernier jeune ». Les temporalités contrariées des migrants irréguliers. *Terrain* (63), 38–53.

Lecadet, C. (2011). *Le front mouvant des expulsés. Lieux et enjeux des regroupements et des mobilisations collectives des migrants expulsés au Mali*. Thèse. EHESS.

Lecadet, C. (2011). Migrants expulsés au Mali : trouver un espace de représentation par le théâtre ? *Cahiers De L'Urmis* (13).

Lecadet, C. (2013). From Migrant Destitution to Self-organization into Transitory National Communities: The Revival of Citizenship in Post-deportation Experience in Mali. In B. Anderson (Ed.), *The Social, Political and Historical Contours of Deportation: Immigrants and Minorities, Politics and Policy* (pp. 143–158). Springer Science+Business Media.

Lecadet, C. (2016). The tirailleurs and the migrants: Malian postcolonial criticism remembers. *International Journal of Francophone Studies*, 19(2), 173–192.

Lecadet, C. (2017). Deportation Ghettoes in Mali: Expelled Migrants Between State Exclusion and Self-Organization. In P. Gaibazzi, A. Bellagamba, & S. Dünnwald

(Eds.), *EurAfrican Borders and Migration Management: Political Cultures, Contested Spaces, and Ordinary Lives* (pp. 109–125). Palgrave Macmillan.

Lecadet, C. (2018). Post-Deportation Movements: Forms and Conditions of the Struggle Amongst Self-Organising Expelled Migrants in Mali and Togo. In S. Khosravi (Ed.), *After Deportation: Ethnographic Perspectives* (pp. 187–204). Palgrave Macmillan.

Lecocq, B., Mann, G., Whitehouse, B., Badi, D., Pelckmans, L., Belalimat, N., Hall, B., & Lacher, W. (2013). One hippopotamus and eight blind analysts: a multivocal analysis of the 2012 political crisis in the divided Republic of Mali. *Review of African Political Economy*, 40(137), 343–357.

Lemberg-Pedersen, M. (2017). Effective Protection or Effective Combat? EU Border Control and North Africa. In P. Gaibazzi, A. Bellagamba, & S. Dünnwald (Eds.), *EurAfrican Borders and Migration Management: Political Cultures, Contested Spaces, and Ordinary Lives* (pp. 29–60). Palgrave Macmillan.

Lentz, C. (2013). *Land, Mobility and Belonging in West Africa*. Indiana University Press.

Lesclingand, M., & Hertrich, V. (2017). When Girls Take the Lead: Adolescent Girls' Migration in Mali. *Population-E*, 72(1).

Lima, S. (2005). La frontière « impossible » ? *Espace Populations Sociétés* (2), 277–291.

Lima, S. (2012). Territorialités en mouvement. *Hommes & Migrations* (1286-1287), 258–267.

Lima, S. (2015). Migrants volontaires et migrants citoyens : les recompositions des associations de migrants originaires de la région de Kayes (Mali). *Afrique Et Développement*, 40(1), 119–137.

Lindsay, L. A., & Miescher, S. F. (Eds.). (2003). *Men and masculinities in modern Africa*. Heinemann.

Link, B. G., & Phelan, J. C. (2001). Conceptualizing Stigma. *Annual Review of Sociology*, 27(1), 363–385.

Lucht, H. (2017). Death of a Gin Salesman: Hope and Despair among Ghanaian Migrants and Deportees Stranded in Niger. In N. Kleist & D. Thorsen (Eds.), *Hope and Uncertainty in Contemporary African Migration* (pp. 154-171). Routledge.

Ludwig, S. (2017a). *La chance: An Ethnography: University Graduates Making Sense of Uncertainty in Bamako, Mali*. Dissertation. Universität Basel.

Ludwig, S. (2017b). 'Opening up *la Chance*': (Un)certainty among University Graduates in Bamako, Mali. In N. Steuer, M. Engeler, & E. Macamo (Eds.), *Culture and social practice. Dealing with elusive futures: University graduates in urban Africa* (pp. 69–88). transcript.

Macamo, E., & Neubert, D. (2012). "Flood Disasters": A Sociological Analysis of Local Perception and Management of Extreme Events Based on Examples from Mozambique, Germany, and the USA. In U. Luig (Ed.), *Negotiating disasters: Politics representation meanings* (pp. 81–103). Peter Lang.

Macé, C. (2019, July 3). Les migrants détenus en Libye, victimes anonymes de la guerre civile. *Libération*.

Maher, S. (2015). *Barça ou Barzakh: The Social Elsewhere of Failed Clandestine Migration out of Senegal*. Doctoral Thesis. University of Washington.

Majidi, N. (2018). Deportees Lost at "Home": Post-deportation Outcomes in Afghanistan. In S. Khosravi (Ed.), *After Deportation: Ethnographic Perspectives* (pp. 127–148). Palgrave Macmillan.

Makhulu, A. M., Buggenhagen, B., & Jackson, S. (Eds.). (2010). *Hard Work, Hard Times: Global Volatility and African Subjectivities*. University of California Press.

Mamadou, C. (2015). *Atouts et limites de la filière coton au Mali*. Thèse. Université de Toulon.

Manchuelle, F. (1989). Slavery, emancipation and labour migration in West Africa: The case of the Soninke. *The Journal of African History, 30*(1), 89–106.

Manchuelle, F. (1997). *Willing migrants. Soninke labor diasporas, 1848–1960*. Ohio University Press.

Mann, G. (2003). Immigrants and Arguments in France and West Africa. *Comparative Studies in Society and History, 45*(2), 362–385.

Mannik, L. (Ed.). (2016). *Migration by Boat: Discourses of Trauma, Exclusion, and Survival*. Berghahn Books.

Marcus, G. E. (1995). Ethnography in/of the World System: The Emergence of Multi-Sited Ethnography. *Annual Review of Anthropology, 24*, 95–117.

Martin, L. (2015). *Deportation and the Dispossession of Time*. Darkmatter.

Massey, D. S., Arango, J., Hugo, G., Kouaouci, A., Pellegrino, A., & Taylor, J. E. (1993). Theories of International Migration: A Review and Appraisal. *Population and Development Review, 19*(3), 431–466.

Mauss, M. (1954). *The gift: forms and functions of exchange in archaic societies*. Cohen & West.

Mbembe, J. A. (1985). *Les Jeunes et l'Ordre Politique en Afrique Noire*. L'Harmattan.

Mbembe, A. (2001). *On the Postcolony*. University of California Press.

Mbembe, A. (2007). On Politics as a Form of Expenditure. In J. Comaroff & J. Comaroff (Eds.), *Law and disorder in the postcolony* (pp. 299–336). The University of Chicago Press.

Mbembe, A., & Roitman, J. (1995). Figures of the Subject in Times of Crisis. *Public Culture, 7*(2), 323–352.

McDougall, J., & Scheele, J. (2012). *Saharan frontiers: Space and mobility in Northwest Africa*. Indiana University Press.

Meillassoux, C. (1981). *Maidens, Meal and Money: Capitalism and the domestic community*. Cambridge University Press.

Meillassoux, C. ([1968] 2014). *Bamako. Urbanisation d'une Communauté Africaine*. Éditions Timbouctou.

Meiu, G. P. (2017). *Ethno-erotic economies: Sexuality money and belonging in Kenya*. The University of Chicago Press.

Menjívar, C., & Abrego, L. J. Legal Violence: Immigration Law and the Lives of Central American Immigrants. *American Journal of Sociology*, 117, 1380–1421.

Mensah, E. A. (2016). Involuntary Return Migration and Reintegration. The Case of Ghanaian Migrant Workers from Libya. *Journal of International Migration and Integration*, 17(1), 303–323.

Merton, R.K. (1938). Social Structure and Anomie. *American Sociological Review*, 3(5), 672-82.

Merton, R. K., Barber, E. G., Kingsley, D. (Ed.). (1976). *Sociological ambivalence and other essays*. The Free Press.

Meyer, C. (2013). Finding the right place. On the rhetorics of field access. In I. A. Strecker & S. La Tosky (Eds.), *Writing in the field: Festschrift for Stephen Tyler* (pp. 21–32). LIT Verlag.

Ministère des Maliens de l'Exterièure et de l'Intégration Africaine (MMEIA). (2014, August 26). *Document de Politique National de Migration pour le Mail (PONAM)*.

Mo Ibrahim Foundation (MIF). (2019). *Africa's Youth: Jobs or Migration? Demography, economic prospects, and mobility*. Ibrahim Forum Report.

Müller, M. (2018). Migrationskonflikt in Niger: Präsident Issoufou wagt, der Norden verliert. In Stiftung Wissenschaft und Politik (Ed.), *Migrationsprofiteure? Autoritäre Staaten in Afrika und das europäische Migrationsmanagement* (pp. 36–46). SWP-Studie 3.

Newell, S. (2012). *The modernity bluff: Crime consumption and citizenship in Côte d'Ivoire*. The University of Chicago Press.

Nyamnjoh, H. (2010). *"We Get Nothing from Fishing" Fishing for Boat Opportunities amongst Senegalese Fisher Migrants*. Master's Thesis. Langaa Research and Publishing Common Initiative Group.

Nyberg-Sørensen, N. (2010). The rise and fall of the "migrant superhero" and the new "deportee trash": Contemporary strain on mobile livelihoods in the Central American region. *DIIS working paper* (22). Danish Institute for International Studies.

Nyers, P. (2003). Abject Cosmopolitanism: the politics of protection in the anti-deportation movement. *Third World Quarterly*, 24(6), 1069–1093.

Nyers, P. (2015). Migrant Citizenships and Autonomous Mobilities. *Migration, Mobility, & Displacement*, 1(1), 23–39.

Okely, J. m. (2008). Knowing Without Notes. In N. Halstead, E. Hirsch, & J. M. Okely (Eds.), *Knowing how to know: Fieldwork and the ethnographic present* (pp. 56–74). Berghahn Books.

Osella, F., & Osella, C. (2000). Migration, Money, and Masculinity in Kerala. *Journal of the Royal Anthropological Institute*, (6), 117–188.

Outtara, B. (2010). *La réinsertion socioprofessionnelle des migrants de retour dans leur pays d'origine. L'exemple des migrants maliens de retour de Côte-d'Ivoire.* International Labour Organization.

Palmberger, M. (2019). Relational ambivalence: Exploring the social and discursive dimensions of ambivalence. The case of Turkish aging labor migrants. *International Journal of Comparative Sociology*, 60(1-2), 74–90.

Parry, J., & Bloch, M. (Eds.). (1989). *Money and the morality of exchange.* Cambridge University Press.

Pereira, N. (2011). *Return[ed] to paradise: the deportation experience in Samoa & Tonga* (MOST Policy Papers No. 21). United Nations Educational, Scientific and Cultural Organization.

Peutz, N. (2006). Embarking on an Anthropology of Removal. *Current Anthropology*, 47(2), 217–241.

Peutz, N. (2007). Out-laws: Deportees, Desire, and "The Law": Notes and Commentary. *International Migration*, 45(3), 182–193.

Pian, A. (2009). *Aux Nouvelles Frontières de l'Europe: L'aventure incertaine des Sénégalaises au Maroc.* La Dispute.

Pian, A. (2010). Trajectoires de rapatriés. *Hommes & Migrations* (1286-1287), 86–97.

Pietilä, T. (2014). *Gossip, Markets, and Gender: How Dialogue Constructs Moral Value in Post-Socialist Kilimanjaro.* University of Wisconsin Press.

Piot, C. (1999). *Remotely Global: Village Modernity in West Africa.* The University of Chicago Press.

Piot, C. (2010). *Nostalgia for the Future: West Africa after the Cold War.* The University of Chicago Press.

Plambech, S. (2017). God brought you home – deportation as moral governance in the lives of Nigerian sex worker migrants. *Journal of Ethnic and Migration Studies*, 43(13), 2211–2227.

Plambech, S. (2018). Back from "the Other Side": The Postdeportee Life of Nigerian Migrant Sex Workers. In S. Khosravi (Ed.), *After Deportation: Ethnographic Perspectives* (pp. 81–103). Palgrave Macmillan.

Pollet, E., & Winter, G. (1971). *La Société Soninké (Dyahunu, Mali).* Éditions de l'Institut de Sociologie de l'Université Libre de Brussels.

Power, C. (2016, 7 July). Samuel Beckett, the maestro of failure. *The Guardian.*

Prothmann, S. (2018). Migration, masculinity and social class: Insights from Pikine, Senegal. *International Migration*, 56(4), 96–108.

Quiminal, C. (1991). *Gens d'ici, gens d'ailleurs: Migrations Soninké et transformations villageoises.* Bourgois.

Quiminal, C. (2002). Retours contraints, retours construits des émigrés maliens. *Hommes & Migrations* (1236), 35–43.

Radziwinowiczówna, A. (2019). Sufrimiento en marcha: estrategias de movilidad de mexicanos deportados de los Estados Unidos. *Apuntes: Revista De Ciencias Sociales*, 46(84), 65–93.

Reason, P., & Bradbury-Huang, H. (Eds.). (2008). SAGE Handbook of Action Research: Participative Inquiry and Practice (2nd edition). SAGE Publications.

Rodet, M. (2009). *Les migrantes ignorées du Haut-Sénégal: 1900-1946*. Karthala.

Rodet, M., & County, B. (2018). Old Hommes and New Homelands: Imagining the Nation and Remembering Expulsion in the Wake of the Mali Federation's Collapse. *Africa: Journal of the International Africa Institute*, 88(3), 469–491.

Roitman, J. (2003). Unsanctioned Wealth; or, The Productivity of Debt in Northern Cameroon. *Public Culture*, 15(2), 211–237.

Rosenberger, S., & Küffner, C. (2016). After the deportation gap: Non-removed persons and their pathways to social rights. In R. Hsu & C. H. Reinprecht (Eds.), *Migration and Integration* (pp.137–152). Vienna University Press.

Rosenthal, G. (1993). Reconstruction of Life Stories: principles of selection in generating stories for narrative biographical interviews. *The Narrative Study of Lives*, 1(1), 59–91.

Rosenthal, G. (2006). The Narrated Life Story: On the Interrelation Between Experience, Memory and Narration. In *Narrative, Memory & Knowledge: Representations, Aesthetics, Contexts* (pp. 1–16). University of Huddersfield.

Roth, M. (2005). 'Ma parole s'achète': Money and Meaning in Malian Jeliya. In S. Wooten (Ed.), *Wari Matters: Ethnographic Explorations of Money in the Mande World* (pp. 116–134). LIT Verlag.

Ruben, R., van Houte, M., & Davids, T. (2009). What Determines the Embeddedness of Forced-Return Migrants? Rethinking the Role of Pre- and Post-Return Assistance. *International Migration Review*, 43(4), 908–937.

Rubin, H. J., & Rubin, I. (1995). *Qualitative interviewing: The art of hearing data*. Sage Publications.

Rudwick, S., & Posel, D. (2014). Contemporary functions of ilobolo (bridewealth) in urban South African Zulu society. *Journal of Contemporary African Studies*, 32(1), 118–136.

Sachverständigenrat deutscher Stiftungen für Integration und Migration (SVR). (2020). *Gemeinsam gestalten: Migration aus Afrika nach Europa: Jahresgutachten 2020*.

Sahlins, M. (1965). *On the Sociology of Primitive Exchange*. Tavistock Publications.

Sarthou-Lajus, N. (1997). *L'éthique de la dette*. Presses Universitaires de France.

Sassen, S. (2016). At the Systemic Edge: Expulsions. *European Review*, 24(01), 89–104.

Sayad, A. (2004). *The Suffering of the Immigrant*. Polity Press.

Schapendonk, J. (2012). Turbulent Trajectories: African Migrants on Their Way to the European Union. *Societies*, 2(4), 27–41.

Schapendonk, J. (2018). Navigating the migration industry: migrants moving through an African-European web of facilitation/control. *Journal of Ethnic and Migration Studies*, 44(4), 663-679.

Scheff, T. J. (2003). Shame in Self and Society. *Symbolic Interaction*, 26(2), 239–262.

Scheper-Hughes, N. (2008). A Talent for Life: Reflections on Human Vulnerability and Resilience. *Ethnos*, 73(1), 25–56.

Schmitt, M., Bitterwolf, M., & Baraulina, T. (2019). *Geförderte Rückkehr aus Deutschland: Motive und Reintegration. Eine Begleitstudie zum Bundesprogramm StarthilfePlus* (Forschungsbericht No. 34).

Schultz, S. U. (2018). Zurück auf Los!? – Abschiebungen als Teil der europäischen Migrationskontrollpolitik in Afrika. *Kurzdossiers Migration*. Bundeszentrale für Politische Bildung.

Schultz, S. U. (2019). Unfulfilled Expectations for Making a Better Life: Young Malian men coping with their post deportation adventures. *Cadernos De Estudos Africanos* (37), 159–181.

Schultz, S. (2020a). *Giving fresh impetus to Germany's collaboration with Africa on migration* (Policy Brief Migration). Bertelsmann Stiftung.

Schultz, S. U. (2020b) 'It's not easy'. Everyday suffering, hard work and courage. Navigating masculinities post deportation in Mali, *Gender, Place & Culture*, 28(6), 870-887.

Schultz, S. (2021a). Mali: Protracted Crises, (In)Securities, and a Glimmer of Hope. *BTI Blog*. Bertelsmann Stiftung.

Schultz, S. U. (2021b). "The adventure is not easy." The Discretionary Politics of Social Suffering and Agency in Post-Deportation Narratives in Southern Mali. *International Journal for Crime, Justice and Social Democracy*, 10(3), 101–114.

Schultz, U. (2014) Über Daten nachdenken: Grounded Theory Studien in entwicklungsbezogener Forschung. In P. Dannecker & B. Englert (Eds.), *Qualitative Methoden in der Entwicklungsforschung* (pp. 75–93). Mandelbaum.

Schulz, D. (1999). Pricey Publicity, Refutable Reputations:"Jeliw" and the Economics of Honour in Mali. *Paideuma: Mitteilungen Zur Kulturkunde*, 45, 275–292.

Schulz, D. E. (2002). "The World is Made by Talk": Female Fans, Popular Music, and New Forms of Public Sociality in Urban Mali. *Cahiers D'Études Africaines*, XLII-4(168), 797–829.

Schulz, D. E. (2006). Promises of (Im)mediate Salvation: Islam, Broadcast Media, and the Remaking of Religious Experience in Mali. *American Ethnologist*, 33(2), 210–229.

Schulz, D. E. (2012). *Muslims and New Media in West Africa: Pathways to God*. Indiana University Press.

Schulz, D. E., & Diallo, S. (2016). Competing Assertions of Muslim Masculinity in Contemporary Mali. *Journal of Religion in Africa*, 46, 219–250.

Schulz, D. E., & Janson, M. (2016). Introduction: Religion and Masculinities in Africa. *Journal of Religion in Africa*, 46, 121–128.

Schuster, L., & Majidi, N. (2013). What happens post-deportation? The experience of deported Afghans. *Migration Studies*, 1(2), 221–240.

Schuster, L., & Majidi, N. (2015). Deportation Stigma and Re-migration. *Journal of Ethnic and Migration Studies*, 41(4), 635–652.

Schutz, A., (1967). *The phenomenology of the social world*. Northwestern University Press.

Schütz, A. (1944). The Stranger: An Essay in Social Psychology. *American Journal of Sociology*, 49(6), 499–507.

Schwiertz, H., & Ratfisch, P. (2016). *Antimigrantische Politik und der "Sommer der Migration"*. Rosa Luxemburg Stiftung.

Schwietering, J. (1946). *Parzivals Schuld*. Klostermann.

Shaidrova, M. (forthcoming). Performing a "Returnee" to fight stigma in Benin City, Nigeria. *Journal of International Migration and Integration*.

Shipton, P. M. (2007). *The nature of entrustment: Intimacy, exchange, and the sacred in Africa*. Yale University Press.

Shipton, P. M. (2009). *Mortgaging the Ancestors: Ideologies of Attachment in Africa*. Yale University Press.

Siekmann, R. (2004). *Eigenartige Senne: Zur Kulturgeschichte der Wahrnehmung einer peripheren Landschaft*. Landesverband Lippe, Institut für Lippische Landeskunde.

Siméant, J. (1998). *La cause des sans-papiers*. Presses de Sciences Po.

Siméant, J. (2014). *Contester au Mali: Formes de la mobilisation et de la critique à Bamako*. Karthala.

Simmel, G. ([1908] 1958). *Soziologie. Untersuchungen über die Formen der Vergesellschaftung*. Dunker & Humblot.

Sinatti, G. (2011). 'Mobile transmigrants' or 'unsettled returnees'? Myth of return and permanent resettlement among Senegalese migrants. *Population, Space and Place*, 17(2), 153–166.

Smelser, N. J. (1998). The rational and the ambivalent in the social sciences. *American Sociological Review*, 63(1), 1–16.

Smith, M. D., Wiseman, R., Harris, P., & Joiner, R. (1996). On being lucky: The psychology and parapsychology of luck. *European Journal of Parapsychology*, 12, 35–43.

Soares, B. F. (2013, June 10). *Islam in Mali since the 2012 coup*. Society for Cultural Anthroplogy.

Soukouna, S. (2011). *L'Échec d'une Coopération Franco Malienne sur les Migrations: Les logiques du refus malien de signer*. Mémoire. Université Paris I Panthéon Sorbonne.

Soukouna, S. (2016). *Les bâtisseurs locaux du lien entre migration et développement : la coopération décentralisée d'Île-de-France au prisme des alliances stratégiques entre mi-*

grants maliens et pouvoirs locaux dans la région de Kayes au Mali Ile-de-France. Doctoral Thesis. Université Panthéon-Sorbonne.

Sow, I. A. (1987). *Dynamique culturelle et transformations sociales. Coopératives agricoles d'anciens émigrés en France : Somankidi-Coura, Sobokou et Lani-Mody.* United Nations Educational, Scientific and Cultural Organization.

Stark, O.; & Taylor, J. E. (1989). Relative Deprivation and International Migration. *Demography*, 26(1), pp. 1–14.

Steuer, N. (2012). "We are just afraid of what others may say about us": Maintaining honour and respect in processes of disclosure in Bamako, Mali. *Medische Anthropologie*, 24(2), 265-287.

Steuer, N. (2013). *Krankheit und Ehre: Über HIV und soziale Anerkennung in Mali*. transcript.

Steuer, N., Engeler, M., & Macamo, E. (Eds.). (2017). *Dealing with elusive futures: University graduates in urban Africa.* transcript.

Stock, I. (2019). *Time, Migration and Forced Immobility: Sub-Saharan African migrants in Morocco.* Bristol University Press.

Strauss, A. L., & Corbin, J. M. (1990). *Basics of qualitative research: Grounded theory procedures and techniques.* SAGE Publications.

Strecker, I., & La Tosky, S. (2013). Introduction. In I. A. Strecker & S. La Tosky (Eds.), *Writing in the field: Festschrift for Stephen Tyler* (pp. 1–20). LIT-Verlag.

Strecker, I. A., & La Tosky, S. (Eds.). (2013). *Writing in the field: Festschrift for Stephen Tyler.* LIT-Verlag.

Streiff-Fénart, J., & Poutignat, P. (2006). De l'aventurier au commerçant transnational, trajectoires croisées et lieux intermédiaires à Nouadhibou (Mauritanie). *Cahiers De La Mediterranée* (73), 129–149.

Streiff-Fénart, J., & Poutignat, P. (2014). Vivre sur, vivre de la frontière: L'après transit en Mauritanie et au Mali. *Revue Européenne Des Migrations Internationales*, 30(2), 91–111.

Streiff-Fénart, J., & Segatti, A. (Eds.). (2012). *The Challenge of the Threshold: Border Closures and Migration Movements in Africa.* Lexington Books.

Stross, B. ([1974] 2000). Speaking of Speaking: Tenejapa Tzeltal Metalinguistics. In R. Bauman & J. Sherzer (Eds.), *Explorations in the ethnography of speaking* (2nd ed., pp. 213–239). Cambridge University Press.

Strübing, J. (2014). *Grounded Theory: Zur sozialtheoretischen und epistemologischen Fundierung eines pragmatistischen Forschungsstils.* VS Verlag für Sozialwissenschaften.

Sylla, A. (2014). *Trajectoires et dynamiques de réinsertion des rapatriés Maliens de la Libye à Bamako.* Mémoire. Université des Sciences Juridiques et Politiques des Bamako (USJP-B), Institut Supérieur de Formation et de Recherche Appliquée (ISFRA).

Sylla, A. (2019). « *C'est devenu si je savais* » : *les trajectoires de réinsertion des rapatriés maliens de la Côte d'Ivoire et de la Libye entre 2002 et 2017*. Thèse. Ministère de l'Enseignement Supérieur et de la Recherche Scientifique.

Sylla, A. & Cold-Ravnkilde, S. M. (2021), *En Route* to Europe? The Anti-Politics of Deportation from North Africa to Mali. *Geopolitics.*

Sylla, A., & Schultz, S. U. (2019). Mali: Abschiebungen als postkoloniale Praxis. *PERIPHERIE – Politik • Ökonomie • Kultur, 39*(3), 389–411.

Sylla, A., & Schultz, S. U. (2020). Commemorating the deadly other side of externalized borders through "migrant-martyrs", sacrifices and politizations of (irregular) migration on the international migrants' day in Mali. *Comparative Migration Studies, 8*(1), 1–17.

Taleb, N. N. (2007). *The Black Swan: The Impact of the Highly Improbable*. Random House.

Taussig, M. T. (1980). *The devil and commodity fetishism in South America*. University of North Carolina Press.

Thiam, S. E. (2014). *Forced Begging, Aid and Children's Rights in Senegal: Stories of Suffering and Politics of Compassion in the Promotion of Rights for the Taalibe Qur'anic School Children of Senegal and Mali*. Doctoral Thesis. McGill University.

Tounkara, M. (2013). *Les Dimensions socioculturelles de l'échec de la migration : Cas des Expulsés Maliens de France*. Thèse. Université Paris-Est.

Traoré, A. D. (2008). *L'Afrique humiliée*. Fayard.

Traoré, K. (2016, December 19). Le Mali dément catégoriquement tout accord de réadmission avec l'UE. *Voa Afrique.*

Trauner, F., & Deimel, S. (2013). The Impact of EU migration policies on African countries: the case of Mali. *International Migration, 51*(4), 20-32.

Trauner, F., Jegen, L., Adam, I., & Roos, C. (2019). *The International Organization for Migration in West Africa: Why Its Role is Getting More Contested* (Policy Brief No. 3). United Nations University.

Tull, D. M. (2021). *Operation Barkhane and the Future of Intervention in the Sahel. The Shape of Things to Come* (SWP Comment C 05). Stiftung Wissenschaft und Politik.

Turnbull, S. (2018). Starting Again: Life After Deportation from the UK. In S. Khosravi (Ed.), *After Deportation: Ethnographic Perspectives* (pp. 37–62). Palgrave Macmillan.

Turner, V. W. (1969). *The Ritual Process: Structure and Anti-structure*. Cornell University Press.

Tyszler, E. (2019). From controlling mobilities to control over women's bodies: gendered effects of EU border externalization in Morocco. *Comparative Migration Studies, 7*(1).

Ungruhe, C. (2010). Symbols of success: Youth, peer pressure and the role of adulthood among juvenile male return migrants in Ghana. *Childhood, 17*(2), 259–271.

Urry, J. (2007). *Mobilities*. Polity Press.

Üstübici, A. (2016). Political Activism Between Journey and Settlement: Irregular Migrant Mobilisation in Morocco. *Geopolitics*, 21(2), 303–324.

Vammen, I. M. (2017). Sticking to God: Brokers of Hope in Senegalese Migration to Argentina. In N. Kleist & D. Thorsen (Eds.), *Hope and Uncertainty in Contemporary African Migration* (pp. 42–57). Routledge.

van Beek, W. (2007). Agency in Kapsiki religion: A comparative approach. In M. de Bruijn, R. van Dijk, & J.-B. Gewald (Eds.), *Strength beyond Structure: Social and Historical Trajectories of Agency in Africa* (pp. 114–143). Brill.

van der Land, V. (2015). *The environment-migration nexus reconsidered: Why capabilities and aspirations matter*. Dissertation. Johann-Wolfgang-Goethe-Universität zu Frankfurt am Main.

van Dijk, R. (2007). The safe and suffering body in transnational Ghanaian Pentecostalism: Towards anthropology of vulnerable agency. In M. de Bruijn, R. van Dijk, & J.-B. Gewald (Eds.), *Strength beyond Structure: Social and Historical Trajectories of Agency in Africa* (pp. 312–333). Brill.

van Gennep, A. ([1909] 1981). *Les rites de passage*. Picard.

van Hear, N. (2014). Reconsidering Migration and Class. *International Migration Review*, 48(3), S100-S121.

van Houte, M., & Davids, T. (2008). Development and Return Migration: From policy panacea to migrant perspective sustainability. *Third World Quarterly*, 29(7), 1411–1429.

van Houte, M., Siegel, M., & Davids, T. (2016). Deconstructing the meanings of and motivations for return: An Afghan case study. *Comparative Migration Studies*, 4(1), 615.

van Hoven, E., & Oosten, J. G. (1994). The Mother-Son and Brother-Sister Relationships in the Sunjata Epic. In J. G. Oosten (Ed.), *Text and tales: Studies in oral tradition*. Research School CNWS.

van Westen, A. C. M. (1995). *Unsettled: Low-income housing and mobility in Bamako, Mali*. Koninklijk Nederlands Aardrijkskundig Genootschap.

Vermont, C. (2015). Capturer une émotion qui ne s'eénonce pas: Trois interprétations de la honte. *Terrain/Théorie, (2)*.

Vigh, H. (2006). *Navigating Terrains of War: Youth and Soldiering in Guinea-Bissau*. Berghahn Books.

Vigh, H. (2009a). Motion squared: A second look at the concept of social navigation. *Anthropological Theory*, 9(4), 419–438.

Vigh, H. (2009b). Wayward Migration: On Imagined Futures and Technological Voids. *Ethnos*, 74(1), 91–109.

Vigh, H. (2016). Life's Trampoline: On Nullification and Cocaine Migration in Bissau. In J. Cole & C. Groes-Green, *Affective Circuits: African Migrations to Europe and the Pursuit of Social Regeneration*, (pp. 223–244). The University of Chicago Press.

Vium, C. (2014). Icons of Becoming: Documenting Undocumented Migration from West Africa to Europe. *Cahiers D'Études Africaines*, 54(213-214), 217-240.

Voirol, O., & Schendzielorz, C. (2014). Verpflichtet auf Erfolg – Verdammt zum Scheitern. Selbstbewertung in Casting-Shows am Beispiel von „Deutschland sucht den Superstar". In R. John & A. Langhof (Eds.), *Innovation und Gesellschaft. Scheitern – Ein Desiderat der Moderne* (pp. 25–45). Springer VS.

Vries, L. A. de, & Guild, E. (2019). Seeking refuge in Europe: Spaces of transit and the violence of migration management. *Journal of Ethnic and Migration Studies*, 45(12), 2156-2166

Walters, W. (2002). Deportation, Expulsion, and the International Police of Aliens. *Citizenship Studies*, 6(3), 265–292.

Walters, W. (2010). Deportation, Expulsion, and the International Police of Aliens. In N. De Genova & N. Peutz (Eds.), *The Deportation Regime: Sovereignty, Space, and the Freedom of Movement* (pp. 69–100). Duke University Press.

Weber, L., & Powell, R. (2018). Ripples Across the Pacific: Cycles of Risk and Exclusion Following Criminal Deportation to Samoa. In S. Khosravi (Ed.), *After Deportation: Ethnographic Perspectives* (pp. 205–229). Palgrave Macmillan.

Wegar, K. (1992). The Sociological Significance of Ambivalence: An Example from Adoption Research. *Qualitative Sociology*, 15(1), 87–103.

Weiss, B. (1996). *The making and unmaking of the Haya lived world: Consumption, commoditization, and everyday practice.* Duke University Press.

Weiss, B. (Ed.). (2004). *Producing African Futures: Ritual and Reproduction in a Neoliberal Age.* Brill.

Weiss, B. (2009). *Street dreams and hip hop barbershops: Global fantasy in urban Tanzania. Tracking globalization.* Indiana University Press.

Whitehouse, B. (2012). *Migrants and Strangers in an African City: Exile, Dignity, Belonging.* Indiana University Press.

Wiedemann, C. (2010). Nützt Migration der Demokratie? Beobachtungen in Mali, im 50. Jahr der Unabhängigkeit. *Blätter für Deutsche und Internationale Politik* (9).

Wiedemann, C. (2013). Der Wulibali. Oder: Marabouts gegen Jihadisten. Über Islam, Demokratie und Krieg in Mali. *Blätter für Deutsche und Internationale Politik* (2).

Wiedemann, C. (2018). *Viel Militär, weniger Sicherheit; Mali – fünf Jahre nach Beginn der Intervention.* Heinrich Böll Stiftung.

Wooten, S. (Ed.). (2005). *Wari Matters: Ethnographic Explorations of Money in the Mande World.* LIT Verlag.

Wooten, S. (2009). *The Art of Livelihood: Creating Expressive Agri-Culture in Rural Mali.* Carolina Academic Press.

Youngstedt, S. M. (2013). *Surviving with Dignity: Hausa Communities of Niamey, Niger.* Lexington Books.

Yuran, N. (2016). A Moralistic Failure: Mandeville and the Obscene Origin of Economic Thought. *Social Research*, *83*(3), 573–595.

Zanker, F., & Altrogge, J. (2019). The Political Influence of Return: From Diaspora to Libyan Transit Returnees. *International Migration*, *57*(4), 167-180.

Zanker, F., Altrogge, J., Arhin-Sam, K., & Jegen, L. (2019). *Challenges in EU-African Migration Cooperation: West African Perspectives on Forced Return.* MEDAM Policy Brief, 2019/5.

Zilberg, E. (2004). Fools banished from the Kingdom: Remapping Geographies of Gang Violence between the Americas (Los Angeles and San Salvador). *American Quarterly*, *56*(3), 759–779.

Cultural Studies

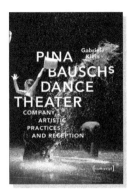

Gabriele Klein
Pina Bausch's Dance Theater
Company, Artistic Practices and Reception

2020, 440 p., pb., col. ill.
29,99 € (DE), 978-3-8376-5055-6
E-Book:
PDF: 29,99 € (DE), ISBN 978-3-8394-5055-0

Elisa Ganivet
Border Wall Aesthetics
Artworks in Border Spaces

2019, 250 p., hardcover, ill.
79,99 € (DE), 978-3-8376-4777-8
E-Book:
PDF: 79,99 € (DE), ISBN 978-3-8394-4777-2

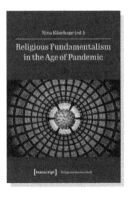

Nina Käsehage (ed.)
**Religious Fundamentalism
in the Age of Pandemic**

April 2021, 278 p., pb., col. ill.
37,00 € (DE), 978-3-8376-5485-1
E-Book: available as free open access publication
PDF: ISBN 978-3-8394-5485-5

**All print, e-book and open access versions of the titles in our list
are available in our online shop www.transcript-publishing.com**

Cultural Studies

Ivana Pilic, Anne Wiederhold-Daryanavard (eds.)
Art Practices in the Migration Society
Transcultural Strategies in Action
at Brunnenpassage in Vienna

March 2021, 244 p., pb.
29,00 € (DE), 978-3-8376-5620-6
E-Book:
PDF: 25,99 € (DE), ISBN 978-3-8394-5620-0

German A. Duarte, Justin Michael Battin (eds.)
Reading »Black Mirror«
Insights into Technology and the Post-Media Condition

January 2021, 334 p., pb.
32,00 € (DE), 978-3-8376-5232-1
E-Book:
PDF: 31,99 € (DE), ISBN 978-3-8394-5232-5

Krista Lynes, Tyler Morgenstern, Ian Alan Paul (eds.)
Moving Images
Mediating Migration as Crisis

2020, 320 p., pb., col. ill.
40,00 € (DE), 978-3-8376-4827-0
E-Book: available as free open access publication
PDF: ISBN 978-3-8394-4827-4

CPSIA information can be obtained
at www.ICGtesting.com
Printed in the USA
JSHW031438160422
25022JS00008B/168